Comanche Trace

Book 4 in the Westward Sagas

DAVID BOWLES

Comanche Trace: Book 4 in the Westward Sagas
© 2019 David A. Bowles
Plum Creek Press, Inc.

Cataloging-in Publication Data

Bowles, David A.
Comanche Trace: Book 4 in the Westward Sagas

p. cm.   ISBN 978-0-9997622-4-0

1. Texas History 2. Austin, Texas—History 3. Texas Rangers
4. Santa Fe Trail—Expedition

PN 6014 S48 2018   FIC BOW

Plum Creek Press, Inc.
P. O. Box 701561
San Antonio, Texas 78270-1561
210-827-4122
info@westwardsagas.com
www.westwardsagas.com

Page Design and Cover Art by Rebecca Byrd Arthur

Printed in the United States of America

Dedication

Wanda Chandler Rohm

"Queen of Quemado, Texas"

1946-2016

and

Karen Thompson Blanchette

Jack's Girl

1948-2018

Author's Note

COMANCHE TRACE is my fourth book in the *Westward Saga Series*. Like the three books before it, each book stands on its own. It is not necessary to read the books in any certain order. The series will continue to be written and published in chronological order. I invite you to ride along with my family of characters or join us anywhere on the trail. I hope you enjoy the ride wherever you start the read.

Preface

COMANCHE TRACE is the story of William Smith, known as "Will" to family and friends. The young Texas Ranger gave up ranging after the Battle of Plum Creek, settling in Austin near family. The story begins the third week of January 1841.

Comanche Indians kill Will's brother, Supreme Court Justice James W. Smith and abduct James' son Fayette. This incredible but true story has two journeys: Will's search for his nephew and the story of a nine-year-old boy's struggle to survive. Maps of their travels can be found at www.westwardsagas.com

David A. Bowles chose to write this story as historical fiction, using real life characters. Some are from his family lineage and their names real, such as great-grandmother Elnora Van Cleve-Brown–the first child born in Austin. The vital statistics of relatives are based on extensive genealogical research. Where historical records are available he used that data; where it was not, Bowles created it in a believable way that the reader will find educational and entertaining.

Names of geographic locations are, as they were during the early years of the Republic of Texas. Comanche Trail was called Comanche Trace, hence the name of this book; the trace west from Austin started at the end of Pecan Street (present day) Sixth and Lamar. It meandered over

Comanche Mountain was renamed Mt. Bonnell. Falls of the Colorado is now known as Marble Falls. Brushy Creek is in Williamson County. The big cave Little Doe refers to is Longhorn Caverns in Burnet County. Spirit Song Rock is Enchanted Rock in Gillespie County and Yellow House Canyon refers to Lubbock.

Bowles' vivid descriptions of places will register with those familiar with the landmarks of old trails, rivers, and mountains.

To ensure accurate descriptions of the journeys in this book. David Bowles and the dogs traveled thousands of miles over ten years researching and writing Comanche Trace.

He followed the Rio Grande from its headwaters in southwest Colorado to where it flows into the Gulf of Mexico. Three summers in New Mexico were spent researching the Santa Fe Expedition. He followed the Santa Fe Trail from Independence, Missouri to Santa Fe twice. Once going the southern route through Mora and Apache Canyon.

The highlight of his travels was taking the Old Spanish Trail from Abiquiú, New Mexico to Rancho Puente, California. He found the 1855 home of John A. Rowland being renovated for a museum. The curator was unaware of Rowland and his partner William Workman's involvement in the Santa Fe Expedition, or his saving Fayette's life and returning him safely to family.

Learn more about author and speaker David A. Bowles at www.westwardsagas.com.

Chapter One

*F*ayette trudged up the rugged mountain trail created years ago by the feet of nomadic Indians. Suddenly, he was gouged in the back with the blunt end of a warrior's spear. He turned to face his tormentor and was poked harder, this time in his ribs. Blood oozed from the head wound above his eye. He struggled to walk faster up the narrow passage, the Colorado River meandered below. Fayette knew the water was deep. His Uncle Will had taught him to swim and jump from the limestone bluffs last summer. Even if he survived this jump, higher than any he'd ever made, could he swim to the other side? It was winter—Fayette knew he wouldn't last long in the cold water. Either way, he was certain his young life was about to end.

Two of Fayette's captors rode ahead, single file, on stolen horses. The other Indians, much younger, walked behind and prodded Fayette along. The leader was a hump-backed Indian with long hair, wrinkles, and few teeth. He wore a buffalo headpiece with deer horns; three scalps were tied to his waistband. One belonged to Fayette's father, Judge James W. Smith.

Fayette's birthday adventure started when his father and uncle took the nine-year-old for a ride along Shoal Creek. They rode unarmed at the request of Fayette's mother. Fayette rode behind his father, holding tight to his waist. They rode Preacher, his father's favorite horse, while Uncle Fenwick rode a sorrel stallion named Deacon.

Uncle Fenwick dismounted to pull back a thick clump of mesquite brush, and then worked his way into the thicket looking for a trap. Someone may have taken it, or a large animal snared by its jaws may have made off with it. Deacon stood untied outside the thicket. Fayette and his father waited near the entrance to a narrow trail a stone's throw away.

Five Indians came out of the brush on foot from the direction of Comanche Mountain. They attacked without warning. An arrow went through the judge's left arm, shattering the bone as it exited just above the elbow. The arrowhead's trajectory lacerated Fayette's forehead as it exited his father's arm. Their horse ran under a low branch and knocked both to the ground. The savages stabbed and mutilated Judge Smith. Fayette, bleeding from his head wound, ran but was quickly overtaken. The Indians assumed Deacon was Fayette's horse. They were unaware that there was a witness to their gruesome crime.

When Fenwick reached Austin, the sun was setting behind Barton Creek where it flowed into the Colorado. Fenwick, using the scant strength he had left, rang the town bell across from Judge Smith's home and courthouse. Angelina Smith raised the bar, opened the door, and saw her brother-in-law bloody and soaking wet. She looked toward Shoal Creek, knowing something terrible had happened. "Where's my son...and your brother?"

She pulled out the pine bench from under the table and sat down. Fayette's sisters Caroline and Lorena climbed down from their sleeping loft. The girls moved quietly to the end of the long bench and listened as he spoke, trying to comprehend what had happened.

Fenwick shook his head. "James is dead. The Indians took Fayette!"

Angelina stood, placed both hands to her thin face, paced toward the door, turned around, and sat down next to Caroline "No…oh no…it can't be so…" She looked at the girls, then asked, "Where did they take my son?" Angelina hugged Caroline and Lorena tightly. Their young minds had yet to grasp their father was dead and their only brother captured by Indians.

Fenwick rose. "I am sorry Angelina, it happened so fast. I was on foot when the Indians attacked. With no weapon…I couldn't do anything." He sat down as tears streamed down his bloody cheeks. "It was awful to see and hear, even from a distance."

"I know you would've done something if you could've. I didn't want that new revolver of James' going off and hurting my boy. I will regret telling James to leave his guns at home the rest of my life!" Angelina touched the deepest scratch on Fenwick's face. "What did the Indians do to you?"

"They never saw me." Fenwick looked at the blood on his clothes, "This is from running through the woods; I fell a few times."

Angelina pointed toward the water bucket, "Lorena, fetch your uncle some water."

The oldest girl carried the long-handled dipper full of water to Fenwick, and watched her uncle swallow it in one gulp.

"Thank you," Fenwick gasped.

Townspeople scurried toward the Capitol as they did whenever the bell rang. They scanned the cedar shake rooftops, but not seeing any dwellings on fire, they knew it must be another Indian attack.

Someone hollered, "Go to Judge Smith's house."

Judge Smith's brothers, Will and Harvey, arrived first. Lorenzo Van Cleve, their brother-in-law who married their sister Margaret, was right behind them. When family friends Joseph Lee and Sheriff Wayne Barton, arrived, they tried to calm the widow and her girls. Everyone realized the severity of the events: Indians had murdered Travis County's highest-ranking public official and had captured his only son.

Indian raids were frequent since the white man built a center of government on their hunting grounds—something President Sam Houston predicted, and newly-elected President Mirabeau Lamar ignored. Austin's leaders attempted to play down Indian depredations in hopes of retaining the Capitol.

The Hall of Congress, which the locals called the Capitol, now vacant, had been turned into a fortress since Congress adjourned. Timbers hauled from Bastrop were inserted vertically into the ground, which created an eight-foot-high wall around the wooden structure. As an extra precaution, a four-foot-deep by four-foot-wide moat was created around the outside fence perimeter. Residents knew to fort-up there in the event of an Indian raid or an attack from the Mexican Army.

Angelina looked up at her tallest brother-in-law and gently touched his arm. "Will, please find my son? Then… bring James' body home to me."

"We'll go after them at first light." Will looked at the men in the room "Are you with me?"

The men nodded their commitment.

Angelina pleaded, "Can't you go now? I don't want Fayette to spend the night…with the savages that killed his father."

Sheriff Barton put his hands on her shoulders, "Angelina, we can't travel in the dark. You know that." He turned toward the men, "We need to pack provisions and all the ammunition you can carry."

"Please bring them home," Angelina begged.

"We will." Sheriff Barton looked at the men, "Won't we?"

They nodded. Joseph Lee said, "We best get home and start packing." Fayette's grandparents, Thomas and Rebeckah Smith, arrived as the sheriff was leaving. Thomas was County Treasurer. Sheriff Barton hugged Rebeckah and Thomas. "I am sorry, Thomas, Rebeckah... for your loss."

"What loss? What happened, Sheriff?" Thomas asked.

"I would rather you hear it from Fenwick. He was there and saw everything." The Sheriff opened the door. "We've got to somehow get more gunpowder and shot, Thomas. If we don't, these damn Indians are going to kill us all."

"I know. Tell the men I'll replace any munitions they use. Lead and powder is on order."

"Tell us what happened, Sheriff!" Rebeckah grabbed his arm tightly.

"Indian attack, Rebeckah. Your son Fenwick can tell you the details. I will be back in the morning with as many men as I can muster." Sheriff Barton held the door for Joseph Lee. Lee nodded goodnight and closed the door behind him.

Inside the cabin, the Smith family intermittently cried and talked excitedly about the attack.

"Listen up," Thomas waited for silence. "Please, Rebeckah and I want to hear from Fenwick! Son, tell us what happened? You were with them. Everyone else just listen up!"

Fenwick told the story of the Indian attack. The Smith's learned that their oldest son James was murdered, and their grandson Fayette wounded and captured. Rebeckah took the loss hard, crying and carrying on. She looked up at the shingled ceiling. "Lord, tell me it isn't true." Thomas Smith sat stoically, his hatred for the Comanche burning in the pit of his stomach. Angelina held the girls tightly and rocked back and forth.

It was late. Condolences and prayers were offered as worried neighbors hurried off to their homes. Few would sleep tonight.

"Will, would you stay?" Angelina asked. He was the first family member to move toward the door to leave.

Will hesitated at the door. William, the handsome twenty-two-year-old bachelor was Angelina's favorite brother-in-law. Will was the least talkative of the Smith family, but when he talked, everyone listened. He served in the Texas Army during the Revolution with Mexico and, until recently, ranged the coastal plains fighting Indians as a Texas Ranger. Will soon tired of ranging—he hung up his gun and badge. He sold his twelve-hundred-acre bounty of land given to him for military service and invested the money in Austin city lots.

"Of course I can stay!" He moved toward the table and sat across from his brother's widow.

"Thank you." Angelina started to cry, "It's my fault! I should've let James and Fenwick take their guns."

"Please don't blame yourself." He reached across the table, took Angelina's hands, and tried to console her.

Chapter Two

Austin, Texas

The Indians made it to the top of Comanche Mountain before sunset. Twenty members of their tribe sat around a roaring fire with food on a spit. Six emaciated horses were hobbled behind their teepees. The men, impressed with the stolen horses, felt the horses' legs, looked at hooves and patted their muscular hindquarters. The women stroked Fayette's red hair. He nervously batted their hands away, making the squaws want to touch it more.

The top of the mountain was flat. Sparse vegetation penetrated the hard limestone, carved by the wind and rain of a million years. The mountain was sacred ceremonial ground for the Comanche. Many successful hunts were celebrated on its mesa. However, this year there was no reason for celebration. Only two buffalo were killed; they usually took ten times that number. The tribe blamed the white settlers for their poor hunt.

The Indians greeted one another excitedly, and then began to dance around the fire in triumph. The leader proudly waved the still bleeding scalp. Fayette lurched for it, screaming, "It belongs to my Pa...don't be doing that!" One of the young Indian braves grabbed his wrists and restrained him. Fayette kicked the Indian in the groin with all his might. The Indian picked Fayette up and slammed him to the ground. As Fayette lie motionless, the Indians continued to celebrate.

When Fayette regained consciousness, every bone in his body ached. He assumed his captors thought he was dead. He ran his hands through his hair, relieved his scalp was still there. Fayette crawled to the largest of the teepees, where the scalps were tied on a ceremonial pole. Using his jackknife, Fayette cut the leather strap that secured his father's scalp. He wanted to free his father's hobbled horse, but fearing it would make noise, decided against it. Fayette moved quietly to the trailhead one slow step at a time. A misstep could send rocks tumbling down the mountain, waking the tribe. He put his father's scalp in his baggy pants pocket. A coyote howled in the distance; or was it an Indian? Fayette prayed it was a coyote.

Hungry and hurting, Fayette managed to descend halfway down the mountain. He began to move a little faster. Suddenly, an Indian named Night Owl, one who did not participate in his capture, came out of the dark shadows. Fayette ran, but Night Owl easily caught up with him and wrapped both arms around the kicking and screaming boy's waist.

"Let me go…leave me be."

"*Kayshaunt,*" said Night Owl, which meant no good to fight. He shook Fayette's shoulders, "No go! You belong to Buffalo Hump now."

"No, I don't!" Fayette tried in vain to break loose.

Night Owl turned Fayette around toward the Indian camp. "Come."

When he tried to break away, the Indian picked Fayette up and threw him over his shoulder like a sack of milled corn.

After a short struggle, Fayette said, "Please let me down. I won't try to run anymore, I promise."

Night Owl sat him down gently.

"Thank you," Fayette said, appreciating not being thrown to the ground again.

As they walked up the trail, neither said a word. Fayette reached for his father's scalp; it wasn't in his pocket. Maybe it fell out during the struggle, he panicked, and then realized it was a blessing. The Indians would no longer have it to taunt him.

Eighteen men rode out of Austin at daybreak. The hastily gathered search party was made up of the Sheriff and three Texas Rangers. The rest were well-armed family and friends. Will led two burros tethered behind George, his large white stallion. One burro carried provisions, the other only an empty packsaddle. The unburdened beast would have the honor of carrying the remains of Judge Smith home.

Fenwick led the search party out of town, west, to the end of Pecan where it crossed Shoal Creek. They traversed quietly several miles up the shallow creek bed. Buzzards, circling high in the sky, pointed the way to the corpse. The Rangers and Sheriff, their rifles at the ready, led the way single-file up the narrow path to Judge Smith's body.

Rebeckah sent a quilt she'd made when James was a baby. It was to be used to wrap her son's body. Thomas Smith, a veteran of the Creek Indian Wars and the Battle of New Orleans, had seen many dead and wounded soldiers. He wasn't prepared to view his son's mutilated body. Judge Smith's left arm was shattered, the arrow still embedded—signs of his defiant struggle on the ground. Small footprints and spots of blood confirmed Fenwick's story.

"Definitely Comanche." Sheriff Barton pointed out the red band of the Comanche handing the arrow to Will, the head covered with the blood of his brother and nephew. Will looked at it and handed it back to Sheriff Barton.

"You alright Will?" the sheriff asked.

Will was upset at seeing the projectile that did so much damage to his family, but he nodded that he was okay.

Sheriff Barton spoke for all to hear, "Tracks leading up the mountain trail." Sheriff Barton motioned for Fenwick to come and get in the conversation.

"Fenwick, I know you were way over there in the brush." The sheriff pointed, "Can you tell us how this band of Indians looked?"

"They each wore purdy much the same, deerskin leggings." Fenwick looked at the sheriff, and then his brother Will. "The one that stabbed James and scalped him…he wore a wooly buffalo headdress. Seemed like horns stuck out of it."

"It's Buffalo Hump!" Will and the sheriff said at the same time.

"Penateka's band of Comanches did this!" Sheriff Barton shook his head. "Should have kilt every damn one of them when we had the chance." He threw the arrow into the brush.

Will mounted up. "We tried, but the renegades scattered…headed in every direction, leaving their seized plunder where it lay."

Most in the search party had fought Buffalo Hump last summer southwest of Austin at the Battle of Plum Creek. The Austin Guards, Texas Rangers, and Militia from all over South Texas dispersed five hundred marauding Indians, killing eighty. The warriors separated by the battle; the white man won were working their way back to Comancheria.

Family members Thomas, Fenwick, Harvey, and Lorenzo Van Cleve returned to Austin with the body. Judge Smith was buried on a hill overlooking the town. Will regretted not attending his brother's burial, electing to stay with the search party until Fayette was found.

Comanche Trace
January 22, 1841

The Indians were gone before the search party left Austin. They followed Comanche Trace to the narrows of the Colorado River where it made a bend to the northwest. Fayette was strapped on an Indian pony, pulling a loaded travois. A young, blue-eyed woman led the pony. She wore a deerskin dress like the other women. Fayette noticed the difference in her skin and hair. Her nose was small; nothing like the other members of the tribe. The wife of Night Owl hadn't looked Fayette in the eye nor spoke to him. Fayette recalled that Night Owl knew a few words of English. *Maybe she taught him those words. Could she be a captive, like me?* he thought.

The tribe stopped at a spring fed creek. Night Owl untied Fayette and gently lifted the boy to the ground. Night Owl and his wife Little Doe seemed to be in charge of him. They gave him dried venison and mush to eat, which he consumed eagerly. Fayette scanned the limestone hills for signs of a search party. *Maybe Fenwick didn't make it back for help.* For the first time, Fayette feared he may never see his family again.

The Indian braves rested as the women took Fayette into a pecan grove where they harvested two large baskets of pecans from the ground.

Fayette managed to slip nuts into his pocket when no one was looking. The women appreciated his help. The men considered pecan gathering women's work. It didn't bother Fayette; his pockets were full of pecans.

While the women made camp, the men with horses went hunting. Night Owl and Big Bear stayed to fish. Throwing their nets into the clear water, each pull brought in fish.

The next afternoon, the Indians made camp on a high bluff above the falls of the Colorado. Water roared between large granite boulders, creating a cloud of mist that formed a rainbow. At the end of the rainbow was part of a broken raft: three large timbers crudely tied together, once part of a flatboat, torn apart as it slammed into the rocks.

Fayette helped Little Doe gather firewood and carried the dried driftwood from the river's bank. He ventured farther each trip until he was near the falls— far enough away to make his escape. He started across the treacherous falls one boulder at a time. From a distance, the granite rocks had appeared closer together. The rock that held the raft was the widest point to jump. The leap appeared to be further than Fayette could jump, the rapids too swift to swim. While pondering his predicament, he slipped on a wet spot, and the decision was made for him. Fayette slid feet first into the water.

He was surprised that the water was only up to his knees. A natural rock ledge was just below the surface; the current was not as strong as it appeared. Large boulders upstream diverted swift water away from the larger rock, creating a small eddy that held the raft against it. Fayette pulled himself up on the raft that was just large enough for him. He pushed off the granite ledge with both feet into the swirling rapids. The raft moved swiftly, faster than anything he had ever encountered. Water rushed over the raft and at times it felt like the raft and he were diving deep underwater. Fayette wrapped his hands tight around the ropes that held the logs together. The raft went through a series of falls, each drop more precarious than the previous. The cold blinding water in his face prevented him from seeing. Fayette hung on for dear life, knowing he was moving rapidly toward home. He floated several miles downstream in a short period of time.

Once in calmer waters, the raft drifted slower until coming to a complete stop in shallow water. Fayette couldn't budge the water-soaked logs. The idea of floating down the river was abandoned as he waded to shore.

A chilly breeze blew out of the north; wet clothes added to Fayette's misery. Searching for warmth, he found a dead tree hollowed out by time and termites. The opening was a tight squeeze, but once inside, he laid back in a somewhat comfortable position. The small confines blocked the blustery north wind and helped retain what little body heat he had left.

Fayette dozed as the shadows of the rocky hills became longer and night fell. The wind howled. He heard rustling above his head. *Was it a possum, coon, or squirrels?* Too tired to care, Fayette remained still while the animals settled in above him.

Chapter Three

The search party followed the tracks of Buffalo Hump and his raiding party to the trailhead at the base of Comanche Mountain. Halfway up the mountain, they found a scalp. Will identified it as his brother's and placed it in his saddlebag. The gruesome find horrified the men but assured them they were on the right trail.

A-top the highest peak in Travis County, they found the Indian's campfire still smoldering.

"It took more than five Indians to make this mess." Will looked around and said, "They were camped here awhile."

"They must've sent a raiding party out while the rest stayed here waiting." Sheriff Barton spit.

"They could see the trail on both sides of the mountain from here." Will gazed over the cliff.

Sheriff Barton looked at Will, "Maybe Buffalo Hump's way of getting back at us for the whipping we gave them at Plum Creek."

"This looks well planned to me," Will said.

"It could be. We won't know till we catch them." Sheriff Barton mounted his horse.

The sheriff thought the Indians went north towards Brushy Creek. If they did, Rangers at Kenney's Fort might have encountered them.

Will had a premonition they went west along the river. He didn't argue with the sheriff. When they found no tracks on the way to Kenney's Fort, Will decided to follow his hunch.

"Wait up!" Will rode up to the Sheriff, "I am going back and following Comanche Trace."

"By yourself?" Sheriff Barton spit.

"I think it best," Will looked back.

"It'll be dangerous, Will! Thomas and Rebeckah don't need to lose another son." Sheriff Barton bit off a piece of his tobacco twist.

"It's dangerous wherever you are. James was killed just three miles from home."

"I'll split the search party in two if you like. Each of us could go the way we think best," Sheriff Barton shifted in his saddle.

"I don't intend to fight Buffalo Hump. When I find him, I intend to give him what he wants for Fayette."

"What you suppose that is?"

"Most likely money, guns, or horses." Will looked toward the mountain, "Whatever it takes. I'm bringing Fayette home alive."

"Good luck, Will." Sheriff Barton tipped his dusty hat and turned his horse toward Brushy Creek.

Will headed into the sun. He didn't know why; he couldn't explain it. It was a premonition; the first he had ever had. It drove him west, seeking the Indians that took Fayette. If he encountered Buffalo Hump and his tribe, he couldn't win a fight. His only hope was to negotiate. That couldn't be done with a blood-thirsty search party. Revenge for what happened would have to wait.

Banks of the Colorado
January 24, 1841

The sun shined bright the next morning, but the wind still whistled as it blew through the hollow tree. Fayette had never been as cold as he was at this moment. He heard a horse nicker, and then the animals nested above him started chattering. *Could it be help, or was it Indians?* His heart pounded—adrenalin raced. *Should I run?* He looked out. It was Little Doe alone on horseback; it sounded like she was crying.

"You must come with me! You will die in the woods," Little Doe pleaded.

Fayette adjusted his position to get a better view. When he did, the hollow tree broke apart, sprawling him on the cold ground as squirrels scattered in every direction.

Little Doe managed to stifle her laugh, "Come. I'll feed you and give you warmth."

She rode slowly up to what remained of the once mighty oak. "No one will hurt you." Little Doe handed him a wool blanket, "Wrap this over your shoulders and get on behind me."

Fayette used the tree stump for a mounting block. Heat from the horse and Little Doe's warm body felt good to the half-frozen boy. She carried him into their teepee where Night Owl and Big Bear were sitting by the fire. They jumped up and spoke excitedly in Comanche. Fayette watched as they pointed at him and then patted him on the back as if he'd accomplished some mystical feat. The Braves left to tell Buffalo Hump.

Little Doe put the shivering boy near the fire on a buffalo robe and laid another robe on top of him.

"I am sorry…I tried to run away…from you," Fayette's teeth chattered.

Little Doe put a finger to her lips, "I told them you fell in the water and drowned. No one knows but me. They now think you possess a special power."

"They think I have power?" Fayette looked up at Little Doe.

"After surviving rapids and the cold of night, tribe thinks your special powers will bring us good luck."

Fayette pulled the buffalo robe up to his neck, "Why didn't you tell them?"

"You risked your life to get away from us. I have no right to stop you."

"Then why did you come looking for me?"

"I had a vision. An old white woman told me where you were and that I must save you from freezing."

Fayette feared punishment. Instead, the tribe treated him as a hero. Buffalo Hump gave him the tribal name of Big Fish. He was fed and allowed to rest until the next morning. For a moment, Fayette forgot he was a captive.

January 25, 1841

As they broke camp the next day, Little Doe told Fayette they were going to a big cave—a place where they would be out of the cold. The tribal elders kept looking at the sky, but Fayette had no idea what they were looking for.

The clouds turned dark blue, and the wind howled in their face. Making it to the cave before the full blast of the Texas Norther hit was important. When they arrived, the men hurriedly pulled brush from the entrance that was larger than any hole Fayette had ever seen. You could pull several teams of horses and a Conestoga wagon inside it. Now he understood why they call it "Big Cave."

The horses were led in first; a black cougar unhappy with being disturbed, exited, growling and hissing, at the intruders. Buffalo Hump gave orders not to harm the big cat, as she protected the cave from evil spirits. Fayette and the squaws were sent outside to gather firewood.

Bits of ice stung his skin as it came down hard from the sky. Night Owl and Big Bear came to carry in the big logs drug to the cave's opening. A roaring fire was built in the first chamber of the cave. Smoke blackened the fifty-foot ceiling with soot as it searched for an outlet. The fire illuminated most of the wide chamber, water dripping into the cavern, echoed off the walls far below.

Fayette lay on a buffalo robe, looking up at the eerie silhouette of dancing flames and the shadows of Indians moving about.

"Little Doe, how far back does this cave go?"

"No one from our tribe has ever found the end. Why do you ask?" Little Doe pulled the robe up to his chin.

"Just curious," Fayette got his first good look into her eyes. He could tell she was not Indian. He asked, "How old were you, Little Doe, when you were captured?"

"I'm not captured! Buffalo Hump found me hungry and cold. I was twelve, he and his wives taught me the Indian ways. Then I married their son Night Owl, brother of Big Bear."

"What happened to your family?"

Little Doe looked down, "I don't know, doesn't matter. I am Comanche now. Wife of Night Owl…daughter of Buffalo Hump."

Three days after separating from the search party, Will came across evidence that a large group of Indians had camped at the falls of the Colorado. *Could this be Buffalo Hump's tribe?* he wondered. Debris in the fire-ring still covered with snow indicated it had started snowing after the Indians broke camp. Tracking the Indians with six inches of snow and ice on the ground would be impossible.

Braving two days of freezing ice in his face, Will kept moving: surviving on deer jerky and stale biscuits. If he stopped to sleep, he and his animals might freeze, so Will pushed on in his search for Fayette. The Indians were two days ahead of him.

The seventh child of Thomas and Rebeckah Smith would turn twenty-three on the third day of April. Will's thoughts turned to Sara. The redheaded girl left behind in Alabama when his family came to Texas. He reminisced about the fun they'd had riding along the Coosa River together. It was where he was born and raised. The only home he knew before coming to Texas. *Maybe I should have stayed in Alabama; married Sara and started a family, like John,* Will mused. John built a good medical practice and a plantation. Thomas Jr. farmed the Coosa homestead. His sister Ann married Brice Burgess, a plantation owner, and now had three children. *They'd all said it never got cold in Texas. If only they could see it now,* he thought.

Brothers James and Will went home to Alabama after the Battle of San Jacinto, excited about the new Republic and the 1,280-acre bounty each received for fighting in the Texas Revolution. They had grandiose plans for their family and Texas. *James is dead. Fayette captured. Fenwick will never be the same.* Will could've stayed in Alabama, but he chose to come to Texas. This was home, where he belonged.

"George, it's your feeding time." Will pulled back on the reins and slowly dismounted. He stretched his body, stiff and saddle-sore from days of riding. It was the twenty-ninth day of January when he reached the San Saba Trail.

With the grass frozen and the feedbag nearly empty, Will made a difficult but humane decision to turn his burro loose to fend for itself rather than watch it starve. He removed his gear, including the packsaddle and bridle, and slapped the burro's bony rump. It trotted off into a clump of nearby mesquite trees. George was fed a small ration of corn by hand. The burro named Sam started making a whinnying nicker, like when it was feeding time. Will went to investigate and saw his burro trying to rear up on its haunches to snatch beans from a mesquite tree. Deer had already devoured those on the lower branches. "Here, Sam, let me help you," Will grabbed a limb.

Will pulled the thorny limbs down where Sam could clench the dried bean pods with its teeth. The burro pulled off the pods and chewed them eagerly. Will pulled what he could reach and then began harvesting them with a broken branch. Now he knew God's purpose for the thorny bush. His horse George thought the long pods of beans were a treat. Will could keep them alive until the ground thawed.

Where could the Comanche take a young boy to trade for horses, guns, or money? Will pondered. Buffalo Hump would be crazy to go to San Antonio, where Indians attempted a hostage exchange last March. The Consul House fight ended in the massacre of many Indians. After the murder of Judge Smith and the abduction of Fayette, any Indian seen around Austin would be shot on sight. They wouldn't go east to Nacogdoches or St. Augustine because there were too many Rangers there protecting the white settlers.

"Santa Fe! They're going to Santa Fe," Will exclaimed, startling his horse and burro. "It's the only place they can sell or barter a white child."

Fayette's Journey
January 26, 1841

After three days underground, the tribe ventured out into the sunshine. It took a while for their eyes to adjust to daylight. Fayette was relieved, knowing he would never be found in the cave. Besides, he didn't like the putrid smell of bat guano or the thought of sharing the cave with a cougar.

The Indians were far from the Colorado River, now moving north at a good pace. The land was easier to travel than the rocky hills behind them. Four horses dragged their loaded travois along a muddy trail.

The Indians appeared to be in a hurry, traveling daylight to dark. Little Doe told Fayette there was a big Pow Wow of Indian chiefs at some springs northwest of their present location.

"How far to these big springs?" Fayette asked Little Doe.

"Ten, maybe twelve days time," Little Doe smiled.

Chapter Four

February 5, 1841

Will camped near a running creek inside Indian country. Fearful of attracting attention, he would not light a fire tonight. He ate the last of his jerky and a very stale biscuit. The animals were tied to low oak limbs, allowing them to graze on the thawed grass. He spread his bedroll on a large flat rock above a spring-fed creek with a fallen oak as his only shelter from the wind. Still in his clothes and boots, Will lay back for his first rest in days. Using his saddle for a pillow, he slept with his revolver resting on his chest.

Will woke to a gunshot, then another. Shots that close together, were either fired from separate guns or a repeating revolver. Only Texas Rangers had the new Colt guns. Will opened his eyes and saw the sun was already up. He'd fallen asleep before sunset and was upset that he'd slept so long. He grabbed his saddle and hurried to his nervous horse.

"Easy George. I know someone is out there. We're going to find out who it is and then make a run for it if we have to."

Riders were coming, following his tracks. *No time to run now.* His loaded guns held six shots between the two weapons. With no room for error, Will moved to higher ground for a better shot. The first rider was a white man with five Indians following him. The last two led tethered horses. *Are they with the white man or chasing him?* Will wondered. As they came into rifle range, the horses suddenly stopped. The white man waved a white flag. The Indians behind him were in no position to attack. They slowly moved closer. He released the hammer of the rifle.

"Willie, is that you?" a voice called. "William Smith, if you can hear me, this is Captain Jack Hays of the Texas Rangers."

"Come on in, Captain Jack," Will hollered.

The burro started whinnying, a bit late. Had it been Comanche warriors, Will would have been scalped by now. Will looked wearily at the Indians, then at the Ranger.

"Don't worry. These Tonkawa Indians work for me," Captain Hays climbed off his horse.

"How did you know, Captain, that it was me camped here?"

"Not a hell of a lot of white men camping out in these parts," Captain Hays said.

"That's for sure," Will shook his head.

The Indians tied the horses. A whitetail doe lay across the back of one horse. Will realized the deer was what the shooting was about. Captain Jack introduced them by their Indian names.

"You're not going to remember. No one does." He pointed to each, "Tell Willie your Ranger name."

"Mathew," the largest Indian said.

"Mark," the shortest Indian said.

"Luke," who wore an English derby said.

"Paul." He wore a long white feather.

"Thomas." He wore a beaver top hat said.

"You, I can remember. Thomas is the name of my brother, father, and grandfather." Will noticed the bullet hole in his top hat.

Captain Hays spoke to the Indians in Tonkawa, telling them to butcher the deer and start a fire. The Tonkawa Indians also spoke English and some Spanish. Hays, as a young Ranger, had gained their trust by learning their language and customs. It was obvious they respected him.

"What brings you here?" Will asked. He placed his rifle on his unmade bedroll.

"Looking for you, Willie," Captain Jack smiled.

"Has Fayette been found?" Will turned.

"Not since we left Austin, two days ago." Captain Jack shook his head. "I am sorry about James. He was a good friend of mine."

"Thank you, Captain Jack." Will studied the man for a moment, "But I know you didn't trail me two days just to offer condolences. Why are you here?"

"Willie, I've come to escort you back to Austin."

"Oh—" Will raised his eyebrows.

Captain Jack pointed toward the fallen oak. "Let's sit," Captain Jack patted Will on the back and said something to the Indians. "Paul will have coffee brewing shortly."

"You think it's safe to start a fire?" Will looked toward the trail.

"No…but, I'm going to have my coffee, Willie."

"You're the only person that calls me Willie."

"It just comes natural to me. William or Will seems so formal," Captain Jack shook his head, "We're too good of friends to be formal. Aren't we?"

"You haven't changed a bit. Still got to have your coffee in the morning." Will sat down on the tree trunk.

Captain Jack sat on the other end of the downed tree, "Coffee is my middle name. You know that."

"Really? I thought Coffee was a nickname because you drink so much of it."

Paul gave them each a rusty tin cup. Thomas brought the large pot and poured each a steaming cup.

"My father named me John Coffee Hays, for his best friend Colonel John Coffee. They fought together in the Creek Indian Wars with your father and my Uncle Andrew Jackson." Captain Jack lifted his cup and said, "Here's to coffee and the men that drink it."

Will turned serious, "Captain, I can't go back to Austin with you."

"I wasn't asking you, Willie. I have orders from the Secretary of War to return you to Austin."

"Dammit, don't call me Willie!"

"Sorry, Will…but I have to take you home."

"I promised Angelina and Mother I would find Fayette and that's what I intend to do!" Will gave Captain Jack a hard stare.

Captain Jack slapped his knee with his left hand, "How in the hell do you plan to find Fayette wondering around Indian Territory alone? Do you even know where you are? Where you're headed?"

"I'm heading west," Will said.

"Where abouts? West?" Captain Jack asked.

"Santa Fe!"

"Santa Fe?" Captain Jack stroked his chin.

Thomas poured them another cup. Paul was cooking bacon and fresh eggs. The smell of it cooking turned Will's attention away from the conversation.

Seven hungry men ate in silence. The only sounds were the crackling of the campfire, an occasional umm, and a compliment to Paul the cook. After the meal, the conversation continued.

"Willie, why do you think the Indians will take Fayette to Santa Fe?" Captain Jack stood and stretched.

Will poured coffee. "If Buffalo Hump's tribe were going to kill Fayette, they would have done it when they killed his Pa."

"I agree with you, but what's Santa Fe got to do with Fayette's capture?" Captain Jack raised his bushy eyebrows.

"Think about it, Captain. Where else could a white boy be bartered or sold?" Will put the coffee pot back on the embers.

"I never thought of that. Those raids on Linville, Victoria last summer and now Judge Smith's murder got the settlers gunning for any Indian they see. One settler near Kenney's Fort took a shot at Thomas," Captain Jack motioned for Thomas to show the bullet hole in his hat.

Thomas, happy to oblige, stuck his index finger through the hole from the inside and wiggled it for Will to see.

"That was close, Thomas!"

Captain Jack said, "Yes it was. I told the settler that Thomas was a good Indian and a scout for the Rangers. He said he didn't care. The only good Indian was a dead one. I had to pull my gun to keep the bastard from shooting at him again. That's the reason I keep the disciples close to me. They know I won't let anyone harm them. "

"Ranging as far as you go, it's good that you have them with you," Will looked at Paul.

"Will, tell me about this idea that your nephew is in Santa Fe?"

"I can't explain it. I just…I have this gut feeling the Comanches will take Fayette to Santa Fe."

"Even if you find them, how do you intend to take Fayette away from at least twenty Comanches by yourself?" Captain Jack stuck his chin out.

"I'll give them whatever they want—money, guns, my horse. Whatever it takes." Will looked toward the rising sun, concerned that good daylight was wasting.

"You know I can't condone paying ransom to the Indians."

"I don't know what else to do," Will looked at Captain Jack.

"You've thought it through. I think you're right—Fayette's valuable to the Indians. They know his family will pay good money for his release." Captain Jack looked approvingly at Will.

"Then you will help me get to Santa Fe?"

"I can't. Secretary of War, Hockley, has ordered Texas Rangers not to cross the Rio Concho. It's part of trying to appease the Comanche." Captain Jack's face showed his distaste of the order, "It's not going to work; we can't keep the white settlers out." Captain Jack shook his head, "No way in hell to stop them now. Wagons are loading up all across the East, putting up signs: 'Gone to Texas.' Farmers are leaving their crops in the fields to come to Texas."

"If you stop me, my mother will never see her grandson again," Will clenched his jaw.

"I spoke to Angelina and Rebeckah. Your family is concerned for your safety."

"How are they?"

Captain Jack reached in his saddlebag and pulled out a handful of mail. "Your family and friends wrote you. While you read their letters, I'll talk to the disciples about roasting us some venison."

The letters begged Will not to go after Fayette alone. They urged Will to come home with Captain Jack and muster up some volunteers to go with him after the Indians. His brothers and brother-in-law were anxious to join in the effort. His mother wrote, "We pray Captain Jack finds you alive and well, and we will hold you in our loving arms soon."

The letters from his family put a lump in his throat. He appreciated their concern for his safety, but it would not change his mind. He was going to Santa Fe to find Fayette.

Captain Jack came up behind him, "It must be nice to have a large family like yours."

"Yes, but sometimes their concern complicates matters." Will stifled a tear.

"Not having any family other than Uncle Andrew and Aunt Rachel, I wouldn't know." Captain Jack looked away and sighed a heavy breath. "You have a good one, and they expect me to bring you home." He looked at Will for an answer.

"I can't go back without Fayette," Will shook his head.

"I understand how you feel, but I've been ordered to escort you back to Austin. I would prefer not to have to arrest you," Captain Jack warned Will with a cold stare.

"You would go that far?" Will looked surprised.

"You've been a Ranger. You know the law—we don't make the laws we just enforce them!"

"Just suppose you hadn't found me this morning," Will suggested.

"What do you mean? I did find you."

"You, I, and the disciples are the only ones that know that! Bad as things are with the Comanche, none of us may ever make it back to Austin!"

Captain Jack looked queerly at Will, then at his Indian guides. He stood up straight with his hand resting on the handle of his revolver. For a moment, Will thought he was going to be shot.

"Let me think about... what you just said." Captain Jack sauntered off.

Will scratched his head, thinking, *What the hell is there to think about? Daylight's burning. Buffalo Hump is already days ahead of us.*

Will unsaddled George and fed him and the burro a mixture of mesquite beans and corn. He tried to keep a wary eye on Captain Jack who was sitting with his back against a large sycamore tree. Will saw only his legs and boots, but he heard the Ranger talking to himself. This strange behavior concerned Will.

Hays came from Tennessee—a nephew by marriage of Andrew Jackson, who had a big influence on his character. Captain Jack had coal-black hair that matched his thick beard and moustache. Years of outdoor living made the lawman look much older than his mid-twenties.

Will started harvesting mesquite beans for the next leg of his trip, wondering which way he would be heading. Would his friend arrest him or take him to Santa Fe? Either way, Will was preparing for a long trip.

Captain Jack summoned his disciples. They sat Indian style in a circle on the ground and had a long discussion in Tonkawa. William thought the Captain looked much like the picture of Jesus in his family Bible. Disciple was a good name for his Indian guides.

Will watched the lively discussion. The Indians nodded in agreement with the captain and sometimes shook their head in opposition. It was obvious that they all respected each other's opinion.

Captain Jack and the disciples rose, obviously having reached an agreement. Paul, the Indian who wore one feather, said something in Tonkawa that made the Ranger smile. Captain Jack was still thinking about Paul's parable as he approached Will. Captain Jack looked like he was in an agreeable mood.

"Captain Jack, what did Paul say that made you smile?

"Paul said the life of a warrior is simple, for all the warrior has to do is follow the orders of his chief." Captain Jack poured another cup of coffee and then raised the well-used tin pot and offered it to Will. "No thanks. I still have a little," Will said.

"Paul never ceases to amaze me with his understanding of mankind. He is one of the smartest men I've ever known." Captain Jack set down his coffee cup. "Paul also said, 'life of the chief is not easy, for the lives of the warriors are in his hands.'"

Will nodded in agreement and looked up at Captain Jack. "I'm curious about something," he said. "I overheard you talking to yourself. If you don't mind me asking, who were you talking to?"

"Something else I learned from Paul," Captain Jack looked toward Paul and then back at Will. "I was talking to my father, the late Harmon Hays. He died when I was just a boy. When I have doubts or questions about things, I seek my father's guidance."

"And he advises you?" Will asked.

Captain Jack sat on the fallen tree. "No, but my asking him questions somehow helps me to make better decisions."

"Then you've made a decision about—"

Captain Jack interrupted, "Yes, I have. Willie, there is no way I can take you."

"I was afraid of that." Will stood, his face flushed. He pitched the cold coffee grinds from his cup on the ground and turned to walk away.

Captain Jack said, "Before you get all lathered up, hear me out. This was a big decision for me. I could get my ass in a lot of trouble for helping you." He pointed towards his Indian scouts, "Thomas and Mathew are going to take you. They know every nook and cranny from here to Santa Fe. The War Department has forbidden any offensive military incursions into Indian Territories. The disciples are not on the payroll," he paused, "If you understand what I mean."

"Spies?" Will asked.

"Disciples," Captain Jack winked.

Will turned toward Captain Jack, the anger gone from his face. "I don't know how to thank you, Captain. When can we leave?"

"In the morning."

"Morning! Why wait? Buffalo Hump has at least two days on us already!" Will rolled his eyes.

"You're going to need grub for at least two weeks. The disciples are making biscuits and dried jerky from what venison we don't eat tonight."

Will plopped down on the fallen oak. "Jerky won't be dry by morning."

"I know you want to head out now," Captain Jack poured himself another cup, "but I can't send you or my men off half-cocked." He sat down on the tree trunk.

"How far is Santa Fe, Captain?"

"Thomas and Mathew say thirty to forty days. Pretty much depends on the weather this time of year." Captain Hays took another swig of coffee. "Damn this coffee gets good at the bottom of the pot."

Will nodded.

They sat watching the flickering fire, each in their own thoughts. The disciples were busy dividing up the supplies. Mathew and Thomas would take the packhorses and all the Ranger's provisions, leaving the others three days of rations to get to San Antonio. Captain Hays would avoid going to Austin for a while, not wanting to be asked whether he found Will Smith or not.

The political wheels of the Republic of Texas were falling off in Austin: President Lamar had bankrupted the new government; the slavery issue had nixed any possibility of annexation by the United States; peace treaties with the Indians were broken, provoking Indian raids and Mexico planned more invasions.

Lamar proposed a trade expedition to Santa Fe. It failed to receive any support from Congress. The President, under the illusion that the citizens of Nuevo México were chomping at the bit to become a part of Texas, planned to send a three-hundred-man expedition to Santa Fe. It would be his final act as President.

Chapter Five

Will ate like it was his last meal, and it very well could be. They shared pinto beans, cornbread, and venison. If they died, it would be on a full stomach. Will learned from the Tonkawa that had he traveled west another five miles, he would have come upon what the Indians called: "Spirit Song Rock." It was a mound of pink granite that reached four hundred sixty feet high with a base a mile wide. Getting around it was Captain Jack's biggest concern. Indians were always near the mountain, for they considered the rock formation to be sacred ground. The mountain sometimes groaned, scaring any that dared to climb it.

"I have something for you." Captain Jack pulled a Colt Paterson revolver out of his knapsack. It was Ranger issued like the pair Captain Jack wore. "This was your brother James' gun and holster." He handed it gently to Will. "Angelina wanted you to have it and all his ammunition."

Will admired the shiny new gun and holster. "Now I have a matching pair," he said, strapping it on.

"I hope you never need two guns. If you do, your fire power's been doubled," Captain Jack smiled.

"The belt fits," Will beamed.

Captain Jack handed him a sack of silver coins from his father. Will pulled the string of the money sack and opened it. "Must be a hundred dollars or more in here! Where did he get so much silver?"

"The town took up a collection. Indians like silver. It's the best thing to barter with," Captain Jack sat down.

"Would you thank everyone for me?" Will asked.

Captain Jack nodded. "When I see them. Hopefully, you'll get back to Austin before me. I'm not going to Austin without you."

"Why did you bring the silver and my brothers' gun if you were going to take me in?"

"I packed them before I was given orders to bring you in." Captain Jack stood and put a strong hand on Will's shoulder, "Sometimes… things just happen for the best or the worst. Only Father Time will tell us which."

Will didn't answer, mesmerized by the Captain's words.

Captain Jack stretched. "I'm tired. Bedding down now, see you in the morning. You can rest well; one of the disciples will be on watch all night."

"Thank you, Captain."

Captain Jack nodded and walked away.

Fayette's captors made camp on Sulfur Creek on the fourth day of February. Warm springs flowed from the creek's bottom, which produced steam and a foul smell like leather tanning solution. Indians believed the warm waters had healing powers. The tribesmen waded into the shallow water. Buffalo Hump found a strong flowing spring and sat on it. His craggy face showed pleasure. The others looked for their own underwater spring to sit on.

They encouraged Fayette to join them as the women went about their chores. He reluctantly handed Little Doe his drop front trousers. He couldn't understand how spring water could be so warm. Once his shoulders were underwater, he enjoyed the spring; it reminded him of Saturday night baths. When Fayette climbed out, he was clean for the first time in weeks, but crying.

"What's wrong, Big Fish?" Little Doe wrapped a blanket around him. "Don't call me Big Fish." Fayette stormed off to their teepee. He laid on his buffalo robe and had a good cry. Little Doe's efforts to console him failed. At that moment, all he wanted was to be with his family.

The next morning, they were moving northwest when Fayette saw a small log cabin. This was the first sign of white settlers since his capture. Smoke billowed from the cabin's stone chimney. The owners were not home when the braves ransacked the house. They found no livestock in the barn but took the bedding and supplies of sugar, salt, cornmeal, and coffee.

Encouraged by signs of settlers, Fayette hoped they would come to his aid. He kept a watchful eye on the thick brush along the ravines that ran through the flatlands. Little Doe led the pony with their belongings.

Fayette saw movement in a thicket, and his heart began to race. He asked Little Doe if he could go into the woods to urinate. She allowed him to go. He went to where he saw the movement.

He heard a "psst" and went toward the sound. He heard it again. It was no animal, but a white man about his father's age, dressed like a farmer.

"Where you from, boy?" The man whispered.

"Austin…the Indians took me on the twenty-first day of January… my ninth birthday."

"What's your name? You got family?"

"I'm Fayette Smith…these Indians killed my father, James Smith. Who are you?"

"Homer Mathews. That was my home you passed a way back. Fayette, go now. Get back to the tribe. I will try to get help to you and your momma soon as I can." The farmer turned and ran.

"She's not my momma!" Fayette hollered.

41

Fayette turned and saw Little Doe watching the farmer run away. She screamed for help as the settler ran toward the thicket. Fayette instinctively chased after him in hopes of escaping. Two Indians on horseback chased them; a well-placed arrow in the back of the settler ended Fayette's hope of escape.

The Comanche found the farmer's horse tied to a low branch of a mesquite tree. Now the Indians had nine horses and another rifle.

They danced around the settler's body, chanting war whoops before mutilating him. Two Braves grabbed Fayette and lifted him up on their shoulders. They chanted Big Fish brave as they carried him around on their shoulders. Fayette was afraid until he realized they thought he was pursuing the settler instead of following him. Fayette was concerned his actions caused Homer Mathews' death, which troubled him.

"Wake up." Captain Jack shook Will's shoulder and said, "We got to move now, while we have darkness on our side."

"What time is it?" Will asked.

"Don't know. It's too dark to see my pocket watch. I hope it's no later than five. I know that's it's time we get to moving." Captain Jack shook Will harder, "Get up. I'll give you details later."

Paul had been on watch and spotted Indians camped southeast of the granite mountain. Captain Jack explained that the Indians most likely had scouts on the mountain and would be able to see them come daybreak.

Captain Jack whispered, "We've got to get west of the mountain before sunrise. We can do it if we hurry."

The disciples had the horses saddled and waiting. Will was about to mount George but saw Mathew shake his head and make the universal walk sign with his fingers. They moved out behind Paul, each leading their beasts of burden. There wasn't a moon, which was good for hiding, although troublesome for walking through rough terrain.

They moved quietly onto an outcropping of granite; each step on a loose rock made noise that threatened to echo through the canyon.

Paul got close enough to count thirty Comanche Indians, but it wasn't Buffalo Hump's tribe. This band had no captives or horses of the white man.

They were within three miles of the Comanche camp. Gray smoke snaked up into the dark sky. They turned north on the east side of the mountain base. The sun appeared over the horizon. The altostratus clouds added a purple hue to the western sky. The shadow of the mountain would keep the Comanche in the dark, for a while.

"Will, do you see that dry creek bed about a mile ahead of us?" Captain Jack pointed.

"I see it."

"I don't think we've been spotted. You, Mathew, and Thomas mount up once I get my men hidden down in the creek bed. You start moving slowly. If you hear gunfire, you'll know it's us trying to stop the Comanche, get going as fast as you can go. Mathew and Thomas will lead you over that hill; try to make it across the Llano River before dark."

"Which way you headed?" Will asked.

"When I see you disappear over that last hill," Captain Jack pointed, "we're going to follow this dry creek bed around the west side of the mountain, then head south to San Antonio."

"Thank you, Captain." Will turned his horse to follow the guides.

"Good luck Willie."

On the fifteenth day of February, Buffalo Hump cantered his stolen steed to a high vista overlooking the shallow canyon. An encampment of hundreds of Indians, tribal leaders from all the Southwest nations, were at the waterhole they called Big Springs. They anxiously awaited Buffalo Hump's arrival. He'd left the tribal council last year with over a hundred warriors on horseback. Now Chief Buffalo Hump returned with twenty.

Buffalo Hump's warriors stood beside him—their faces smeared with war paint. They wore feathered headgear and held tribal spears; short bows and quivers were on their backs. The foot warriors stood erect in their war bonnets, proud to follow their leader. The Indian women and Fayette cautiously approached the overlook and looked down on the encampment below.

Nomadic Indians had used the springs for hundreds of years. This was the last watering hole on the Llano Escondido until Yellow House Canyon. From a distance, hundreds of teepees looked like cornstalks neatly stacked in a farmers' field to dry. Now Fayette could understand what all the primping was about. This was a big event!

They began the descent into the canyon where hundreds of horses grazed. Women and children scurried about in the excitement of their arrival. The men chanted and beat drums. Buffalo Hump stopped by a stand of trees. He dismounted and gave final orders to his tribe, advising his tribal members how to make their grand entrance. Buffalo Hump put them in order of importance; Fayette and Little Doe were last in line.

When the small band of Comanche advanced to within a hundred yards of the camp, Buffalo Hump raised his hand—the order for everyone to stop. Night Owl rode out in front, raised a buffalo horn, and blew it for attention. The Indians in camp responded by forming two lines that led into the camp. Buffalo Hump's tribe entered between the lines. Children pushed forward to see the famous Indian Chief. Once they saw the white boy with flaming red hair, their attention turned to Fayette. They stared at him, pointing and gesturing. He tried to ignore them.

The chiefs sat in a circle on grass mats and shared a long pipe. It was Indian custom to smoke the pipe of peace before business was discussed. Each chief wore his ceremonial war bonnet and enemy scalps tied to his waistband—except for one. Old Wolf was not a warring Indian. He should have been named Old Fox. He looked like an Indian but thought like a white man. Old Wolf had a lot of experience dealing with the Comancheros and most of the tribes of the West. It was the Bent Brothers, Charles and William, owners of Bent's Fort that taught Old Wolf the white man's ways. He couldn't read or write, but he knew the value of gold, silver, buffalo hides, and horses. Too old to hunt buffalo or round up wild mustangs, he found it more profitable and enjoyable to sell and trade commodities.

The Indian children were curious but wanted nothing to do with the redheaded boy. Fayette sat near the teepee he shared with Night Owl and Little Doe. He whittled on a stick with his jackknife and shared stories with Little Doe. From his position, he saw all the activities going on around him: boys playing with a ball and girls playing tag with one another. The Indian village seemed to have more activity than Austin.

The difference, Fayette realized, was Indians placed their teepees within a few feet of each other. The settlers in Austin had large lots for each cabin; some had fences while others only had stakes in the ground, designating their space on Earth. Indians shared their space with their tribesmen; there was no ownership of the land beneath them. This was the great divide between the two cultures—Indians couldn't fathom the concept of land ownership by an individual.

Fayette saw Preacher wandering away from camp. The horse didn't like to be hobbled. It learned to slide the rawhide hobbles off his pasterns and then stepped out of them. Fayette didn't say anything. He hoped the stallion could somehow make it back to Austin.

Night Owl and Big Bear eventually saw the untethered stallion drifting from camp. The brothers tried unsuccessfully to get a rope around the horse's neck. Preacher reared up in defiance; he wasn't through grazing and didn't want a rope on him. Their attempts only exasperated the strong-willed stallion. While everyone watched the stallion going mad, Fayette crawled into the teepee and found a canvas bag of sugar. He put two hands of it in his pocket and hurried out to get Preacher under control.

The Indians had guns raised to fire. Fayette made eye contact with Preacher. Its eyes had turned blood red, nostrils flaring.

Big Bear raised his rifle to fire saying, "Horse…crazy!"

"No, don't kill him!" Fayette screamed.

Fayette approached the stallion and motioned to the children who had gathered to get back. He walked up, whistling the tune his father had taught him. Preacher twitched his ears, shook his long mane, and cantered toward Fayette. Preacher was rewarded with a taste of sugar from Fayette's hand. The Indians couldn't believe such a small boy was able to control a wild stallion so well. Fayette lovingly rubbed Preacher's neck and nose and then compensated him with more sugar. Night Owl came near with a rawhide rope.

"No, rope… Preacher doesn't need a rope right now." Fayette put a hand up for Night Owl to back away.

Night Owl reluctantly backed away.

Fayette walked toward a cluster of teepees and Preacher obediently followed. The Indians made way for them.

Chief Old Wolf enjoyed watching Fayette handle the stallion. He liked Preacher's composition: a big strong horse from good breeding, unlike the scrawny wild mustangs of the desert.

The tribe of Old Wolf lived peacefully with the Mexicans and Americans around Bent's Fort. Never involved in hostilities, they wished to be trading partners with all.

Old Wolf had no desire to fight Buffalo Hump's war against the Texans. The chief attended the Pow Wow to listen and profit. He knew the Indian Wars in South Texas took its toll on the tribes. They needed horses and guns. Old Wolf had enough to outfit every Brave at the Pow Wow.

Old Wolf needed a stallion to improve his herd of wild mustangs. He assumed Fayette belonged to the white squaw and offered Buffalo Hump six horses for Little Doe, Fayette, and the chestnut stallion. Buffalo Hump explained that he'd raised Little Doe to be his youngest son's wife. Old Wolf understood Little Doe was family. He traded six horses for the stallion and Fayette. When Little Doe discovered that Buffalo Hump had traded Fayette to Old Wolf for horses, she stormed into his teepee. Little Doe berated the chief during a tribal conference in front of his peers. This was such an extreme embarrassment that Buffalo Hump told her in Comanche that if she didn't leave, she would be sold, too.

Little Doe high-tailed it out of the Tribal Council Meeting angrier than she came in. She found Night Owl telling stories behind a windbreak of salt cedars on the opposite side of the waterhole. When she approached, the young braves that Night Owl was entertaining knew her wrath and made a beeline for their teepees. Night Owl had never seen Little Doe so angry. Fayette heard her screaming at Night Owl from across the waterhole. He realized the argument had something to do with him. Curious, he ran to the windbreak and quietly worked his way into the center of the thicket. Fayette squatted under the thick cover of cedar and tried to figure out what the ruckus was about. Little Doe always came to Fayette when he cried; she had become his surrogate mother since his capture. Once Night Owl left, the boy went to Little Doe, and she opened her arms to him.

Little Doe held Fayette tight and shared her feelings of how much she had wanted a son, and that he reminded her of the little brother who was killed the day she was captured.

Fayette said, "I thought you were—"

She put a finger over her lips. Fayette now knew that the Comanche had captured her too.

"We must not talk…of that." Little Doe looked at Fayette, "You promise?"

Fayette nodded his head. He had so many questions to ask. *Where was she from? Why didn't she and Night Owl have children?*

They looked up and saw Night Owl standing only ten feet in front of the big rock where Little Doe sat. Night Owl looked sad but said nothing. He shook his head, turned, and walked away.

Little Doe screamed "No!" She rocked and wailed.

Fayette tried to comfort Little Doe as she had comforted him. He didn't understand why Night Owl hadn't tried to console Little Doe.

The Pow Wow over, teepees down, the Tribal Council adjourned. Days of heated discussion about the white man's encroachment on Indian lands reached no consensus. Buffalo Hump wanted war. Old Wolf didn't and convinced a majority of the chiefs that a large army of Mexicans would soon overtake the Texans. He suggested waiting and letting the Mexican army fight their battles. If Mexico defeated the Texans, Mexican treaties would be restored. Besides, even if the Texans beat the Mexicans back again, their might would be greatly diminished, and then the Indians could easily conquer the Texans.

Old Wolf's opposition infuriated Buffalo Hump. He wanted revenge for his losses and to drive the white settlers out of Comancheria. Buffalo Hump vowed to fight alone if need be. Suffering buyer's remorse for trading the stallion and Fayette for six ponies, Buffalo Hump asked to keep the boy. Old Wolf needed Fayette to be the stallion's handler and denied his request. The trade created a schism in Buffalo Hump's family. Night Owl and Little Doe were mad at Buffalo Hump for trading the boy; the childless couple had taken Fayette into their teepee as well as their hearts.

The Indian guides led Will over the last rise. Now only the tip of the granite mountain was visible. As they stopped to look back, they heard rapid gunfire. The shots came faster than Will could count.

"Should we go back and help the Captain?" Will asked, looking first at Thomas then Mathew.

The firing started again. The horses, recognizing the sound of battle, nickered and stomped their hooves. Mathew put up a hand for silence and listened intently to the firing: ten more rapid fired rounds and then silence. Mathew spurred his horse and motioned for Will to follow. Thomas stayed concealed behind a Huisache tree, watching and waiting should the Comanche advance toward them.

Will rode up to Mathew and asked, "Don't you think we should check on Captain Jack?"

Mathew shook his head. "Captain…good."

"How do you know?"

Mathew didn't answer. He motioned for Will to follow and moved his horse into a faster gait. Now off the granite formation, soft soil allowed the horses to run. They found a shallow ford to cross at the Llano.

While waiting for Thomas, Will asked, "Mathew, how did you know it was the captain's gun we heard?"

"I know sound of Captain's gun. He only man that can shoot that fast." Mathew looked up. "Here come Thomas. We cross river now."

Will and his guides crossed the Llano River and made camp in a thick grove of pecan trees. The winter grass, lush from the moisture of the recent snow, provided the best grazing the horses had since leaving Austin.

At daybreak, on the fifteenth day of February the Tonkawa guides led Will west, staying south of the Rio Concho to avoid Indian Territory. The vast uninhabited country became arid; trees were scarce as the land became flat. Their movement could be seen for miles. Mathew kept them in low places when he could. Thomas followed, always on the alert. They entered the land of the Apache, who hated white people as much as the Comanche. Thomas served as the hunter, bringing in rabbit, prairie chickens, and deer for Mathew to cook. Food was plentiful, but water was scarce. They continued west to the Pecos River where the river snaked north to its headwaters in the Mora Valley, twenty miles east of Santa Fe.

Traversing the Pecos on the third day, they spotted Mescalero Apache Indians above the Canyon. They followed above the rim for two days, watching and waiting. Mathew and Thomas knew they were there but showed little concern. Will tried to do the same. When they stopped to make camp, the Apache made camp above them. They beat their drums and chanted, which was the Apache way of intimidating their enemy.

The next morning, the canyon trail came closer to the top of the rim. The Apache were now only fifty feet above them. At mid-morning, the Apache took a position in a curve of the canyon trail. The leader held up his hand in a gesture for Will and his guides to stop.

"What do they want?" Will asked.

"All we have. But we only give them what is fair…for crossing their land," Mathew said.

"What do you think is fair, Mathew?"

"It depends. We must wait. Apache will tell us what they think is fair."

Mathew stopped his horse, pulled a white rag out of his haversack, and held it high. The three Apache horsemen disappeared from the rim above as two could be seen approaching from their rear. Will grew tense; Mathew and Thomas seemed unconcerned, like being surrounded by Apache was an everyday experience.

"They come to trade. You have silver; count one piece for each Apache," Mathew said.

Will had six cinco pesos in his pocket. They only saw five Indians; the three from the rim had found an easy trail down. The other two following Thomas closed in. Now they were boxed in by water, canyon walls, and five Indians. Thomas dismounted and asked Will for the coins.

"Six cinco pesos…an extra for good luck." Will, handed the coins to Thomas.

"Never let Apache see your fear," Mathew whispered.

Thomas and Will waited as Mathew and the Apache negotiated passage. Mathew handed the silver coins to the leader, who looked approvingly at them. The Apache would provide protection through Apache Canyon just southeast of Santa Fe—for thirty pesos.

Chapter Six

By March 1841, Austin's population had dwindled to just under a hundred people. Those that remained still grieved for Judge Smith and prayed for the safe return of Fayette. Family and friends feared Indians had captured Will. Fayette's mother and grandmother held firm to their Christian faith, confident that God would answer their prayers. Every traveler brave enough to pass through Austin was approached and begged to be on the lookout for their sons. Travis County Commissioners appointed family friend Joseph Lee to the unexpired term of Judge Smith. The Austin Lyceum, an organization of local professional men, had surrendered its charter to make their assets available to assist Judge Smith's widow in finding Fayette.

President Lamar took a leave of absence for health reasons, which delayed the Santa Fe Expedition. The trade expedition was well advertised and reported in America's expansionists newspapers. Some reported it was larger than the Lewis and Clark Expedition a quarter of a century earlier. When news of the expedition reached Territorial Governor Armijo he considered it a well-planned invasion of his territory under the guise of a trade mission.

Fifty merchants signed on, anxious to sell their wares in Santa Fe, unaware of the hostilities awaiting them. The expedition leaders carried a list of Texans abducted by Indians. Fayette was on the list.

Many of Austin's original settlers headed back east, fearing more Indian depredations and attacks from the Mexican army. They left their dreams on the banks of the Colorado. With no purpose other than a center of government, the future of Austin was bleak. The hardy souls that stayed were determined that Austin would remain the center of government for the Republic of Texas.

Little Doe made deerskin britches and moccasins for Fayette. By March, Fayette's clothes, relics of his past, were threadbare. Discarding the clothes his mother had made was difficult, as was saying goodbye to Little Doe. She saved him from freezing and nursed him back to health. It was obvious she loved him. Fayette would miss her.

Little Doe put a hand on Fayette's shoulder, "You must obey Old Wolf. He is mean. If angry—he will kill you! His wives are also mean." She knelt and whispered, "If you want to get back to your people, wait until you get to Old Wolf's camp. There is a trail to a place called Independence. When you see many wagons, run to them. Your people will help you," She hugged Fayette.

Fayette looked at Little Doe. "Can't you and Night Owl come with me?"

Little Doe glanced at Night Owl, and then looked at Fayette. "We are with our people. You belong to Old Wolf." She pointed toward his caravan, "Go now, he is waiting."

Fayette slowly walked toward Chief Old Wolf proudly sitting astride his father's horse. The old chief hollered something to one of his five wives. She ran up to the boy, pushing him along faster. Fayette resisted and was swiftly kicked in the seat of the pants. He looked toward Little Doe for help, but she was gone.

On the third day of March, Will, Thomas, and Mathew followed their guides into the narrow walls of Apache Canyon. In the distance, smoke rose from chimeneas of Santa Fe. The Apache leader and a brave turned to block the trail that led out of the canyon. They demanded six more pieces of silver for passage.

Thomas said, "We pay no more!"

The leader drew his tomahawk; the tribesmen went for their short bows. Will drew one of his revolvers and fired five well-placed shots. The leader and one brave died along with their ponies. The braves in the rear scattered for the cover of the jagged rocks of the canyon walls. Thomas dismounted and quickly retrieved the coins from the leader's deerskin pouch.

Thomas said something to Mathew in Tonkawa; they both laughed.

"Thomas, what did you say?" Will asked.

"You shoot like Captain Jack!" Thomas smiled, revealing only two front teeth.

Thomas held out the coins to Will. Will shook his head and said, "You earned them. You keep them."

Thomas accepted them graciously and said, "We go now…Apache come soon with many warriors!"

Now out of the canyon and into the open desert floor, Will felt safe knowing anyone approaching could be seen for miles. On the outskirts of Santa Fe, he said goodbye to his guides. Their job done, Thomas and Mathew would rendezvous with Captain Hays and the other disciples at Ranger Headquarters in San Antonio. Thomas reminded Will that no one was to know who took him to Santa Fe.

Will rode into the dusty town that appeared larger than San Antonio. It was laid out like San Antonio with a river running through it. The buildings were made of adobe rather than limestone. It was sundown. The church bell tolled. Well-dressed families scurried toward church for Mass, glancing at him suspiciously. Governor Manuel Armijo had warned the citizens of Santa Fe of a pending Texas invasion. The two Colt Paterson revolvers Will wore confirmed their suspicions.

An old woman with a black cross smeared on the center of her forehead shook her fist at Will and called him names. She spoke a language he didn't understand, but he knew she wasn't glad to see him.

Will tied his horse and burro to a cedar hitching post with a water trough. Dirty and dusty from many days of travel, Will entered the open lobby of the only inn on the square.

The man behind the desk had a black cross on the center of his forehead, too. He smiled and said, "Buenas Noche...Señor."

"Do you have a room?" Will asked.

"How...many rooms?" the middle-aged man with salt and pepper hair asked.

"It's just me," Will said.

"I have a small room. It is comfortable for one person," The innkeeper grabbed a key.

"I have a horse and a burro."

"Ramon, the stable boy, is my son. He is at church serving as an altar boy. If you will feed your horse and burro and put them in the corral tonight, Ramon will take care of them in the morning. My name is Miguel Miranda, I am the proprietor of La Posada. What did you say your name was, Señor?"

"Will Smith."

The innkeeper gave Will a suspicious look. "Please sign our register, Mr. Smith. Where did you say you're from?" The innkeeper looked nervously at Will's guns.

"I didn't say, but I'm from Austin."

"The Capitol of Texas! You have come a long way. What brings you to Santa Fe on the first day of Lent?"

"Ash Wednesday?" Will raised his eyebrows.

"Yes, that is why the inn is full. It is the day of ashes; the pilgrims come."

"It's the start of Lent already?" Will shook his head.

"Yes, Señor Smith, we Catholics celebrate the resurrection! You do believe in Christ?"

"Yes, I do."

"Then you must come worship with us this Sunday," Miguel handed him the key.

"I would like that—if I'm still here. Thanks for the invitation," Will looked at the large key.

Miguel nervously cleared his throat, "Do you have instructions for me Señor Smith? From Austin?" Miguel stood waiting for an answer that didn't come. "Maybe information...you carry for the compatriots of Nuevo México?" Miguel stood behind the counter; he smiled, waiting patiently for an answer.

Will asked, "Where's my room?"

Miguel pointed. "Your room is at the end of the hall, Señor Smith. We will talk again tomorrow, yes?"

"Maybe," Will said as he turned toward the open lobby.

Will hurried to get his animals tended before dark. He lugged his gear to the four-by-eight room. The only outside view was an eight-inch square opening toward the stables. The hinged hole cover was made for a gun portal rather than for the view. The cot was small but adequate, with enough space for his gear underneath. It would be Will's first night sleeping off the ground since leaving Austin.

Fayette walked every step of the way since leaving Buffalo Hump's tribe at Big Springs. His deerskin moccasins were so thin that he lined them with bits of buffalo hide cut from his robe. It was difficult for a nine-year-old to stay up with horses and grownups. The squaws beat him with sticks and threw him in a patch of prickly pear cactus for not staying up. They were furious because Old Wolf paid more for him and a horse than the chief paid for all his wives.

Fayette thought of running but was too tired to try. Old Wolf and his tribesmen didn't know of his previous attempts. The Indians wouldn't expect a young boy to attempt running away in the desert. *Would Preacher be able to find the way home?* Fayette wondered. Preacher had wandered away many times and always came home. *How would I mount such a large animal? Maybe from a tree? Would I be able to hang on without a saddle?* So many things to think about. Fayette remembered his father saying, "When you're not sure what to do, do nothing until you figure it out."

The Indians ignored Fayette's frequent questions about where they were going and how much further it was to Old Wolf's camp. He was surrounded by people with no one to talk to.

As they marched into the sun, Fayette's mind wandered. He thought back to his family and friends in Austin. He recalled with fondness the fresh-baked pies his mother made, dropping further behind. Tired, he sat down in the sand. The heat from the ground felt good to his aching body. Fayette stretched out. He couldn't go on, falling into unconsciousness on the desert floor surrounded by sagebrush and cactus.

Fayette dreamed of being picked up by an angel and swished away to Bullocks Inn where family and friends gathered around him. Mrs. Bullock fixed a smorgasbord of delicious treats. He ate his fill of pecan tarts and peach pie. He swam in Shoal Creek with cousins and ran through the tall grass on the banks of the Colorado.

A rooster crowing woke Will from a deep sleep. He heard a young boy singing in Spanish near the stables. *It must be Ramon, the innkeepers' son.* Now fully awake, he pulled on his trousers, boots, and buckled on a gun. Time to check on his horse and burro.

Will entered the covered stables and saw Ramon talking to his horse. Ramon appeared to be about fifteen. He wore a straw sombrero and baggy linen pants tied at the waist. The matching shirt had big buttons up the front. The ashen cross of Lent was still on his forehead.

"Ramon, George doesn't understand Spanish," Will said.

"Then I will teach him." Ramon rubbed the stallion's nose, "Jorge is a strange name for a horse, Señor Smith."

"I named him after George Washington, who rode a horse that looked just like him." Will stroked George's sturdy hind flanks and gave his horse the usual once-over, looking for cuts or injury from the trail. He found a loose shoe and several scratches that would quickly heal. The shoe needed replacing.

"In school, I have seen the picture of the American Presidente on his white horse. He does look like him." Ramon went about raking up the straw and horse dung.

William handed Ramon a peso, "I rode him hard; the burro too, take good care of them."

"Sí, Señor Smith. I take good care of your animals. Father says you come from Austin, Tejas."

"Yes, but we call it Texas now." Will saw a hammer and anvil on a nearby workbench, "My horse needs shod, can I use your blacksmith tools?"

"Sí, Señor Smith. The tools are for our guests to use. I will help you," Ramon leaned his rake in a corner of the split rail corral.

Ramon ignited kindling for the forge. Then he carried a bucket of water for cooling the hot metal shoes. Will removed the loose shoe.

Ramon admired Wills' revolver. "Why do you wear only one of your guns Señor Smith?"

"How would you know how many guns I have?" Will asked.

"The padre told the congregation last night that you had come. Wearing two of the guns of a Texas Ranger. We have only seen pictures of this new gun in the American papers," Ramon pointed at Will's holstered revolver.

"You want to hold it?"

"Sí, Señor Smith! May I?"

Will pulled it carefully from the holster and handed it to Ramon, "Careful now; it's loaded and there is no safety."

The boy held it as if his priest handed him the Baby Jesus from the foyer of San Miguel Church. Ramon handed the gun back to Will and said, "If you have two such guns, why do you wear only one?"

"Because, I think I am in a friendly place." He looked at Ramon, "I am in a friendly place, aren't I?" Will looked for an answer that didn't come. Ramon shrugged his shoulders, like he didn't know how to answer. Will thought, *Why would the priest mention his arrival to the congregation?* He remembered the old woman who hissed at him—the hatred in her eyes.

Will turned his attention back to shoeing his horse.

Ramon placed more logs on the fire. "Señor Smith, when will your army come?"

"It's just me, Ramon, I have no army." Will lowered the finished hoof and picked up the other rear hoof. "Why would you think I have an army?"

"The newspapers and the padre say the Texas Army is coming. That there will be bloodshed in our streets," Ramon pumped the foot bellows of the outdoor fire pit.

"I know nothing about that!" Will put down the other rear hoof and moved to George's left front hoof. He stood and looked at Ramon; the boy was obviously fearful of the Texas Army.

"It is true. The Mexican army is on the way to defend us from your army!" Ramon stopped pumping, "Everyone in Santa Fe is talking about it. Ask my father. He knows."

"I will as soon as I finish this last hoof and clean up."

When Will entered the lobby, he heard men talking excitedly, unable to keep their voices down. "He is here, Señor Dryden, as we speak. I see him with my son Ramon in the stables!"

"Miguel, you're certain he is a Texas Ranger?" Will heard someone ask.

"Si, you showed me pictures of the new pistol of the Ranger. He has two, Señor Dryden."

"This Mr. Smith didn't ask for me?"

"No, Señor Dryden. He asked for no one. That is why I sent for you last night. As you told me to do when men come from Texas."

"You did the right thing sending for me when you did."

Another voice said, "We need to talk to this Mr. Smith."

"Here I am gentlemen," Will leaned on the small registration desk. He saw the Mexican innkeeper in a back room, but not the others whose voices he overheard.

"Please join us, Señor Smith." The innkeeper was embarrassed that his guest had heard them talking about him.

Once behind the curtain, Will realized he was in the family kitchen. Miguel Miranda introduced his wife Lupe and daughter Bella. The daughter was busy with both hands patting out tortillas as her mother cooked them on an open grill. The pungent smells of roasted cabrito and fresh tortillas overwhelmed Will's senses. He nodded a feeble hello to Lupe and tried to speak to Bella but was so taken back by her beauty that he couldn't. It was obvious the Texan was as attracted to the brown-eyed Señorita as she was to him.

Miguel introduced the men as Texas Commissioners: William Dryden—a Santa Fe Lawyer, William Workman and his partner John Rowland—businessmen from Taos, a village seventy miles to the north of Santa Fe, high in the Sangre de Cristo Mountains.

"Glad to meet you, gentlemen." Will removed his hat and shook hands with each man graciously, "My name is William Smith. Everyone calls me Will. What are commissioners from Texas doing here?"

They looked at one another to see who would answer. Mr. Dryden spoke, "Same as you, I suppose?" Mr. Dryden nervously turned his felt hat with his hands.

"I am here to find my nephew, Fayette Smith. Comanche's killed his father, Judge James Smith, back in Austin and abducted him."

Will steadied himself by grasping the back of a wooden chair at the end of a long hand-carved pueblo table.

The innkeeper noticed Will looked pale. "Please sit down Señor Smith. It is an honor to have a Texas Ranger with us," Miguel Miranda pulled the chair out and gestured for the others to sit at his family table.

"I'm no longer ranging. I gave it up after the Battle of Plum Creek…to pursue business ventures in Austin."

"Still, we are honored to have you at our table! We have heard much of the men who wear the star. My wife and daughter have prepared desayno for us."

"What's des—"

"Breakfast," John Rowland said.

Will was impressed with John Rowland. The businessman sported a neatly trimmed moustache. He had the blue eyes of an Anglo but dressed impeccably as a Mexican rancher.

"Judge Smith was your brother?" Mr. Workman asked in his British accent, "You weren't sent here by President Lamar?"

Bella poured each man coffee from a large pot. Will nodded his thanks to Bella. She accepted his appreciation with a smile that revealed beautiful white teeth.

"No, Mr. Workman. I am here in hopes that the Comanches that captured Fayette may try to sell or trade him here."

The men seemed disappointed at Will's answer. Mr. Workman said, "We're sorry for your loss Mr. Smith. We'll do what we can to help find your nephew."

The men nodded in agreement. John started the conversation, "We are far removed from Austin and most anxious to hear about Texas. Do you have any news from the capitol?"

"I left Austin the morning of January twenty-second with a search party. The fourth session of Congress had pretty well wrapped up its business by then." Will looked at Rowland, then at Miguel. "Your son Ramon says everyone in Santa Fe thinks Lamar is planning an invasion of Santa Fe."

"You don't?" Mr. Workman looked at Will in disbelief.

Will shook his head, "I don't see how. Congress didn't appropriate money for the military. The Rangers and local militia are doing all they can just to keep the Indians away from the capitol."

Mr. Dryden gestured for John to hand Will the wrinkled newspaper he carried.

The headlines of the Independence, Missouri newspaper dated February 3, 1841, read: "Texas to Invade Santa Fe." Will read it.

"First, I've heard about that." He handed the paper back to John. The men looked at each other as if the Texan was hoodwinking them.

"Then you weren't…sent by the President?" Mr. Workman asked.

"That's what I said."

"Then what brings you to Santa Fe?" Dryden asked.

"I told you I came on a premonition that I would find my nephew here!"

Bella was intently listening to every word the men said as she served more huevos and hand-pulled cabrito. This young widow had married shortly after her quinceañera ten years earlier. Her husband who had been a sheep rancher died of cholera five years after they'd wed. They had no children. "Mr. Smith, or whatever your name is, you are in great danger," Mr. Dryden said.

"I believe Mr. Smith," John said. "Why would he lie about such a thing as his brother's murder?"

"I agree," said Mr. Workman.

Ramon came running into the lobby hollering, "Papa, the soldiers are coming. They come from the Governor's Palace."

The innkeeper whispered, "Ramon, listen to me. How many soldiers did you see?"

"Three Papa…they are in the uniform of the governor's soldiers."

Miguel backed away from the table, motioning for everyone to be quiet. He went to his desk behind the registration counter in the lobby.

The sound of the soldiers' boots on the saltillo tile echoed through the lobby. Those in la cocina listened intently to the conversation that continued in Spanish. Will watched the other's expressions for a hint of what was being said by the Mexican soldiers. It wasn't good. The commissioners took defensive positions out of sight, with guns drawn. Bella and her mother instinctively pulled back a cowhide rug that covered a trap door. As the mother held the door up, Bella led Will quietly down the steps to a cellar directly below.

Once the door lowered and the rug was placed over it, they were in total darkness. The musty smell concealed the stench of hundreds of buffalo robes awaiting the next wagon train north. Will started to speak, but Bella touched his face and placed a soft hand on his lips. Her touch lingered on his lips. She fumbled for a phosphorus match on a shelf. Finding it, she lit a candle. Will stared at her in the dim candlelight. She was the most beautiful woman he had ever seen. She placed a finger to her lips. He nodded that he understood. They listened to the harsh words of the soldiers speaking to her father in Spanish. Will knew they were talking about him and not in a good way.

The cellar was cold and damp. It provided storage for the inn's staples. Large burlap bags of beans, rice, and cornmeal were stacked neatly in chest-high rows. Casks of brandy, wine, and mescal aged in wooden racks from the floor to the ceiling.

Bella led Will to a stack of pinto beans. They sat and waited, listening but not fully understanding the sounds heard above them. Fear and cold made Bella shake, the light linen dress gave her little protection. Will removed his woolen shirt and put it over her shoulders. She nodded her appreciation. He gently put his arms around her. Bella snuggled into his arms, taking comfort and warmth from his manly embrace. It had been many years since she had been in the arms of a man.

Time had no meaning in the darkness of the cellar. Bella slept while Will thought about his predicament and the danger he unknowingly brought to Bella's family. The Mirandas could have given him up to the soldiers, but they chose to protect him. *Was there to be an invasion?* he wondered. *How could Texas invade when they couldn't defend the capitol city from a small band of renegade Indians?*

Light from the trap door suddenly brightened the cellar as it creaked slowly upwards. Will recognized a man's shiny leather boots descending the rickety stairs. The lower legs of a man were all he could see. Will touched Bella's arm gently to awaken her, then pulled her down behind the stack of beans. He drew his revolver and waited. It was not her father. The shadow this man cast was of a tall, slim man. Will pulled the hammer back.

Bella touched his arm, shaking her head to hold his fire.

"Who is there?" Bella asked.

"John Rowland...Bella, I must talk to Will."

"I'm here." Will instinctively moved to a better defensive position.

John said, "Will you're in great danger. Governor Armijo has more troops coming for you."

"Why? I'm just trying to find my nephew! I have no quarrel with anyone."

"We believe you! I have a plan. Please come out so we can talk in a lower tone."

Will said, "How do I know I can trust you and your friends?"

John said, "If you couldn't trust us, you would be in jail by now waiting for a firing squad in the plaza."

Will looked at Bella. She nodded that John was right. He slowly placed his revolver in its holster, then stepped into the dim light from the kitchen above.

John asked, "Bella, would you light a lamp?"

Once there was light in the cellar, they moved crates and boxes to form a makeshift table. Bella went upstairs to prepare food. It had been nearly twelve hours since the three Mexican soldiers came looking for the Texan. Mr. Miranda provided the soldiers much food and brandy in an effort to prove the inn's loyalty to the government. The soldiers were sleeping off the effects of that loyalty.

"Why are you and the others willing to help me? You could've turned me over to the soldiers this morning and gone about your business."

"We are all in this complicated mess together."

"I am not involved with anyone," Will said.

"You are now—whether you like it or not! We need you, Mr. Smith… Texas needs you."

While they talked, Bella brought tortillas, beans, and roasted chicken down for them in large pueblo bowls.

John took a deep breath, " How is the family doing?"

"Mother is…much worried…that the soldiers will burn the inn." Bella shrugged and rolled her eyes. "Father is on the roof watching the plaza and the main road into town." She started to cry, "My poor brother Ramon has been out on the road to Santa Cruz watching for the soldiers. If you see him, please tell him to come home and eat." Bella touched Will's arm and said, "Will, I will pray that you make it safely to Taos and find your nephew."

"Thank you, but why am I going to Taos?" When an answer didn't come from Bella, Will looked at John.

"I'll tell you later. We got to go now!" John put his hat on.

Bella and John hurriedly moved neatly folded blankets and quilts from shelves against a back wall. It took all of them to move the shelving and open a large door. Behind the door was a tunnel four feet high and four feet wide.

"Where does this take us?" Will asked.

"To the river, please hurry! The others will be waiting."

Bella touched Will's cheek, "We will meet again soon …if it is meant to be."

Before Will could say what he was thinking, John grabbed his arm and pulled him into the dark hole.

In the darkness of the tunnel, they found it easier to crawl than to crouch and walk. John Rowland told how his wife's grandfather built the tunnel many years ago for the family to escape Indian raids.

"So, you are kin of the Miranda's?" Will asked.

"Only by marriage. Miguel is my brother-in-law. His wife Lupe is my wife's younger sister."

"That makes Bella—"

"Niece…Bella is my niece," John said, "and no, she is not married!"

"You're asked that often, I suppose?" Will said as he bumped his head on a wooden support beam, "Ouch! How much further?"

"I don't know," John said.

Will grabbed John's arm, "You don't know? You are leading me through this dark tunnel, and you don't know how far it is?"

"Relax, we can't get lost. There is only one way in and one way out."

They heard running water. The river must be close. They made a short turn and felt a comfortable breeze, relieved to be at the river. Thick brush placed in front of the exit hole to hide the tunnels existence had to be removed. Moonlight glittered on the narrow stream. They heard a horse nicker and the creak of a slow moving wagon. Will saw the silhouette of a man driving a small farm wagon. A woman cradled an infant. George nickered, smelling the presence of his master. His burro started to bray. Both were tethered behind the wagon.

"They brought my horse and burro!"

John said, "Hush, don't say another word. Just do what I tell you. Maybe we can get out of Santa Fe alive."

"Is it that serious?"

"Yes, it is. My brother Tom is in a Mexican prison for corresponding with his friends in Texas," John said.

They found a shallow place to wade across.

The wagon stopped at a stand of red willow trees. John pulled back the canvas that covered the cargo area and motioned for Will to get in.

He hesitated for a moment before climbing in. Once under the cover, the wagon started moving.

Will felt for his saddle, his carbine, and the other colt revolver under the canvas cover.

"Everything that was in your room is in this wagon," John whispered.

"Thanks. Who loaded it?" Will asked.

"Mr. Dryden. It's his wagon. Workman and I helped," John said.

"Did you find the…"

"The money. Yes, we counted it—one hundred and twelve dollars in silver," John said.

"It was my brother's scalp that I was concerned about."

"Scalp…you were concerned about a scalp?"

"It was in my saddlebag," Will said.

"Trust me: no one would take a scalp. Please just be quiet 'til we are far from town."

The wagon bounced along the Taos Trail. Will tried to sleep. Each time he came close to dozing off, the wagon hit a rock or hole in the road. He rolled on his side and peered through a small space between the sideboards. A full moon illuminated the knee-high sagebrush.

"John, you awake?"

"I am now."

Will turned onto his back and rested on his elbows, "I would like to know what our next move is?"

"Our goal is to make it to Santa Cruz before daylight; from there it's about…"

"Hush, riders coming," Mr. Dryden interrupted them.

From under the tarp they groped for their guns. John listened intently to the clip clop of the approaching riders. He raised two fingers, indicating it sounded like two horses. Will looked through the small open space between the sideboards of the wagon bed. He nodded and raised two fingers, indicating to John he could see them.

Both riders wore Mexican sombreros. They were well-armed with holstered pistols and wide blade knives. Their flashy attire suggested they were not men of the ranchero, but of the cantina. Will saw them pass a bottle; it was obvious they were drunk and looking for trouble. Both were short in stature—one fat the other slim. Both wore moustaches that curled at the ends. It was hours before sun up.

The fat one slurred, "Buenos días, Señor y Señorita." He took a gulp from a bottle of mescal.

Mr. Dryden said, "Yes, it is a good morning, gentlemen. We must be on our way now," He shook the reins.

The other man grabbed the harness of the lead horse, startling it. "Why are you in such a hurry amigo?" The horse shook its head trying to break free from his grasp. The bandit held the harness tight. "What is it you have in your fancy wagon, Señor, that you do not want us to see?"

The fat one rode to the rear of the wagon and yanked back the canvas. He was confronted with three gun barrels in his face. His sobriety quickly returned when he realized he was no longer the predator, but the prey.

Will stood up in the wagon. Both revolvers were aimed at the bandit in the rear. John had the bandit in front covered. Neither offered any resistance.

"Buenos días to you. Now amigos, off your horses!" John motioned with his pistol.

Will jumped to the ground and tied their horses to the wagon. The bandits looked up at the buckboard and saw another set of guns pointed at them.

"Off with your guns and knives. Put them in the wagon, pronto," John said.

"Why you do this to us?" The rotund bandit said after placing his gun on the wagon bed.

"We intend to teach you and your friend not to go poking your noses into other people's business," John said.

Will removed the carbines from their scabbards and added them to the pile of weapons.

"Now your boots," John demanded.

"Please not my boots; my feet are fat. I must have them made in Santa Fe."

"Then do as I say, and you may get them back," John said.

"Anything you say, Señor."

"Your clothes." John waved his gun.

"I beg you, not my clothes, please!"

"I know. You have your clothes made by a tailor in Santa Fe," John said.

"How did you know, Señor?" The fat bandit laid his shirt and pants on top of the pile of weapons.

The slim bandit protested, "I can't undress. The woman. She is watching." He pointed toward Mr. Workman who was dressed like a woman so as not to be seen leaving Santa Fe.

John, Will, and Mr. Dryden started laughing when Mr. Workman stood up and dropped the blanket from his shoulders and removed the veil. He then tossed the "baby," which was a river rock wrapped in swaddling, at their feet.

"No women here now, so get your clothes off. Put them in the wagon, now!" John said as the others tried not to laugh again.

Dryden said, "Workman, you make the ugliest damn woman I ever saw!"

Workman looked around, "I think we're far enough from Santa Fe to be who we are."

"Sure glad you said that; I don't want anyone thinking you're my woman." Dryden laughed.

Will, now impatient, asked, "What about them?" He pointed at the two bandits in their stained long johns and dirty socks.

Mr. Workman asked the bandits, "Are you Catholic?"

"Sí, Señor we very good Catholic."

"Do you know Padre Martinez at Santa Cruz De La Canada, the Catholic Church up the road?" Mr. Workman asked.

"No. It has been many years since we attended church," the fat bandit said.

"That's what I figured," Mr. Workman said.

Forty-one-year-old William Workman reached under the buckboard of the wagon, pulled out a hand-tooled leather satchel and asked,

"Do either of you speak or read Latin?"

"No, Señor. We have never heard of this tribe."

"Good, you are a little closer to getting your belongings back." Mr. Workman pulled out a piece of stationery, pen and ink, and utilized the wagon's tailgate to pen a letter.

William Workman was born in Cumberland, England around the turn of the nineteenth century and educated there. He sailed to America in his twenties and headed west in his thirties. He became the partner of John Rowland, and like Rowland, married a Spanish woman and became a Catholic and a naturalized citizen of Mexico. Now a prominent merchant of Taos, he was considered the best educated man in Nuevo México. He and Padre Martinez had become fast friends. They corresponded often by letters written in Latin.

This letter asked Padre Martinez to help find Will Smith's nephew. He told the padre about the bandit's feeble attempt to rob them and prayed that the padre could save them from burning in hell.

"That ought to do it." Mr. Workman sealed the letter. "John, Will, saddle up and scout the road ahead. I'll talk to these gentlemen who will give their confession of faith to the padre today."

Mr. Workman approached the bandits tied to a rear wagon wheel. They squatted low by the rear wheel as if they were hiding.

"If you want your gear and horses back, this is what you must do," Workman said.

Mr. Workman explained in fluent Spanish that they were to talk to no one at the church other than Padre Martinez. Each should confess their sins to the padre after giving him the unopened letter. If he felt their confessions were sincere and the donation to his church sufficient, Padre Martinez would take them to their horses and gear.

Will and John mounted and rode out ahead of the wagon as Mr. Dryden climbed onto the buckboard.

Workman untied the bandits and said, "Sit on that big rock and watch us. When you can no longer see our wagon, start walking toward Santa Cruz." He climbed on the wagon next to his best friend William Dryden.

"Buenos días, Señors." Mr. Dryden shook the reins and the horses moved forward.

Chapter Seven

As daylight broke on the fifth day of March, Will and John rode slowly into the village of Santa Cruz ahead of Dryden and Workman in the wagon. They gazed at the flat rooftops and the open courtyards for signs of the Mexican army. The only creature stirring about was a spotted mongrel dog that snarled as they approached. It tucked its tail and ran behind an adobe wall when Will hissed at it. Three White-Leghorn hens scratched in the red dirt for morsels of yesterday's tortillas.

Santa Cruz De la Canada Mission was built in 1730. The adobe village that grew around it was called Santa Cruz.

John cautiously entered the sanctuary. Will stayed with the horses and burro. Although John was Catholic, married a Catholic, and raised his children in the faith, he never felt comfortable entering a Catholic church. Maybe his Protestant upbringing back in Pennsylvania caused his reluctance. John never knelt at the altar. He blamed an old injury from an Indian battle for his inability to kneel.

That Indian battle was one of many fights John and his brother Tom encountered during their eighteen years in the mountains. The brothers ventured west—trapping beaver and hunting buffalo and bears, and then sold their robes and hides at Bent's Fort. Now John was a prosperous businessman. He owned a flour mill, distillery, and general store in Taos.

John, Thomas Rowland, William Dryden, William Workman and some twenty other settlers were supportive of Nuevo México being part of the new Republic of Texas.

Governor Manuel Armijo was incensed that they would support the Texans. Armijo arrested Thomas Rowland for treason and then ransacked his home and took liberty of his personal property. The settlers who supported Texas' annexation of Nuevo México also supported the success of President Lamar's Santa Fe Expedition.

William G. Dryden called on President Mirabeau Lamar in October of 1839 when his administration was gearing up for the start of the Fourth Congress. Dryden naively led President Lamar to believe that the people of Nuevo México would welcome annexation by Texas. It was an assumption on Dryden's part based solely on his close affiliation of like minds. People like him who spoke English—Anglos from Europe, America, Canada, and Texas.

William Dryden's knowledge of law and world affairs impressed the newly elected President and his Vice President, David Burnet. They appointed Dryden as Texas' commissioner of Nuevo México. Dryden recommended his friends John Rowland and William Workman as fellow commissioners. President Lamar and Vice President Burnet appointed them solely on Dryden's recommendation—without their knowledge or consent. Dryden rode back to Taos with a handwritten proclamation from President Lamar seeking the citizens of Nuevo México support in annexation. The presidential appointment Dryden was so proud of would cost him and his friends dearly.

John found the sanctuary empty, except for a black cat that rubbed its fat body against his boot tops. As he exited the church, Dryden and Workman arrived with the wagon and the bandits' gear.

Dryden asked, "Where's the padre?"

"Not in the church," John said.

Workman said, "You men best stay here and keep an eye on the road."

"You think the Mexican army would follow us this far… looking for me?" Will inquired.

Workman said, "Yes, I do. And beware, this is where Governor Armijo worships." Workman climbed down from the buckboard, "I know where the padre can be found. If you'll take the bandits' possessions to the stables, I'll find the padre."

Dryden said, "I'll come with you."

"I would prefer you didn't." Workman turned and started walking toward a small adobe home away from the churchyard.

The three men looked at each other, puzzled by Workman's unusual response. He usually took Dryden with him wherever he went.

"Padre, it's your friend William Workman." As he knocked on the blue frame door, he heard people moving about; then an interior door slammed shut. A woman's voice said something in Spanish that Workman didn't understand, but he knew she didn't appreciate his knocking.

"Are you alone?" Padre Martinez whispered.

"Yes, I am alone. Dryden and Rowland are with the horses and wagon at the front of the church."

"Please, come in Señor Workman. It has been some time since I had the pleasure of your company," Padre Antonio Jose Martinez slowly opened the ornate Spanish door and looked around cautiously as if they were being watched by the devil. Workman followed the padre inside. He still wore a white-linen sleeping shirt. The padre sat behind his impressive hand-carved desk and motioned for Workman to sit in one of the two matching high-back Pueblo chairs.

"Welcome back from your trip to Durango," Workman sat down, "I hope your journey was fruitful."

"Yes, but I am happy to finally be home." Padre Martinez glanced toward the closed door.

The middle-aged priest was born in nearby Abiquiú on the Martinez family ranch. He quickly bored of herding sheep and educated himself by reading books in his father's extensive library. He married young, but lost his wife and baby before his twentieth birthday. His grief turned him to the Bible and eventually priesthood. He studied in Durango, Mexico. In 1826, Martinez became the priest of Taos and Santa Cruz.

Workman may have been the best educated Anglo in Nuevo México, but Padre Martinez was the scholar of the native populations. At first, he didn't like the Anglos who came down the Santa Fe Trail in their large freight wagons, but Padre Martinez took a liking to Workman. They argued about Manifest Destiny. Padre believed in Devine Destiny and supported all the vows of his priesthood, except celibacy. He felt strongly that every man should take a wife and procreate, regardless of their vocation. He didn't flaunt his wife and children but was proud of his family.

"How are your wife and the baby?" Workman asked.

"They are well, thank you for asking...and your family?"

"Growing, Padre. I will soon need your services to marry my eldest daughter."

"I would be honored to perform the ceremony, here at Santa Cruz or Taos, if you wish a church wedding."

"I will get back to you with details as they develop." Workman paused. He pulled a handkerchief from a vest pocket to wipe a tear from his eye.

"What is it that troubles you so?" Padre Martinez made a temple with both hands.

Workman sighed, "I haven't told Maria that I may be in prison soon...along with Thomas Rowland."

Padre Martinez nodded. "I've heard of Thomas' imprisonment and that his Brother John and you will be next. You must tell her, so your family can prepare."

Workman's voice cracked as he asked, "Padre, will things ever get better?"

"We can only take this political turmoil one day at a time. As I told you when we last spoke, you should seriously think about going into exile before it is too late."

"But where can I go, Padre?"

"Far from here. I have friends who can help you in California."

"If it weren't for my business and the family, I would have left months ago," Workman said, "Please send me the names of your friends in California when you have time." Workman stood.

"Go take care of your family," Padre Martinez said slipping a sealed envelope in Workman's pocket, "The information you need is in my letter."

"I know you must get ready for Mass, Padre." Workman glanced out the window, his companions stood talking and looking restless.

"Is there something else you need to tell me?" Padre Martinez asked.

"Yes there is, Padre. Two bandits tried to rob us this morning on the way here."

"They tried?" Padre Martinez looked amused and interested in the story but indicated with his hands that it must be told quickly.

"They will be here after Mass, coming to you humbly dressed, in need of salvation. They have a sealed letter from me, as I wasn't sure I'd see you. If you feel they are worthy of forgiveness, their horses and gear have been stored in your stables. Do as you wish with them."

"I look forward to meeting these sinners." Padre Martinez smiled.

"Pray for us, Padre." Workman opened the door.

"I will, Señor Workman. Go now in peace."

Workman joined the men who had taken shelter from the morning sun under a large cottonwood tree.

"We best get going!" Workman climbed on the wagon.

Dryden didn't reply. He shook the leather reins and the horse stepped into a trot. Dryden was upset that he hadn't been invited to meet the popular but notorious Padre Martinez.

Riding in silence, Workman read Padre's letter written in Latin. Workman took a deep breath, folded the letter, and put it back in his vest pocket.

Workman broke the silence, "Dryden, I consider you my best friend. You're the Godfather of my children. That makes us family don't you think?"

Dryden said, "I suppose it does."

Workman leaned toward Dryden, "The reason I didn't take you to meet the padre is that he wouldn't have talked to either of us if I had."

"Why would he be afraid to talk about the Mexican bandits in front of me?" Dryden shook the reins.

Workman's face turned red, "It's not about the bandits. I don't give a shit about their salvation."

Dryden shook the reins again. "Then why did you write the letter to Padre Martinez? I thought you were hell-bent on their salvation."

"That was part of it. I needed a reason to call on the padre and that was a good one."

"Yes, it was." Workman laughed, thinking about the bandits walking into church in their dirty underwear.

Dryden asked, "What's going to happen to us?"

"I don't know, Dryden. I'm not staying around Taos to find out."

"You have too much invested to leave." Dryden slowed the wagon to ease around a washout. "Your home, a thriving business, and all your friends are in Taos." Dryden's voice cracked with emotion.

"I was in hopes my friend might come with me?" Workman said in a way that sounded like a question.

Dryden said, "You're serious?"

Workman nodded. "Yes, I am."

They rode in silence. The only sounds a creaking wagon and hoof beats of horses anxious to get home.

They were called Tres Amigos. Dryden, a lawyer, met Workman and Rowland in their early days of trapping. Dryden drew up their first business partnership.

They stopped at Cieneguilla Crossing on the Rio Grande. The river along with who governed the lands on either side caused most of their problems. The native people on both sides of the Rio Grande had always been content sheep and goat ranchers, surviving under the flags of Spain and Mexico with little government interference. Now they feared the new Republic of Texas was planning an invasion of their homeland.

Will sat tall in the saddle as his horse and burro drank from the river. He looked up at the mountains to the north. John was off his horse, kneeling to fill a gourd with water.

"John, how far is this Taos?"

"Just a few miles north, straight uphill from here. We best rest a spell before the test of man and beast."

Will helped Workman unharness Dryden's horses from the wagon.

"Thanks, Will, I appreciate your help," Workman said.

"Mr. Workman, I know you're trying to help me, but I don't—"

Workman interrupted, "Will, we are safe from Armijo's men for the moment. Let's sit and talk." Workman pointed to the shady side of his wagon.

"Come join us? Soon as you're finished," Workman said to Dryden and Rowland.

The horses were staked in the marsh near the river's edge to graze. Workman opened a grub box and retrieved some deer jerky and hardtack biscuits. Dryden and John sat down, backs to the rear wagon wheel.

"This meal will have to do until we get to the trading post," Workman said.

"When will that be?" Will asked, trying to chew the dried jerky.

"About sunset," John answered, as Workman struggled to choke down a bite of jerky.

Mr. Workman cleared his throat and said, "Fellas...we need to talk. I have shared some information with Dryden already. We've discussed the ramifications of this expansionist movement being made by the Republic of Texas," He paused. "I'll tell you what I know about our situation and it isn't pretty."

John said, "What could be worse than my brother Thomas being thrown in prison?"

Workman cleared his throat again. "John you'd be in prison already if you weren't married to Padre Martinez's cousin." He tried to cough, "Governor Armijo has ordered the Texas Commissioners be arrested—that's us!" He pointed at his partners. Then he looked at Will, "Armijo has posted a reward of a thousand pesos for your capture, Will," Workman stared at him, "Dead or alive."

Nothing was said as they thought about what it meant. The Governor of Nuevo México had declared war on them.

"That's a handsome reward," John choked on his jerky.

Workman said, "Yes, it is. The reward will be paid to anyone who brings in Will's head and Colt pistols."

"This Armijo fella wants me dead and the three of you in prison." Will shook his head. "Damn these Mexicans are a mean bunch of bastards!" He stood up, "All I want to do is find my nephew and get the hell out of here. I don't give a damn who controls this country."

They sat in silence, thinking about their families, unaware that Armijo's soldiers had gone to Workman and Rowland's haciendas to arrest them. Fortunately, they were in Santa Fe. They were lucky they had not encountered the governor's men on the road to and from Santa Fe.

John said, "It looks like we have stepped into one big pile of shit."

"How in the hell did it come to this?" Will turned and looked up the mountain trail they had yet to climb.

"I am sorry, Will." Dryden said, then looked at his partners, "It's my fault." His voice cracked with emotion, "I shouldn't have called on President Lamar when I was in Austin."

Workman said, "It's not your fault, Dryden!"

"It is." Dryden wiped his eye with a dirty knuckle, "I let my sense of importance overload my common sense."

"Don't be blaming yourself." John stood and put a hand on Dryden's shoulder.

"I just got carried away talking to the president." Dryden looked up at John and Will standing, then down at Workman, "I never met a president before. I rattled on about how beautiful Taos was, how friendly the native people were, and how we were creating a utopia on the high desert right in the middle of the mountains."

"You never told us that." Workman looked at his friend, "What did President Lamar say to that?"

Dryden leaned over toward Workman, "He asked me if Taos was as pretty as Austin." Dryden smiled, "I told him just as pretty…and then some." Dryden continued, "That's when the president asked me to form a commission of progressive thinking businessmen. I told President Lamar and Vice President Burnet about you two. We were made commissioners right then and there."

"What about the proclamation to the people of Nuevo México you carried back?" John asked.

"President Lamar penned those words as I waited. Of course, I made some suggestions here and there."

"No wonder Armijo thinks we are the instigators of this expedition," John said.

Workman said, "We wouldn't even have known about it had I not read about it in the Independence paper."

Dryden shook his head, "Now everyone knows about it."

Workman got up, "President Lamar thinks he is sending a trading party to Santa Fe and the natives will welcome them with open arms." Workman began to pace, and then he turned toward Dryden, "Hellfire! Governor Armijo and the Mexican army are preparing for an invasion."

"I said I was sorry, Workman." Dryden looked at him.

"Dryden, I know you did. You were just doing what you thought was right at the time. I might have done the same."

"No one is blaming anyone," Workman stopped in front of where Will stood, "Will, you haven't said anything. What are you thinking?"

"I think a lot of people are going to get killed for no good reason."

"That's why you've got to get to Austin and stop this damn wagon train before it starts," Workman raised his eyebrows.

Will clinched the side rail of the wagon so tight his knuckles turned white. Then he gazed up at the trail. "Soon as I find Fayette, I'll head back." He turned to walk away.

Workman said, "You've got to go now! The last we read in the paper, the expedition was planned for the spring. This is the first week of Lent." Workman became agitated, not used to anyone turning his back on him while he talked, "John, help me explain this to him."

Will turned and said, "No one has to explain anything to me. I understand your problem, but it's not my problem. My only concern here is finding my nephew." Will turned toward the river.

John followed, "If Fayette is in Nuevo México, I will find him and return him to Austin."

Will stopped walking, turned toward John, and said, "I can't leave without Fayette."

"One thing I know Will, is that a dead man can't find Fayette."

They walked back toward the wagon.

Will didn't respond; he knew John was right. Captain Jack Hays who was now in San Antonio—if the Indians hadn't killed him—was the only person who knew of his plan to go to Santa Fe. If he was killed or imprisoned, who would be left to find Fayette?

"What makes you think you can find my nephew?" Will turned toward John.

Workman spoke, "Padre Martinez is not our political ally, yet. We've been trying to sway him to our way of thinking. He's told me he sees the advantages of aligning with Texas. His followers want to be governed by people that speak Spanish and understand and respect their customs."

Will looked at Workman, "What's this padre got to do with finding Fayette?"

"Everything!" the three commissioners said, almost in unison.

Will looked surprised at such a positive response.

"How is he going to find Fayette?"

John said, "Padre Martinez is not only our priest, he is the voice and leader of all the native people. When he speaks, they listen. His parishioners will spread the word. If Fayette is alive in the territory, he will be brought to us."

Will looked at John and asked, "Can I trust this padre to find Fayette?"

Workman answered, "Yes, you can. Padre Martinez will prey on the fears of his parishioners about this invasion from Texas."

"How's that?" Will asked.

"He will imply that by returning Fayette to his family, the Texans will call off the expedition—which only you can make happen."

Will remembered how Captain Jack Hayes made major decisions like this. "Excuse me, I need to think." Will walked to a large Cypress tree on the riverbank and sat down under it.

"Where's he going?" Dryden asked.

Workman said, "Maybe he wants to pray about it?"

"Glad to know he's a Christian." Dryden nodded.

"Let's get harnessed and saddled up. We've been here too long already." Workman stretched.

As Dryden and Workman harnessed the horses to the wagon, Dryden said, "We've been friends a long time. I want you to know that I am going to stick with you wherever you go."

"Thank you, Dryden. I feel the same about you."

John had both horses saddled when Will approached him.

"Thanks, John, for saddling George for me."

"Check the cinch for yourself? Can't have you falling off on this trail. It's a long way to the bottom."

John and Will rode ahead of the wagon as Workman and Dryden followed.

"Workman, do you think Will can make it back to Austin alone?" Dryden asked.

Workman said, "He made it to Santa Fe alone. He should be able to, if someone doesn't kill him for the reward money."

Dryden changed the subject, "What do you think of us going back east—maybe to St. Louis or New Orleans?"

"I was thinking more like California—where land is cheap. They tell me you can grow anything in California." Workman looked at his friend.

Dryden smiled, "Never been to California, heard a lot about it though. I think that would be as good a place as any to make a new start."

Chapter Eight

Somewhere in the mountains of Eastern New Mexico, Fayette woke to the smell of fresh horse dung. He was tied in a travois pulled behind a pony in gastric distress. He was blistered from severe sunburn, a condition the Indians called the white man's weakness. Indians didn't understand what little tolerance a redhead's skin had to the blazing sun. The desert took its toll on Fayette, leaving him unconscious and delirious for days.

The oldest wife of Chief Old Wolf applied a gooey substance from the leaf of an aloe vera plant. It would have provided immediate relief had it not been applied so harshly.

Old Wolf rode up to check on Fayette. As the chief and his wife discussed Fayette's condition, Preacher stomped the ground and nickered. The horse realized it was Fayette strapped in the travois. Fayette recognized the sounds of his father's horse.

"Please bring Preacher to me," Fayette said in a raspy voice.

Old Wolf ordered the horse brought to the travois. Preacher shook its head excitedly, frightening the Indians gathered near Fayette. Having seen Preacher riled, they gave the stallion ample space. It stood gazing at the badly burned boy, flesh peeling from Fayette's nose and cheeks. The horse nosed the Indian blanket back, trying to get a better look at Fayette.

Chief Old Wolf motioned for his wife to untie Fayette's restraints. Fayette strained to rub Preachers nose and managed a hoarse whisper, "Good boy."

The presence of the horse gave Fayette the will to live. Old Wolf watched and listened intently as the boy whispered to Preacher. The horse made sounds like it was trying to talk to Fayette. The chief, a wise man, saw that a human and an animal could have feelings for one another. The use of horses was new to the Indians. First introduced to Old Wolf's fathers' generation by the Spaniards, he only learned what little his father knew of horses. From Fayette, the chief could learn more. Old Wolf ordered Fayette's travois attached to Preacher.

Happy to have Fayette near, Preacher gave the Indians no problem attaching the travois behind its legs; something the horse had never experienced before. Fayette was soon well enough to ride behind Chief Old Wolf. Tribal members resented the preferential treatment their chief gave Fayette, whom he traded their horses for—horses they could be riding instead of having to walk.

At the end of the day, while the others made camp, Old Wolf and Fayette would sit under the shade of trees where Fayette would explain the use of praise, repetition, and reward. Old Wolf would look at Fayette in disbelief, having only known to beat beasts of burden into submission. Preacher was allowed to roam free. Fayette assured Old Wolf the horse wouldn't run away.

Old Wolf asked, "Big Fish teach Preacher to come when I want."

"Please don't call me that name," Fayette blurted out.

"You teach me to talk to horse. I give you…new Indian name."

"I don't want a new name. My name is Fayette. Fayette Smith, that's my name."

"You like name Fayette Smith more than Big Fish?" Old Wolf shrugged his shoulders.

"That's the name my father gave me. It's all I have to remember him by." Fayette stood and said, "I need to check on Preacher now," Fayette avoided facing Old Wolf, knowing that Indians didn't think well of men who cried.

Preacher saw Fayette wading through the lush meadow of mountain grass. The horse ran up to him and shook his long mane. They greeted, the horse nuzzled Fayette while he rubbed Preacher's nose. The horse was all the family he had for now. He was blessed to be with his father's favorite horse.

Fayette spotted a motley group of men coming out of the cedar and pinion trees. They traversed slowly down the fall line directly towards him. His heart raced. *Could it be a search party looking for me?* They rode strange looking horses and led a caravan of twelve burros. The pots and pans tied to the pack saddles clanged and rattled. The men rode mules, which plodded the trail carefully, stepping gracefully over every obstacle. Six multi-colored goats and a dozen sheep free ranged behind the noisy caravan.

Old Wolf walked down and now stood beside Fayette, smiling and waving. Whoever they were, they knew each other. The sun made Fayette squint as he tried harder to see all the wares dangling from the burros' pack saddles.

Fayette asked, "Who are they?"

"Comancheros, Fayette." Old Wolf patted Fayette on his shoulder.

"Ouch," Fayette grimaced from being touched on his blistered shoulder but appreciated being called by his name.

"What's a… Coman…chero?" Fayette struggled to say.

"They trade with anyone for anything. Mostly they trade with Comanche."

"Are they Comanche?" Fayette looked up at the chief.

Old Wolf laughed, "No one knows…they don't know." He waved at the men, "Their mother doesn't know who the father is."

Fayette didn't understand the jest about the Comanchero parentage, but thought they were an interesting group to behold.

The leader wore a dirty sombrero that was much too small for his bushy head of reddish-brown hair. It was held on by a lanyard with the knot tangled in his beard. He wore well-oiled leather pants, boots, and silver spurs that jingled as he dismounted from his mule.

"Hola, Old Wolf." The leader removed a worn leather glove and shoved it in his back pocket.

The men greeted each other like old friends, with back slaps and bear hugs.

"Old Wolf, who's the gringo?"

Old Wolf pointed, "Chico this is Fayette Smith; he is a member of my tribe."

"Looks like you tried to cook him alive. Take it from me Old Wolf, gringos don't cook up too good. Besides, they taste salty."

Chico's comment scared Fayette. He stared at this strange-looking man. Chico's thick, curly beard hung down to his chest. His fat round face reminded Fayette of a baby buffalo he once saw.

"Just trying to have a little fun. I meant no harm." Chico took off his hat. He knew the boy had to be someone special because he was standing next to the chief.

Chico introduced the others: Blanco, a skinny white man with green eyes and dirty blond hair; Blackie, a big black man; and Mescal, who wore the trappings of an Indian. The men just nodded hello and let Chico do the talking.

"Old Wolf, can we make camp here in the meadow near you?"

"You have whiskey for Old Wolf?"

"I got your favorite, Old Turley's Lightning," Chico paused, "distilled by your friend, Simon Turley: last year's batch!"

"You and animals make camp...up wind from my teepee." Old Wolf pointed to a high place about a hundred yards up the fall line.

Chico asked, "Old Wolf, you don't like the smell of my four-legged critters?"

"No, it's the two-legged critters' smell I don't like." Old Wolf smiled.

Chico looked hard at Fayette, then at the chief. He turned quickly toward a burro tethered behind his mule. He opened a leather pouch on the burro's back and pulled something out. Chico pitched it toward Old Wolf, who caught it easily with one hand. Fayette had feared for his life, thinking Chico had gone for a gun. Everyone broke out laughing, except Fayette, who laughed when he realized they were joking.

Old Wolf said, "You. Make camp. Eat with us." He held the bottle of whiskey high, "Bring more whiskey."

Fayette and Old Wolf walked toward camp. Preacher followed closely behind.

Chico turned to his companions "See that good looking stallion following them—no rope, no lead on its head. I'll have a horse like that someday."

Old Wolf's wives prepared a feast in honor of their guests, which included fried corn, cactus pear stew, and an assortment of nuts and berries. Indian bread pudding simmered over ashen coals as two braves slowly roasted a large deer.

Drums beat loudly, to signify the start of the feast. Chico, Blanco, Blackie, and Mescal entered the camp each leading two burros loaded with shiny new wares from over the mountains.

The Indian braves watched the cornucopia-laden burros with skeptical interest. The women and children couldn't hide their interest in the trader's goods. They wanted to touch and feel every item. A hand-held looking glass was fought over. Few Indians had ever seen their face. More than one Indian was disappointed with what they saw. Imported coffee was offered at a dollar a pound, but no one had dollars—only hides, horns, wild honey, and sexual favors were available to trade.

As the night wore on, drinking and dancing intensified. The younger squaws offered their services for things they wanted. Fayette had seen this ritual at the tribal council of the Big Springs. A Comanchero would enter a teepee with trinkets and exited pulling up his baggy pants. He watched and waited, pretending to be asleep, rehearsing in his mind his escape.

A waning crescent moon hid behind a listless cloud. Fayette looked around the camp. It appeared all were in a drunken state of sleep.

This escape would be made with Preacher to the Colorado River far to the east. Fayette watched the sunset over a craggy mountain of red rock. He studied pilot points to the east that could be found in the dark. They pointed the way to the Colorado River.

Fayette crept up close to Preacher and grabbed its nose to prevent the usual nicker. Preacher didn't make a sound. The horse just shook his head like it knew what was happening. Fayette untied the horse and they slowly walked away.

Fayette stopped to get his bearings at a ravine. The cloud that covered the sliver of moon drifted away, allowing enough light to reveal a pile of boulders. Happenstance had placed the rocks in such a way as to allow Fayette to mount Preacher.

Once on their way, they traversed slowly down the steep incline. At the bottom, Fayette's pilot point was no longer visible. He prayed they were headed east.

Preacher became nervous as they entered a ravine that went up the side of the next mountain. There wasn't a trail; they would blaze a new one in the darkness. The ravine came to an abrupt end. A large rockslide had sealed it off. Fayette jumped off Preacher and led him in search of an exit.

Fayette found an opening and entered. Preacher spotted the yellow eyes first—a reflection of moonlight from the eyes of a cougar posed on a boulder. The cat leaped on Preachers bare back. The horse instinctively reared up and then bucked, trying to throw the predator to the ground. In the melee, Fayette was slammed against the rocks and knocked unconscious. The last thing Fayette remembered was seeing Preacher running out of the small entrapment, the cougar on its back, gnawing and clawing.

The sun had risen when Fayette began to stir. He had taken a blow to the head. He was disoriented but able to slowly stand and walk.

Moving to shade, Fayette sat down to ponder his predicament. Thirsty, he must find water. The cougar couldn't have survived without it. *Where could water be?* He knew how to find water because his father had taught him. Water always flows down into the valley. It reveals itself with tall trees and green grass. Find the trees and the green grass and you will find water.

Fayette worked his way out of the rocks and found a trail down the mountain. Walking toward the direction the sun came up, Fayette spotted birds overhead and watched as they disappeared in a small valley about a mile away.

As he followed a narrow path, he heard the running water of a mountain stream. Fayette found a large flat rock that protruded out over the water's edge. He laid on the rock to sip the cool water directly from the stream. The water was so clear that Fayette could see the river rocks on the bottom, three feet below.

Three speckled trout darted upstream. He saw a large one jump. Fayette found a shallow place in the stream that was difficult for the fish to navigate and caught two large trout with his hands. First, he cleaned them with his jackknife and then found a dead branch from a pinion tree, which he whittled for kindling to start a fire.

Fayette ate what fish he could and placed the rest in the forked branches of a red willow tree. Fayette fell asleep on the rock, listening to ripples of running water. He woke to the sounds of a tree rustling in the wind. But there was no wind.

He opened his eyes and instinctively looked towards the sound. A mama bear had found his fish. Fayette got up and hollered at the bear that was now standing on its hind legs, reaching for his fish. Fayette picked up a rock and threw it hard.

"Go catch your own fish, you damn bear!"

The bear wanted no trouble and ambled off; her young cub followed. It was the first bear Fayette had seen up close and he hoped the last.

Chapter Nine

*W*ill reached the mesa as the sun began to set. He stopped to watch, mesmerized by what he saw. A deep gorge cut through the west side of the valley, winding north into the Rockies. The Rio Grande flowed gently through the gorge hundreds of feet below. It glistened like a golden thread, meandering to the end of the horizon. Knee-high purple sage covered the valley floor.

The valley was a gigantic bowl in the earth, created by volcanic eruptions millions of years ago. Now, it was encircled by a wide ring of snow covered mountains as puffy white clouds nestled amongst the Sangre de Cristo peaks. Mountain winds gently rearranged the clouds. Their shadows created contrasting shades of color on the mountains.

John rode up to Will. They both gazed across the gorge of the Rio Grande. They were quiet and their horses stood like statues. An approaching wagon broke the silence. Workman and Dryden pulled up and set the handbrake. The men watched the sun struggle to cast one last glimmer of light on the gorge.

Will's voice cracked, revealing the awe of what he just witnessed "Which...way to... Taos?"

"We'll be home soon." John coaxed his horse into a fast trot down a dusty trail. Will and the wagon followed. They arrived as darkness fell on Taos. The Trading Post was a fortified compound of buildings that belonged to John Rowland and William Workman. John's wife Maria Martinez Rowland ordered the gate opened. They entered a walled fortress with gun towers and armed sentinels.

"Thank God you are alive, John!" Maria's voice quivered as she embraced her husband.

"What's wrong Maria? Why are you so upset?" John asked.

"Everyone, please come quickly into the sala grande," Maria motioned them forward, "we have many guests waiting for you. Please hurry Señor Workman…Señor Dryden…and this must be Mr. Smith. Bella has told me much about you."

Will stopped, "How could she?"

"My niece Bella is here, now. She came just an hour ago. Welcome to our Hacienda. " Maria hurried them inside.

The sala grande was a large room for fandangos and family gatherings. Small fireplaces burned sweet-smelling pinion at each end. Their guests, neighbors and friends waited—mostly couples of Anglo men and their Spanish wives—wanting to hear the events of the day, which might change their lives forever.

Will looked for Bella and hurried to her and embraced her, "Bella, how did you get here?"

"I came the back way. Please, I must tell everyone what I know at the same time." Bella motioned for him to sit.

Will took a seat but couldn't take his eyes off Bella, who returned his glances with a smile. He had learned from her Uncle John that Bella means beautiful in Spanish. *An appropriate name for such a lovely woman,* will thought.

Maria welcomed everyone, making introductions in Spanish and English, but intentionally did not recognize Will.

She introduced Bella, who had become emotionally distraught. With comfort from her Aunt Maria who she called Tia, Bella began.

"I bring you news from Santa Fe and a message from Governor Ar…mijo." Bella's dislike for Armijo showed when she pronounced his name. "My Brother, Ramon, was arrested this morning…by the Mexican army…they tortured him," she sobbed, "He is only fourteen years old."

Maria put an arm around her niece and said, "I will tell them, if you wish."

"Por favor…Tia." Bella sat down next to Will and he took her hand to comfort her.

Bella gave Will's hand a gentle squeeze. Her presence stirred emotions he had never felt before.

Maria explained the Mexican army captured her nephew Ramon Miranda and made him divulge information that implicated his father Miguel Miranda in the Invasion of Santa Fe. Miguel surrendered to the authorities to secure the release of his son.

"Arrest warrants have been issued for my husband and his business partner…William Workman." Maria paused, "They wish to hang Señor Dryden…for treason." She took a deep breath, "My poor sister's husband, Miguel, will not be released until they surrender." She sobbed. "The soldiers have already come. Searched my house…and accused us of treason against the Mexican government." Maria totally broke down in tears.

John rose to comfort his wife. When he held Maria, she asked him to finish for her. Which he did. He tied up loose ends, the best he could, without revealing William Workman's communication with Padre Martinez.

In closing, John said, "Those who can't live under Mexican rule should consider leaving Nuevo México immediately."

Maria looked at John in disbelief at what she heard. She was born here. Her family had roots back to the earliest Spaniards to arrive. Lifelong friends lived here. She couldn't leave them or the beautiful hacienda they had built. "No! I will not leave my home!" Maria stormed out of the room.

Embarrassed by his spouse's reaction in front of guests, John knew better than to say anything to his strong-willed wife. She would have more to say when she came to bed. He would hear her out in silence and then calmly explain to his wife what Workman had learned from her cousin Padre Martinez. The priest and John's wife's relationship was never discussed. If asked, the family didn't deny the kinship. A feud over property rights, many years before Maria's birth, had created a schism in the family.

John adjourned the meeting by saying, "It's been a long day, amigos. We should eat. The food is waiting." He pointed toward the long pine table in the back of the room. "Then rest and consider our options another day."

Bella made a plate for Will and herself. She asked him to sit with her on leather cushions by the fireplace in the sala grande. They ate as Mariachis played string instruments and sang for the guests.

Bella was mesmerized by Will's hazel eyes which were rare in Mexican Territory. She said, "Will, your eyes are full of sadness." She touched his hand discreetly.

"I'm sorry…I just dread leaving without finding Fayette."

"I know you wish to find him, but you must leave before the soldiers find you."

The music became louder, making it difficult to hear. Will asked, "Is there somewhere quiet where we can talk?"

"Sí we can go to the weavers' room. The fire should still be burning. The weavers have gone home. It is a quiet place where we can talk."

They crossed the courtyard to the storerooms away from the main house. In the weavers' room were four large looms across a long but narrow workspace. Here, Pueblo Indians spun wool into coarse thread to weave Indian blankets. The fire was nearly out, so Will placed logs on the embers while Bella lit candles.

They sat on a stack of finished blankets and held hands.

Will said, "Bella I'm so glad to see you again."

"I'm glad we're together again even if just for a few moments." Bella moved into Will's arms.

"Are you cold Bella?"

"Not now that I'm in your arms." Bella snuggled closer, "Will, why aren't you married?"

"I just haven't found the right girl. I had a girlfriend once when I lived in Alabama."

"Who was she?"

"Her name was Sara."

"What happened to her Will?"

"We moved to Texas. Some of our neighbors came with us. Her family stayed in Coosa, Alabama. I'm sure she's married by now." Will gave Bella a gentle squeeze, "I never had the feelings for her that I have for you, Bella." Will embraced and kissed Bella for the first time. "You said we would meet again. How did you get here before us?" He kissed her neck. They kissed and touched each other passionately; he gently cupped her breast.

Bella gasped, enjoying his kisses, "I came on horseback up the Miranda Valley." They kissed again. "It is faster...but a wagon can't... go that way."

Bella pulled away, gasping for breath. "It has been a long time since a man has made me feel this way. I'm...so confused." She stood up. "I must help my tia clean up. I hear the guests leaving. Tia will come looking for me, as she worries about me. I will see you in the morning."

"Promise?"

Bella nodded her head nervously. "Please wait here for a few minutes. I don't want the guests to know we were alone. Your room is in the corner, three doors down."

"I will be thinking of you in my dreams," Will let go of her hands.

She pulled the door latch and turned for what she thought was her last kiss from the gringo from Texas. She kissed Will passionately and then ran toward the sala grande. He stood there alone, longing for more.

Will was sequestered near the distilling room. The small room had one door and no windows. From outside, the room appeared to be part of the distillery, which is why his hosts had chosen it for him. It was built for the seven-foot-tall Navajo Indian who tended the stills during the winter. His comfortable, oversized bed made up for the lack of a window.

For added security, Will pulled a writing desk in front of the door. It was not heavy enough to stop an intruder, but it would slow their entry. Will fretted about the bounty on his head; he had arrested men that killed for less.

Bella entered the sala grande and found Maria Rowland in a much better mood. "Where have you been?" Maria asked, already knowing the answer.

"We were talking," Bella picked up a plate.

Maria smiled. "I just asked where you were. You're a grown woman who has been widowed for nearly five years. You don't have to tell me anything."

"I'm so confused, Tia. I don't understand what is happening to me."

Maria took the plate. "Will is the first man I have seen you attracted to. He reminds me of my John. It was love that I felt the first time I saw him. I knew he was the man I wished to spend the rest of my life with."

"Tia, please tell me what I should do? Will is leaving in the morning. I may never see him again."

"I can tell that Will cares greatly for you and you for him. I have never seen you smile as you did sitting with him tonight. I think you are in love with him, Bella."

"You think so?" Bella picked up more plates. Maria approached her and looked deep into her eyes, "I've never seen you look so happy."

"I just met him, Tia. He's leaving in the morning. What should I do?" Bella pleaded.

"It is like when I met John. I knew he was the only man for me."

"Should I go to him, Tia?"

"If it were my John that was leaving…I would want to spend every minute in his arms until he leaves in the morning." Maria touched Bella's arm, "You must never tell your parents what I say."

"Never, Tia, would I do that."

"I have put night clothes on your bed. Go now and make yourself ready for the one you love."

"I love you, Tia." Bella kissed her aunt on the cheek.

"No one must know but us," Maria said.

Bella went to her room to wash up and change from the clothes she rode in from Santa Fe. There was no time to pack for her urgent journey. Maria had laid out a beautiful white sleeping gown.

Bella ruffled up the bedding of her bed, using pillows to make it appear she was in bed. She wrapped an Indian blanket over her shoulders and then tip-toed out of the house, crossing over to the row of warehouses. She moved in the shadows to avoid the eyes of the sentinels. A slight dusting of snow was falling.

She knocked lightly on Will's door. His blood raced as he instinctively reached for his revolvers. With a gun in each hand, Will moved away from the wooden door to the protection of the thick adobe walls.

"Who is there?"

"It is Bella; I must talk to you."

"Are you alone, Bella?"

"Yes, I'm alone."

He hurriedly moved the desk and slowly opened the door. Will looked around the empty courtyard and gently pulled Bella inside his room.

They embraced passionately. Groping, she unbuttoned Will's shirt. He removed the blanket from her shoulders. Will heard the sound of gravel and snow crunching on the walkway outside his door. He turned for his guns on the desk and pushed the desk back against the door.

Bella said, "It is the sentinel. He is here for our protection. We are safe…for now."

"Are you sure Bella? The bounty for me…is tempting." Will placed his guns back on the desk and turned to see Bella sitting on the bed.

Bella extended both arms. "The guard is my cousin. We are safe." She took his hand and he sat next to her. He didn't know what to do—but Bella did.

They'd met only the day before. The fast-paced happenings since created a close relationship out of necessity and survival, regardless of the language and cultural differences. As the wick in the candle became short, two hearts became one—their fears set aside for the passion of the moment. Each knew they could be arrested by Mexican soldiers at any moment and that this might be their last time together.

Across the snow-covered courtyard in the library, the Texas Commissioners shared a bottle of brandy and discussed their future.

Dryden sighed, "I created this problem. Only I can correct it."

"Just how in hell do you plan to do that, Dryden?" Workman took a sip of brandy.

"I have pondered our situation for some time." Dryden instinctively rose from the table to make his point, "President Lamar doesn't want a war with Mexico," Dryden put his knuckles on the table. "According to Will, Texas is near insolvency. Its army has disbanded. Lamar's Presidency is over. The new president will most likely be Sam Houston."

"What if David Burnet is elected the next president and not Houston?" Workman raised his eyebrows.

"Most Texans feel Houston is their only hope. Old Sam just might be able to clean up this financial mess Lamar created. Houston doesn't need a war any more than Santa Anna wants another fight."

"Dryden, I think you are right." Workman stood to pour another glass of brandy, "This trouble isn't between Texas and Mexico, it's about two mean little bastards' egos."

William Dryden laid out a plan which all agreed may work. They would enlist Padre Martinez's assistance to negotiate with Governor Armijo. The padre was the only person the egotistical governor would listen to. Dryden would surrender to authorities, admitting his complicity with President Lamar to annex Nuevo México. If Armijo released Thomas Rowland and Miguel Miranda immediately, they would assure the governor that should a Texas invasion occur—they would not be a part of it. The reward for Will would be rescinded. He would go back to Austin to persuade Lamar to reconsider the expedition.

Morning came too soon for Will and Bella. They had no regrets. Both felt as if it were meant to be. They would be together for eternity. Will had reservations about leaving her.

Someone brought breakfast. They knocked lightly and then left the tray at their door. Bella retrieved it; the couple devoured their breakfast, giving them the strength to make love one more time.

Wrapped in each other's arms, they laid exhausted on the bed, gazing up at the large vigas that supported the earthen roof. Bella and Will were deep in their own thoughts and fears of the future.

"Take me to Texas with you?" Bella asked.

Will thought about how much he wanted to take her with him. Then the reality of his situation sank in. "You understand I am a wanted man, with a large bounty on my head." She rolled on her side, not wanting to hear what he was saying but knowing he was right. Will rolled with Bella as if they had been lovers forever. "It wouldn't be safe. I'll come for you when it's safe. I promise."

Bella turned toward him and sat up, "I will worry every moment. Until I know you're safe." Bella removed a medallion that she wore around her neck and gave it to Will. "You wear the medal of St. Benedict. It will protect you. When you touch it, I hope you will remember me."

Will slipped the medal over his head and kissed it. "Bella, I will always remember you."

He opened his saddlebag, "This star was carved by my brother Fenwick from a silver coin: a Mexican cinco peso. I want you to have it…to remember me."

A knock at the door interrupted them. "Will we need to get you safely out of Taos," John said.

"I will be right out," Will answered, his eyes still on Bella.

Will dressed hastily, and then looked into Bella's sad eyes as he tucked in his shirt.

"I pray for your safety." Bella stood on her toes for one last kiss. Will moved to the door, bags in hand. Bella stood wrapped in a white sheet. To Will, she looked like a Roman goddess that he'd seen in a book. He wanted to remember every feature of her being: the smell of her hair, her smile, and her brown eyes, now misty with sadness. He slowly opened the door. John was waiting.

John said, "Your horse is saddled. Supplies and grub are on your burro. Eduardo, my wife's cousin, and I will get you to the trail to Bent's Fort." As they hurried toward the stables, snow and gravel crunched under their feet.

John hollered in Spanish to the sentinel on the wall. The all-clear signal was given, and a burly gatekeeper pushed opened the heavy double gates of the compound. Three horsemen and a burro rode slowly out onto the main road. Edwardo led, and John and Will quietly followed, not wanting to attract attention. The trail was now covered with a light dusting of snow. Once out of the village of Taos, they spurred their mounts toward Three Mile Creek. They hid amongst tall pinion trees and allowed their animals to rest and drink from the half-frozen stream named for the distance from Taos.

"The weather looks good, Will." John looked at the sky "Once over Raton Pass, you'll be far from anyone who could know who you are. Travelers coming the other way won't know of the bounty. We're requesting that Governor Armijo rescind the reward for you."

"Will he do that?" Will raised his eyebrows.

"I think so. Once Dryden surrenders, we'll tell the governor that only you can get word to Lamar not to invade Nuevo México. "

John handed Will a sealed envelope addressed: President Mirabeau Lamar, Capitol of the Republic of Texas, at Austin.

"What's this?" Will looked warily at the envelope.

"It explains in detail the situation here in Nuevo México. We ask President Lamar to cancel his expedition. Attached are letters of our resignations."

Will carefully placed the documents into his saddlebags. "Thank you, John. For everything." Will straddled his horse, "I want to ask a favor of you."

"What's that?"

"I want you to be my best man. I'm coming back to marry Bella!"

"I would be honored," John said. He climbed on his horse. "We'll do everything we can to find your Fayette and return him to Austin."

Will turned toward Raton Pass. The Santa Fe Trail was the long way back to Texas, but it was the safest route.

He regretted not bringing Bella but knew he'd made the right decision. If the trip wasn't safe for him, it wouldn't be safe for her. Since coming to Texas, Will had lost a brother, his nephew Fayette had been captured, and more than a dozen good friends had been killed by Indian depredations. His youngest brother Fenwick would never be the same after witnessing the gruesome mutilation of their brother, James.

Will planned to pen a letter to Bella when he reached Bent's Fort. As he rode along the rocky trail, he made a mental list of all the feelings he had for her. Riding from sunup 'til sundown gave a man time to dream. Will imagined the great life Bella and he could have together: *A special woman like Bella needs a fine house and furnishings, not a dirt floor cabin like mine. Maybe I can take her to Alabama. She would like the Coosa River with its fertile river bottom. I could study to be a doctor like my brother John. Our children would have plenty of cousins and a fine education in Coosa.*

He suddenly realized he couldn't send a letter as it would compromise the safety of the Miranda family.

Chapter Ten

Will made it to Raton Pass in three days, halfway to Bent's Fort, but still a long way from home. From the highest point of Raton Pass, Will observed a solid white mass on the trail. It was miles away, slowly moving north. *Snow?* he wondered. *Maybe a caravan of wagons?* If it was, they were headed toward Bent's Fort. It took most of the day to overtake the white sea of movement. When he got near, the sounds of thousands of bleating sheep intensified. Will, his horse, and the burro were annoyed by the noise and smell. The sheep appeared to be herding their wooly bodies along the trail without any human direction. At places, the herds' width was a quarter-of-a-mile wide, and the length was twice that long. The large wooly critters made way for the intruders' presence. They continued on, following each other—as sheep do. If spooked, the flock bleated even louder as they jumped over one another. The last thing Will wanted was to stampede this large flock of wooly backs.

He saw riders trying to tighten the breadth of the herd on each side of the trail. The vaqueros had been in the woods rounding up strays. His presence in the middle of this island of sheep was complicating their efforts. Will pulled back the reins, and Sam and Deacon stopped in their tracks. The sheep continued around him until he was behind the herd.

Someone stood. He'd been there all along, crouching in the sea of sheep. The herdsman waved. Will waved his hat in the air for all to see. Others started rising from the flock, waving, one by one: four vaqueros on horseback with dogs herding the sheep.

The sheepherders didn't know Will was a wanted man. If he joined them, he would have some protection from bounty hunters. The herdsmen appeared friendly. Will hoped they spoke English.

Besides, Will couldn't get around the sheep if he wanted to. When the last ewe ambled by his horse, he stayed back, but close enough to help if needed. The herdsmen seemed to appreciate his concern for not spooking the herd.

As the shadows of the mountains grew longer, the herdsmen began to turn the flock towards an open meadow, which was not an easy undertaking, but it was well executed. The meadow was a natural clearing created between two peaks. The closeness of the peaks prohibited sunshine, retarding any growth of vegetation.

Two strange-looking wagons camped on a knoll near a running creek. Two men waved everyone in, including Will. It was the sheepherders' camp. A short young man in a derby hat appeared to be in charge. *A sheep rancher,* Will assumed.

The rancher greeted the men in Spanish. Everyone appeared to be in good spirits. The herdsman said something to the rancher in Spanish that Will didn't understand. The rancher had an accent—definitely not an Irish brogue, but he did have the ruddy complexion of an Irishman. Will learned that the man's father was Irish, but he was raised by his mother's French Canadian family, which accounted for the French-Canadian accent.

"You from the States?" The rancher asked.

Will started to say Texan but decided to just nod his head in agreement.

"You speak English?"

"It's all I know," Will said.

"Damn glad to have someone around who speaks English, for a change because the herders only speak Spanish. My cook, Navajo, speaks a little English." The rancher scratched his blonde whiskers and said, "My name is Lucian Bonaparte Maxwell. My friends call me Max."

Will shook Max's hand. "Just call me…ah…Bill."

"Welcome…Bill." Max pointed at the man he spoke to earlier, "Carlos, my herdsman, says you helped with the herd today. I appreciate that. Would you join us for some grub that my cook has prepared?" He pointed at the Indian kneeling by the fire. "Navajo doesn't take too kindly of people turning down an invitation to eat his cooking."

The Indian stood to welcome Will. He was the tallest man Will had ever seen. He was at least a head taller than Big Foot Wallace—a very tall Texas Ranger Will had served with.

"I would be honored to join you, Max, and enjoy Navajo's cooking."

The big Indian stared at Will and looked deep into his eyes. His enormous hand grasped Will's outstretched hand. The Indian shook it in an unfriendly way that disturbed Will.

"Glad to meet you, Navajo," Will said.

They supped on flame roasted mutton, camp beans, and biscuits. Afterward, they sat around the campfire. Carlos sat by the fire playing his harmonica. Max opened a crock of Turley's white lightning and offered Will a cigar. He declined both. Knowing that sobriety was in his best interest at the moment.

"Bill, you don't drink, don't smoke?" Max shook his head, "Are you a man of the cloth?"

"No, just a man that likes to keep his mind clear."

Max stretched out on his bedroll. "I like that," Max said. He blew a large ring of smoke and asked, "you Catholic?"

"No." Will was becoming nervous about all of Max's questions, so he decided to become the interrogator.

"Max, how did you, being such a young man, come by all these sheep?" Will looked around, "Sheep as far as I can see."

"Winters get mighty cold here in the mountains. Not much to do if you don't have a woman," Max shifted trying to get comfortable and continued, "except play poker and drink whiskey." He took another swig from his crock. "I won hundreds of them damn four-legged critters…

about four years ago. They multiply like jackrabbits; I don't know how many I have. When you have this many, you can't count them. Carlos thinks there is about two thousand head. We'll know after they're sheared. They'll be counted one by one as they're put out to pasture."

"When will you shear them?" Will asked.

"When we get them to Bent's Fort," Max said.

"When will that be?"

"A week or so after Easter, or when Carlos is sure the winter storms are over. Can't let these little woolies freeze to death cause we sheared them too soon," Max said.

"The Navajo shearers meet us at Bent's Fort. It's a sight to watch all these critters inside the walls of the fort. The shears snipping away, wool flying everywhere...like it's snowing." Max imitated the motion of snowflakes falling.

"They shear um close...to get all that precious wool they can. The shearers get a part for the shearing. My herders take a share and I keep the rest."

Max explained wool was bringing thirty cents a pound in St. Louis. The big Spanish Merino ewes and rams he owned could produce ten to twelve pounds per year. He could get three dollars for their wool and still have his sheep. Ewes lambed at least once, sometimes twice a year. Many had twins.

Max said, "Sheep ranching is kinda like whoring—you sell it and you still have it!"

"That's funny, Max." Will stood and stretched, "Mind if I bed down near your camp?"

"Not at all! You're welcome to ride to Bent's Fort with us if that's where you heading?"

"I appreciate the offer, but I have business in Independence. I'll need to get on the road ahead of your sheep in the morning. I'll get my bedroll now and spread out near the fire."

"Be careful of that big ram, Bill." Max pointed toward a large horned sheep, "He might think you...is a ewe!" Max had his last laugh of the night.

When Will went to get his bedroll, he noticed Navajo looking at his gear but not touching anything. "You come from Taos?" Navajo asked. He towered over the 6'2" Will.

"No…from Santa Fe," Will answered.

"You go… way…of… Taos?" Navajo asked.

"No, why do you ask?"

Navajo didn't answer the question. "You…sleep good. Navajo… watch!"

Will interpreted the Indian's statement more like a warning than reassurance that he would be safe. "See you in the morning." Will picked up his bedroll, laid it out near the campfire, and bedded down for the night. He kept wondering why the big Indian didn't like him.

Will woke to the smell of breakfast and coffee boiling in a large coffee pot that hung from a wooden tripod. Max stood, intently looking at Will's gear. Will thought the interest in his provisions was strange. Max and Navajo were having a lively conversation. Will couldn't make out what they were saying, but it appeared serious.

Max approached Will. "Bill, you got any coffee in your provisions? We're a bit short."

"I do and its fresh ground." Will retrieved a two-pound bag of freshly ground coffee.

Max opened the linen bag and smelled its contents. Then Max poured a handful of ground coffee in Navajo's palm. The Indian smelled the coffee, then stuck his finger in his mouth, dabbing the wet finger in the coffee. Navajo licked it off his finger, nodded to Max, and then went back to cooking.

"It's good coffee, I've made a couple of pots from it." Will looked at Max, "Brews up good."

"Where did you get it?" Max asked.

"Santa Fe. Why do you care where I get my coffee?" Will raised his brow.

Max said, "It's not about coffee, it's about honesty. You lied to us. I don't want anyone in my camp I can't trust."

"What have I lied about?"

"You told us you didn't come through Taos," Max said.

"What makes you think I did?" Will looked Max in the eye.

"The coffee you have can only be bought at Rowland and Workman's Trading Post in Taos and nowhere else. Navajo roasts the beans for John Rowland and he adds a secret ingredient that only he knows."

"Oh…" Will looked down at his feet.

"Besides, you wear the medal of St. Benedict and you're not Catholic. What's your real name anyway?" Max tossed the bag of coffee at him.

"I would rather not say."

Max pointed to the trail "Then get your gear… and clear out!"

Will stammered, "I'm…I'm sorry. I…had good reason."

"There is never a good reason for lying!" Max turned away.

Will felt dejected and embarrassed because he knew what Max said was true. He regretted telling an untruth to his host. Lives were at stake so he did what he thought was right at the time. Will was not used to deception and clearly wasn't very good at it.

Will's goal was to make it to Timpas Creek before dark. John Rowland's map noted Timpas Creek was halfway between Raton Pass and Bent's Fort. It also mentioned Comanche Indians frequented the area. He hadn't seen as much as a jack rabbit since leaving the sheepherders. He stopped to unpack his revolvers, which he knew could identify him. It was a risk Will was willing to take because he knew his single-shot rifle would do little good against the short bows of the Comanche.

By the tenth day of March, Will was north of the Raton Pass on the Santa Fe Trail. He looked out over the open grassland with views for miles and saw movement in a large break of juniper a quarter of a mile to the east. Will saw the horses—first two, then another, and another—but not riders. Four horses were being led single file through the thicket, most likely an Indian hunting party. He rode on like he wasn't aware of their presence.

Will slowly wandered off the trail into a thicket of his choosing. If they followed, then he would know they were hostile Indians. Will dismounted, dropped George's reins, and signaled the horse to stay. The burro tied to George couldn't wander. Will climbed a large boulder. He carried all his ammunition, a gourd of water, and buffalo jerky. The rock, the size of a small cabin, was surrounded by salt cedars, which was sufficient for cover, but open toward the trail. He laid out his percussion caps for the colt revolvers, loaded his rifle, and five rounds in each cylinder of his pistols. From his elevated position, Will had a fighting chance against four Indians.

The sun beat down on the rock, making the surface hot to the touch. Without a whisper of breeze, Will's shirt became soaked with perspiration. He wiped sweat from his brow with the back of his hand.

The first brave came into sight riding a paint horse—the others close behind. They had short bows of warriors, not the long bows of hunters. The young braves had a lively discussion, and then the leader pointed the direction of Will's tracks. Thinking their prey was on the move, unaware of their presence, the Indians followed the trail toward the boulder. The prey—now the predator—watched and waited.

Will had a bead on the leader; he took a deep breath, finger on the trigger. When his target came within twenty yards of his sights, he pulled the trigger. The sixty-nine caliber flintlock boomed, echoing through the canyon. Birds and animals scattered. George nickered at the boom but didn't move.

Blue smoke lingered, revealing his position. When the smoke cleared, Will saw the Indian he shot sprawled on the ground. Expecting a full charge from the other warriors, he reloaded the Springfield

Flintlock and waited. The Comanche usually charged after the first shot. They knew the white man's long gun only held one round. With short bows, the Comanche could usually eliminate a lone gunman before he could reload.

The anticipation of the attack took its toll. *What are they up to? Waiting for more warriors? It's me against three of them. I can take them if they will just make a move.* They wanted Will to make the first move. Time was on his side. Experience had taught him to wait. The shrill call of a quail came from a clump of salt cedar. Another call came from the other side. Will knew the quail calls came from the Indians. They split and were circling for the kill. The young braves had tired of waiting. Will was anxious.

An Indian darted out of a cedar break only twenty yards in front of his position, zigzagging from tree to tree directly in front of the boulder. Will fired his rifle and missed. The Indian rushed Will's position. He tried to scale the front side of the boulder. A knife was the warrior's only weapon. Will grabbed both colts and fired down at the Indian. The second shot took him down. The other two Indians scaled the rock from the rear and also attempted to attack with knives. Will quickly dropped them with the remaining shots. They died not understanding how the white man could have fired so fast.

Will reloaded and waited for the smoke to clear. The Indians made only the gurgling sounds of death. There was no movement. Will descended from the boulder, loaded his gear on the burro, and stopped to view his kill. Impressed by the accuracy and the effectiveness of the new Colt Paterson Revolvers, he felt no pity or guilt. Will had turned as savage as the Indians who had killed his brother.

Chapter Eleven

*F*ayette was alone in hostile Indian Country, far from anywhere. He knew that beyond where the sun comes up every day was Austin. He continued to follow the twists and turns of the mountain stream one way and then the other, because it provided him with water. He had to get out of the canyon but everything looked the same and he became lost and confused. Fayette thought if he could get up high on a mountaintop, then maybe he could see the wagon trail or a settler's cabin. He searched for a way up, but the rock walls always forced him down.

Time no longer mattered, or what month it was. Barefoot, his clothes threadbare except for his buffalo robe, he survived on pinion nuts and bugs. The spear Fayette whittled for protection, he hoped would skewer his next meal. Captivity seemed a better option than what Fayette now endured. He would gladly return to the Indians, if only he knew where they were.

A loud boom echoed through the canyon. Fayette instinctively ducked behind a boulder, fearing he was the target. Not sure where the gunshot came from, he hunkered down and listened. All Fayette heard was his heart pounding in his chest. He breathed heavy and thought about his predicament. He remembered his father's words: "When you don't know what to do—do nothing until you have sorted out all your options."

Fayette thought that the Indians may have fired the shot, or it may be a search party was looking for him. Tired and hungry, he fell asleep, but was awakened by sounds of a broad axe. White men cut and split wood for their fire, but the Indians had yet to learn the advantages of burning split wood. Fayette recognized the sounds of a white man's axe.

Venturing cautiously toward the sound of human activity, Fayette saw whiffs of smoke coming from a hollow. He followed a game trail toward the smoke and found a fallen timber that had once been a towering pine now downed by a bolt of lightning.

Fayette scaled the giant tree trunk for a better view. He heard the excited bray of mules and a barking dog. The wood chopping stopped.

Someone pulled back a robe and exited the dwelling, followed by a large dog. He walked like a man and swung a man-size axe. The person appeared to be alone, except for the dog, three mules and several goats running about. The carcass of a deer hung from an Aspen tree.

Fayette was relieved the deer was the target of the shot fired earlier. *Time to meet this goat man,* Fayette decided. He scooted down the girth of the mammoth trunk. Near ground level, he leaped and landed hard, falling forward on his hands. He stood to face the barrel of a rifle and a growling dog.

"Please don't shoot…I mean no harm."

"You're just a boy!"

"Yes, sir. I…was nine…my…last birthday," Fayette stuttered.

"You got no shoes." The man lowered his gun, "Your feet cold?"

"Don't know…I can't feel anything," Fayette looked down at his bare feet.

"I'm Jeremiah, this is my dog Caleb." Jeremiah reached toward Fayette, "Shake my hand so Caleb knows you aren't a threat to us."

Caleb was the largest dog Fayette had ever seen. It had long shaggy black and white hair. You could barely see its golden eyes, for the hair. If it wasn't for the white in its coat, it would resemble a bear. What tail remained wagged excitedly. Caleb greeted Fayette with a slobbery kiss. They became instant friends.

"This way." Jeremiah ambled down the trail towards his camp. Fayette and Caleb followed. Jeremiah reminded Fayette of the cedar-choppers who had cleared land for Austin. His face couldn't be seen for the beard and moustache. He wore a coonskin hat with the ringtail still attached, and a bowie knife was attached to his belt. His buffalo coat had sleeves and a collar that buttoned. The pants had pockets front and back. He wore a deerskin glove on his left hand, the right one was tucked in his back pocket. A powder horn and shot bag on a leather lanyard hung loosely around his neck. He was not a large man but fit and dressed for the outdoor life he lived.

Milk goats greeted them at the lean-to. They bleated, nudging Fayette and Jeremiah for attention.

"When did you eat last?" Jeremiah asked.

"Don't remember. I ate a few pinion nuts and some beetles yesterday."

"I'll fix you something a bit tastier." Jeremiah smiled.

Fayette told how he came to be lost in the mountains. Jeremiah listened as he warmed yesterday's stew. After eating several bowls, Fayette laid back on the comfort of a bed of bear robes. He shut his weary eyes and quickly drifted back to Austin. Dreaming of a reunion with family.

Thirty-year-old Jeremiah Busch was the youngest of Fredrick Busch's children. The Busch family was one of the founders of St. Louis. Fredrick Busch and Sons were known as the town's oldest and best tailors. Jeremiah had, along with his four older brothers, toiled in the shop. Jeremiah learned the family trade, but quickly tired of it. Having heard tales of the West, he yearned to see the other end of the Santa Fe Trail. A romance gone awry was his excuse to escape the humdrum life of a tailor. Jeremiah sought adventure as a mountain man.

While Fayette recuperated, Jeremiah crafted him deerskin boots, pants, and shirt. His previous tools of trade provided the tailor warm and comfortable clothing. Jeremiah found solace in sewing for Fayette. The work he once despised now provided him with a distraction from the everyday struggles of mountain life.

Fayette didn't wake for two days, except to eat or relieve nature's call. Caleb had patiently shared his bed with Fayette. It was time to get up. The dog licked his face. With a yawn, the boy rubbed Caleb's ears. The smell of venison strips smoking over the campfire aroused his hunger.

"What smells so good?" Fayette stretched and yawned.

"Making venison jerky," Jeremiah said

After eating his fill of venison stew and sourdough biscuits and cream gravy, Jeremiah showed Fayette the boots and clothes he made.

"You made these for me?" Fayette held the boots to his chest. "Thank you, Jeremiah."

"You need to wash before trying them on." Jeremiah pointed toward a small table he'd made from the green saplings of an aspen tree. Steam rose from the tin bucket. "Soap and water awaits you, my boy!" Jeremiah looked at Fayette's' dirty hair. "Be sure to wash your hair. I'm going to trim that head of yours."

The smell of pine-tar soap brought back memories of Saturday nights in the bathtub.

His Pa would say, "Fayette don't forget to wash where the sun don't shine." Fayette tried to wash the memory of his father's violent death from his mind.

"Damn...Injuns!" Fayette blurted out.

"What's wrong?" Jeremiah asked.

"Nothing's wrong." Fayette vigorously scrubbed his scalp.

Jeremiah trimmed strands of red hair that hung over Fayette's sunburned face, leaving what covered his head and shoulders for protection from sun. He fitted Fayette for a coonskin cap. Deerskin gloves completed Fayette's mountain wardrobe.

Feeding mules, milking goats, and checking beaver traps were Fayette's chores around camp. Playing fetch with Caleb and watching the antics of the goats prevented boredom.

Jeremiah had learned mountaineering and trapping by devouring every book or newspaper story he could read on the subject. With book learning and the tales he'd heard, Jeremiah signed on with a Santa Fe bound caravan. His initial job was as an "outrider," the wagon masters' first line of defense against Indian attacks.

Twenty-four wagons left West Port in the spring of 1838. They took the lower route of the Santa Fe Trail. It ventured southwest through Cimarron Springs, crossing Mora Creek. Jeremiah drew a map in his journal of the place he chose to make his home, returning after the caravan made it safely to Santa Fe.

Jeremiah settled in a small basin on the east side of the Sangre de Cristo Mountains, which faced the Mora Valley. From camp, he could see buffalo roaming the gentle hills of the valley below. The river provided abundant fish and beaver to trap. Deer, elk, and bear could be shot from camp. Trading posts in Santa Fe or Taos were less than a hundred miles away.

Fayette studied Jeremiah's writings on mountaineering and trapping. Fortunately, he'd learned to read at an early age. Fayette was the first to read Jeremiah's manuscript. The author envisioned a book published for greenhorns going west.

Now an experienced outrider, Jeremiah could negotiate Fayette free passage. Jeremiah realized it was time to go home. He had seen the West, trapped its game, and proven his manliness. Now with a manuscript of his adventures, which included saving a nine-year-old boy, he was ready to go home.

Jeremiah missed his family, the tailor shop, and the comforts of civilization. Fayette afforded him the opportunity to go home not in defeat, but in triumph. Reuniting an Indian captive with his family would be a rewarding experience. His family would approve his heroic efforts. The public would want to read his story.

Fayette gained weight and grew stronger each day. Both were anxious to begin their arduous journey. The Columbines bloomed in the valley, signaling that winter was over. After the season's pelts and supplies were loaded on the mules, Jeremiah secured his lean-to as if he was coming back. He knew he wasn't. He left a note for the next trailblazer, and then noted in his journal: "Left for Santa Fe the third day of April 1841. Fayette Smith is with me."

Above the timberline, snow still covered the mountains. Warmer than usual weather had started the spring thaw. Frosty nights re-froze the days' runoff—especially on the shady side of the mountain where icy spots were created on an already treacherous trail. While going to Santa Fe on the wagon trail would've been easier through Apache Canyon, it was twice the distance.

Going through a narrow crevice single file, Jeremiah led the first mule with the other two mules tethered behind the first. Fayette and Caleb coaxed them along from the rear as needed. The trail made a sharp turn to the left. All Fayette could see was the rear end of the last mule. Jeremiah was in front, a distance of about fifty feet. Suddenly, the earth shook, making a rumbling noise. Fayette instinctively backed up against the canyon wall—protected by a natural ledge over his head. He watched tons of dirt and rock tumble in front of him, down hundreds of feet to the canyon floor. It was only a few minutes before the last rock tumbled. When it was over, Jeremiah and his mules were gone. An eerie silence prevailed, and the crows stopped crowing.

The trail was gone. Caleb now covered in the yellow dust of the mountain, found Fayette. They cuddled under the ledge. It happened so fast. One minute the mules were in front of him—the last one an arm's length away. Three mules and Jeremiah were gone. The mountain had devoured them.

Caleb barked. Fayette, dazed and partially blinded by thick dust, followed the dog down into the canyon. Caleb ran about sniffing the large pile of debris. The mound was larger than a two-story house. Fayette dug where he could with his bare hands. He called for Jeremiah again and again. There was no sound except Caleb's whimper. Fayette tried to calm the dog and by doing so calmed himself.

Fayette woke to reality the next morning. Dawn's first light crept slowly into the canyon. It cast a pale glow on the mountain. The unfamiliar surrounding confused Fayette. He saw where a large piece of the mountain broke away, taking Jeremiah and the mules with it. Yet, they were saved by a rock ledge, which Fayette didn't even know was there.

Lying on the rubble, Caleb inched closer to Fayette for comfort. The dog, too large to hold, snuggled close. Fayette felt for its ears in the dog's shaggy head of fur. As he rubbed the ears gently between his fingers, Fayette felt the dog's tense muscles relax.

I am just a boy. What to do? No food and a hungry dog, Fayette thought.

Their last meal was breakfast the day before. *Do I look for the Indians? Would they even take me in after losing Preacher?* Fayette got up from the mound of dirt and dusted yellow dust particles from his clothes. Caleb's tail wagged, giving Fayette confidence to start the day.

If they were to escape the canyon, Fayette would have to make his own trail. They stopped at the upper side of the giant mound of dirt. Fayette tried to say goodbye to Jeremiah but was interrupted by Caleb's barking. The dog saw something in a pinion tree.

"What is it, Caleb? Do you see something?"

He stood next to the excited dog and looked up for a critter that wasn't there. It was the first time Caleb had gone on point and not spotted something. Fayette walked away from the tree. Caleb got in front of him, blocking his way and making a fuss. Fayette went back and again looked up into the tree. Halfway up the thirty-foot pinion tree was a haversack dangling from a small limb, as if someone had deliberately placed it there.

Fayette climbed the tree to get it. He pulled the limb towards him, and the limb's movement dislodged the canvas bag. The heavy sack fell to the ground with a thunk. As Fayette climbed down the tree, Caleb sat obediently before the sack.

"Good boy!" Fayette rubbed Caleb's head.

Fayette was crying by the time he untied the sack. It held biscuits and freshly smoked jerky. Inside a side pocket was Jeremiah's Journal. Fayette shared a large piece of Jeremiah's smoked jerky with Caleb. Fayette sat down beside the dog and read Jeremiah's journal.

Fortunately for Fayette, Jeremiah wrote meticulous notes and made detailed maps in his journal of his travels. He found a map of an alternate trail up the mountain, which could be climbed on foot.

"See Caleb, Jeremiah is still with us." Fayette looked up.

Caleb released a bark that Fayette needed to hear.

Fayette and the dog made the mountains crest before dark. They found a small cave on the other side that provided shelter for the night.

The next morning, they ate the last of the jerky and hardtack biscuits. Wandering down the mountain, they stopped at a clearing with a view of the valley below. Water from melting ice pooled in a puddle quenched their thirst. Fayette saw smoke in the distance. Its source didn't appear far from his vantage point, but it was. They followed a game trail along a small creek for hours. Seeing the smoke was not possible from the thick timbers. Fayette gauged the location of the smoke by the sun's position and a high vista to the east.

The sun was setting behind the Aspens. Fayette had lost all hope of finding the camp of the unknown. Disappointed, he sat down on a log to think. What food we had is gone. I don't know where we are. What should I do? Caleb barked, one of his senses alerted the dog to something in the woods. The dog didn't try to run towards it, as when he had a varmint up a tree. Caleb continued to emit a low growl. They both heard the sound of twigs breaking in the woods. It was that eerie time of day—just before sunset. Shadows of the tall pinion and aspen trees made the forest dark, yet the sky beyond remained blue.

Fayette held the anxious dog with both arms as it continued its low-pitched growl. Then Caleb saw something and charged off into the darkness of the woods. Fayette followed the dog's trail and found Caleb sitting on the chest of a terrified hunter.

"Good dog Caleb," Fayette said

"Get him off of me," the hunter screamed.

Fayette recognized the voice of Chico, Old Wolf's friend, leader of the Comanchero. His mule stood with a deer carcass strapped across its back.

"Chico it's me Fayette. From Old Wolf's camp."

Chico said, "I know. The chief sent us looking for you and the horse." Chico raised his head. "Get this damn dog off me!"

Fayette said, "Caleb...off!"

Caleb whined like he didn't want to let Chico up.

"Off, Caleb!" The dog grudgingly removed his large framed body from Chico's chest and went to Fayette.

"You got a good way with animals to be such a young'un." Chico brushed pine needles from his pants.

Fayette nodded. "Animals have always been my best friends."

Chico looked beyond where Fayette and Caleb stood. "Where is that fine stallion you rode off on?"

"A cougar attacked him. It was on top of him, the last I saw." Fayette was about to cry, "I don't know what happened to him after that."

Chico knew, but chose not to tell Fayette. He found the skeletal remains of a large horse in a gully. Strands of horse hair and the story Fayette told assured Chico the horse he wanted was dead.

"Where did you get the clothes? They even got pockets." Chico looked Fayette over. Caleb growled at him.

"Whose mongrel dog is that?" Chico looked at Caleb.
"He's not a mongrel. He's a *Bouvier des Flandres,* a Belgium dog bred to pull carts."

Caleb growled; Chico backed away. "Well, excuse me," he said to the dog.

Fayette explained how Caleb and Jeremiah Busch found him: took him in and sewed the clothes he wore. He told Chico of Jeremiah being buried in a landslide on the mountain.

"Caleb and I been together since," Fayette put his arms around the dog.

Chico asked, "No sign of this Jeremiah after the landslide?"

"Just his haversack. Caleb found it in a tree." Fayette showed Chico the empty sack. "Jeremiah was taking me home," Fayette shook his head.

"Where is home?" Chico asked.

"Austin. Do you know where that is?" Fayette asked.

"Can't say I do." Chico started walking, Fayette and Caleb followed, not knowing or caring where he was going.

"I reckon my grandpa would pay you a big reward if you were to return me to Austin," Fayette said.

Chico said, "How much you think he would pay?"

"I don't know. Once Grampa told me I meant the whole world to him."

Chico didn't answer. He just kept walking. It seemed to Fayette that Chico kept walking faster, as if he was trying to walk off and leave them behind. Fayette stumbled and fell on the rough terrain, then ran to catch up, not wanting to be alone again.

"Why do you walk so fast?" Fayette gasped.

"It'll be dark soon. The boys will be hungry and worried."

It was dark when they saw flames flickering in the sky. Blackie, Blanco, and Mescal were surprised to see Fayette alive, assuming he died with the horse.

Mescal asked, "The horse?"

Chico shook his head and handed the mule's reins to Mescal. The half-breed said nothing but looked disappointed. He led the mule to a tree to unload the deer. He used a rope to hoist the deer onto a low limb. When the mule was out from under the weight of the deer carcass, it let out a bray of gratefulness. Mescal skinned the gutted carcass and cut off a hindquarter for their evening meal.

Fayette and the dog stretched out on the ground. He heard them talking about him and going to Texas, just before falling asleep.

Chico said, "I know Old Wolf doesn't want the boy back without the horse."

"Then why bring him to our camp?" Blanco asked.

"He followed me. Says his grandfather in Austin has money. That he is a treasurer, whatever that is?"

Blanco laughed, "Chico...you don't know? A treasurer is someone who keeps other people's money like a banker."

Mescal smiled, "That's what it means Chico. The one who watches the treasure is called the treasurer."

"Is that so?" Chico looked at Blackie, "I've always wanted to rob a bank."

Blackie tended the hindquarter rather than look at Chico.

"No shit!" Chico looked at Fayette lying on the ground. "He may be worth some money after all."

Chico woke Fayette. They ate venison with beans and biscuits. Fayette gave meat to Caleb when no one was watching.

"Boy, how far is it to this place you call Austin?" Chico looked at Fayette.

"It's east of here a ways to the Colorado. Then you just follow the river down to Austin. It's on the banks of the river. You can't miss it." Fayette made it sound easy.

"You could point the way then?" Chico looked at Mescal and Blanco.

Fayette nodded. Chico asked the others what they thought about going to Texas. They talked about what Fayette's family might pay. They knew the price for a young white boy in Taos would bring at least sixty dollars at auction. Taos was closer than Austin. No decision was made before the liquor jug was uncorked. The Comancheros drank while Fayette slept—Caleb beside him, alert to the men's every move. For the moment, Fayette was safe.

Fayette woke first. He decided to make himself useful by gathering firewood and making kindling to throw on the simmering coals. Fayette was excited that the Comancheros were talking about taking him home. Chico woke slowly; the effects of last night's liquor still lingered in his body. He stumbled around like a man twice his age, looking for his coffee pot. Not finding it, he became enraged.

Fayette picked the wrong moment to expound on the virtues of Austin as he excitedly exaggerated the size of the deer and buffalo herds.

Chico hollered, "Will you shut up about Austin?"

The outburst startled Caleb. The dog snarled, revealing its teeth. Fayette didn't respond. He placed another log on the fire, hoping Chico would be in a better mood later. For now, he would stay quiet. One by one, the others rose slowly, like it hurt to move.

They ate last night's leftovers. Fayette fed the remaining scraps to Caleb, satisfying the dog's hunger.

Blackie looked at Caleb, "What about the dog? We gonna take him with us?"

"Why not? That's a fine dog," Blanco pointed at Caleb.

"I don't like dogs," Blackie said.

Fayette looked at Blackie, "I'll make sure he doesn't bother you."

Blackie was more interested in trying to roll a smoke than listen to a child. Chico sent Fayette off for wood they didn't need, wanting to talk to Blackie without Fayette around. Everyone but Blackie was for taking Fayette to Texas. The decision became a big argument between the men.

"Why are you so dead set against going to Texas?" Chico asked.

"If you go to Texas, it will be without me," Blackie said.

Chico got in Blackie's face "This is our big chance! We can get ten times as much money from his grandpa as we can in Taos." He turned towards the others.

"That be good for you and the others, but not me," Blackie said.

"Why is that?" Chico titled his head.

"I'm a runaway slave! I came to Mexican Territory to be free. Now Texas is trying to take over the territory. If that happens, I could be sent back to my master," Blackie shook his head defiantly, "that... ain't going to happen!"

Chico said, "You never told me that."

Blackie looked at Chico wide-eyed, "Why would I tell anyone? They could take me back for the reward money. You, Blanco, or Mescal do anything for money."

"We wouldn't do that to you!" Chico smiled his sinister smile.

"You're willing to sell that white boy to the Indians! Why wouldn't you do the same to me?"

"You're my friend Blackie. I wouldn't do that to you." Chico laughed.

"I've seen you kill men for less," Blackie said.

Chico turned and walked toward the others and said loud enough for all, including Fayette, to hear. "That settles it. We aren't going to Texas!"

When Fayette heard that, he dropped the armload of wood he carried, and ran toward Chico, screaming and hitting at him. "You said you would take me to Austin!"

"No, I didn't!" Chico pushed back.

"But, you promised," Fayette stammered.

Chico's cold stare and his hand resting on his gun handle convinced Fayette to back off. Afraid, he took off running, Caleb followed behind. It would be the last time Fayette ever ran. Chico caught Fayette, pulled out his Bowie knife, and yanked off the boys' boots. Fayette screamed in agony as Chico cut both heel tendons to the bone.

"You won't be running from me no more!" Chico turned and left Fayette where he lay.

Blackie was the first to see Chico with the bloody knife in his hand. He said, "How stupid can you be killing the boy? He's worth more than every pot and pan we got."

"I didn't kill him. I just cut his tendons. He'll live." Chico threw his bowie knife into a tree trunk.

Blackie and Mescal rushed to Fayette. Caleb wouldn't let them near him. Mescal managed to grab the dog and hold him while Blackie helped Fayette.

"Damn it to hell! Why did Chico do this?" Blackie tightened his belt around Fayette's right leg, making a tourniquet between the knee and his ankle.

"It's just the way Chico is. You never know what he'll do next," Mescal held onto Caleb.

They carried Fayette back to camp. Caleb no longer resisted their efforts.

Chapter Twelve

Mescal tied Fayette on a burro tethered behind the mule Blackie rode. It would be a two-day ride to Santa Fe. The makeshift tourniquets stopped the bleeding. Fayette fell in and out of consciousness as the short-legged burro bounced along the rocky trail. Investing a few pesos in their most valuable asset seemed logical to Blackie, Mescal, and Blanco. Chico was in denial of the severity of the injuries he'd inflicted. No one spoke, afraid they might upset him again. Chico always had an explosive temperament. After attacking Fayette so viciously, they suspected he might be out of his mind. Liquor and untreated syphilis may have deteriorated an already sick brain.

Mescal and Blackie decided it was time to break away from Chico and Blanco. They no longer felt safe and Fayette needed protection.

The town of Santa Fe was preparing for market days, the week-long celebration that started every year the Saturday before Palm Sunday. They arrived on Friday evening and unpacked their wares in the best spot for trading. Fayette was placed on the center of the canvas tarp that held tin cups, pots, and pans. Other traders began to arrive. Most were native craftsmen who made everything from straw brooms to flat iron hardware. Chico looked for small items that could be carried back to the northern tribes. New things such as metal pots and pans were replacing dried gourds and buffalo stomachs for carrying water. The Indians found the flat bottom pots easier to cook with.

Chico bartered beaver pelts for ornate hinges and locks, forged and hammered by the village blacksmith. He knew who would buy them. It wasn't the Indians; they had no doors. It was the newly arriving Anglos who would pay top dollar for the hardware.

Bella Miranda was shopping among the vendors in the plaza for fresh nopalitos when she saw a gringo boy and his dog lying on a dirty canvas. Bloody rags were wrapped around the boy's feet. She could tell he didn't belong to the vagabond he was with. He had hazel eyes and red hair—just as Will had described. She was certain the boy was Fayette.

She approached the boy. He looked up at her with sad eyes. "What's your name?" Bella asked.

Before he could answer, Chico moved between them saying, "May I help the beautiful Señorita?"

His manner and cold stare frightened Bella. She managed to say, "Such a precious boy. Is he yours?"

"Yes, he is," Chico said in Spanish, sounding more like the boy was his possession than a family member.

Bella smiled at Fayette. His lips quivered. She heard no words, but his eyes begged for help.

She rushed home and called for her mother and father.

"What is it Bella?" her father asked.

"You look so frightened," Her mother embraced her.

"Will's nephew Fayette is here! I saw him. His hair is red, his eyes are just like—"

"Where is he, Bella?" Miguel grabbed his sombrero.

"In the plaza. The first group of traders you see." Bella grabbed her father's arm as he turned to go and said, "He is with the Devil who threatened me with his eyes. I can tell the boy is afraid of him."

"How would you know?" her father asked.

"The boy shook when the Devil spoke to me. I could tell. He needs our help," Bella said.

Miguel went to the square and found Chico, but he did not see the boy. Fayette was nowhere to be found. Miguel returned to the inn.

"The boy wasn't there. Only the Anglo they call Chico. I know him, Bella. You are right. He is no good. I once bought his buffalo robes. He cheated me out of a robe and then stole a bottle of brandy."

"I will find him!" Bella removed her apron and placed it on a wooden peg.

"No, Bella. It is too dangerous," her Father called out to her.

She paid no attention to his pleas as she headed to the outdoor market.

Holiday worshippers flocked to Santa Fe for Holy Week. The inn was full. Families from the farms and rancheros camped under their wagons. Bella impatiently worked her way through the crowd to the wares of the one they call Chico.

"Where is the boy? The one you say is your son," Bella demanded.

"I didn't say he was my son," Chico said politely, not wanting to scare off buyers.

"It doesn't matter. Where is he?" Bella asked.

Buyers with pesos in their hands, fearing a fight, backed away. Chico saw Bella's presence disrupting his business. Feigning a pleasant voice, he asked her to leave and not return. His cold stare revealed he was a demon.

Bella frantically searched the plaza, asking anyone who would listen if they had seen the young Anglo boy with red hair. She was told he was seen on a burro lead by a black man and followed by a half breed known as Mescal. The men rode mules and led three burros—a strange looking dog followed them out of Santa Fe toward Santa Cruz.

Bella went home in frustration—without Fayette.

Fayette developed a fever and crimson blisters all over his body. Blackie and Mescal thought the symptoms might be an infection from his wounds. Mescal heard of a Pueblo Indian with special healing powers. They called him Crow. He lived near the Village of Chimayó northwest of Santa Fe. They found the adobe hut of the curandero on Nambe Creek. He was a soft-spoken Pueblo Indian. His beady eyes had seen many moons. He once resided inside the Taos Pueblo in the home of his wife's family. It was his father-in-law, the Pueblo chief, who first recognized Crow's healing powers. The chief bestowed the title of Curandero of the Pueblo on him. Word of Crow's ability to heal reached the adobe fortresses of the white man. Crow ventured outside the walls of the pueblo village to assist them, finding the Anglos paid better than his people.

Crow helped two of his wife's barren sisters have healthy baby boys. They grew up to look just like him. Excommunicated from the Pueblo, the medicine man took refuge near the falls of the Rio Nambe. He acquired an Apache bride as a gift from her father for treating his rattlesnake bite. Crow outlived three more wives and now lived alone, enjoying his solitude.

Blackie started to untie Fayette.

"Not here. We take him to the mud that heals." Crow pointed toward a hill behind his hut.

They traversed up a narrow trail, following it to a flat spot where steam came from holes in the ground. High walls of multicolored rock protected the mud holes from the winds. The medicine man placed his hand in the mud holes. He did this several times until he found just the right one.

He wiped the mud on his pants and pointed, "Take off his clothes. Put the boy in this one."

"In the mud?" Blackie asked.

Fayette protested, "I don't want to be put in there!"

Crow looked at Blackie, "It's the only thing that will save him."

"Aren't you gonna look at his feet? That's why we brung him," Mescal sounded agitated.

"I have seen enough; he has the pox."

"Pox! I had that when I was little!" Mescal moved away from Fayette.

"You good then. You no catch the pox," The medicine man looked at Blackie.

"I never had nothing looked like that," Blackie said.

"You go away," Crow swished him away from Fayette. "If you live twenty-one moons," Crow pointed at the sky, "come back for boy."

"And if I don't?" Blackie looked wide-eyed at Crow.

"Don't come back." The stoic Indian grinned, revealing only three jagged front teeth. Blackie didn't appreciate his Pueblo humor.

Crow agreed to care for Fayette for a peso a day, twenty-one pesos paid in advance. Blackie and Mescal only had ten pesos but traded a large pot for the difference. Fayette was now so sick he couldn't care whether he was in mud or not. Once in the mud, it clung to his blistered body like a warm poultice, providing comfort. When Fayette was awake, Crow spoon fed him a thick broth from an earthen vessel.

After a day in the mud, Crow moved Fayette to a hot spring to soak. Once the mud on his body had been washed away, he was led to a small hut made of aspen saplings tied together with straps of buffalo hide. The hut was built over two steaming pools of crystal-clear water from natural underground springs. Buffalo robes made a roof and vents for the sides. The steam produced by the hot springs could be controlled by opening and closing the robes as needed. When Fayette first entered the hut, the steam was too thick to see. Crow led a shuffling Fayette to a bed of pelts as Caleb waited patiently outside the hut's entrance.

Easter passed and the Santa Fe Plaza was now empty. Chico realized Blackie and Mescal weren't coming back. Incensed they'd abandoned him. Chico took to the bottle. Blanco decided Chico was a lost cause. While camped on the river north of Santa Fe, Blanco asked for his share of profit from the market and told Chico he was leaving. They got into a heated argument. Knives were drawn. Both died in a pool of blood.

Blackie succumbed to the pox. Mescal buried him where they camped. The only survivor of Chico's band of traders made it back to Crow's home. Mescal found Fayette over the pox, his wounds partially healed, still barely able to walk.

Crow looked at Mescal, "You know there is much money being offered for the boy."

"How do you know?" Mescal asked.

"I know of such things. Padre Martinez has told everyone to be looking for this boy. They say you should take him to the trading post of John Rowland in Taos for the reward."

"I've been to his trading post. I will take him there." Mescal said.

On the twentieth day of March, Mescal led his mule and the burro Fayette rode through the gates of the trading post. Caleb followed. Mescal had seen Chico dicker with the proprietors of Taos' only trading post. This time the illiterate half-breed would do the negotiating. The merchandise was a white boy barely able to walk. Mescal would leave Fayette on the burro until the deal was done.

John Rowland was away on business. When the store clerk saw the pale looking red-headed boy, he knew it was Fayette, the boy from Texas. He ran to the main house, summoning Maria Rowland who hurried to the store. "Boy... what is... your name?" Maria asked between gasps, winded from excitement and hurrying from her kitchen.

"Fayette Smith, I am from Austin, Texas. This is my dog, Caleb."

"Get the boy down," Maria ordered the half breed.

"Not 'til the deal is done." Mescal shook his head.

Maria told the clerk in Spanish to bring the bag of silver coins from the safe. The long-legged young Spaniard hurried to the store.

Everyone in the compound came to see the red-headed boy from Texas with a French name. He was as they'd been told: a boy with fiery-red hair, freckle-faced, and eyes the color of the sky. In this part of the world, a person of this description was as rare as a white buffalo.

Maria went to the boy who was still straddling the burro and touched him. Fayette knew her touch. It was the loving touch of a tender woman. The attractive Mexican woman looked and dressed like the woman at the market in Santa Fe. Fayette was unaware it was her much younger sister.

The store clerk, accompanied by company bookkeeper Peter Duncan, came with a canvas bag of coins. Maria counted out sixty dollars in silver. Both of Mescal's hands were full; he had no idea how much it was or what it could buy. Content, Mescal put the silver in his haversack and lifted Fayette to the ground. Caleb now beside Fayette, his stub of a tail wagging, sensed they were surrounded by good people.

Maria saw Fayette struggling to walk. She turned toward Mescal and screamed, "What have you done to this boy?"

"Just saved his life is what I done," Mescal said.

Maria looked into Fayette's eyes and asked, "Is that true?"

Fayette nodded.

"Then thank you, Señor. Go now in peace, knowing you have done a good thing."

They watched Mescal ride out the compound gate.

"Come. I will fix you something to eat," Maria said.

Fayette said, "Do you have something for Caleb?"

"I'll fix you both something special." Maria helped Fayette to her kitchen.

Maria made fresh tortillas and carne guisada, which he and Caleb quickly devoured. She enjoyed watching Fayette eat the meal she prepared. The Rowlands had cooks and servants, but when it came to family or close friends, she preferred to cook for them. It gave her the opportunity to express her love for family. Maria missed all her grandchildren. Fayette would fill that void in her life.

Maria Encarnación Martinez married John Rowland young. They had grown children, and many grandchildren, who lived across the Sangre de Cristo Mountains on the Spanish land grant of her family. They usually came to visit after their sheep were shorn. Maria sent word to stay away from Taos for now, fearing her children might be implicated with the Texas loyalists.

"Why are you looking at me?" Fayette asked.

"You look like your Uncle Will."

Fayette's eyes opened wide, "You know my Uncle Will?"

Maria instinctively put her hand over her mouth.

"How do you know my Uncle Will?" Fayette asked.

"He came looking for you the first week of Lent," Maria said.

"He is here?" Fayette looked at Maria.

"No, Fayette. He headed back to Texas."

"Why didn't he wait for me?"

"He couldn't. The Mexican army was searching for him. If they found him, they would kill him. They think he is a spy for the Texas government. It is very complicated here. You must trust no one, Fayette. In time you will understand. Never speak of your uncle to anyone! Do you understand?" Maria put a hand on his shoulder.

"Yes ma'am," Fayette agreed even though he didn't understand.

"Why don't you call me Momma Maria?"

Fayette nodded his head but was confused; nothing made sense. He had a roof over his head and someone who cared for him. Maria knew his uncle. She wanted him to call her Momma Maria. He felt safe.

Within a week, Fayette knew everyone's name inside the compound. The store clerk Estevan Martinez, a second cousin of Momma Maria, kept Fayette busy stocking shelves and sweeping the floor. Nights were fun in the grand sala after dinner, with singing and dancing. Fayette enjoyed the music of Spanish guitars. He didn't understand the lyrics but enjoyed the happy melodies.

Momma Maria would hold Fayette in her arms, translating the ballads to English. He watched the fire in the fireplace, which he kept stoked with wood. Fayette never wanted to be cold or hungry again.

Chapter Thirteen

Maria heard the commotion of her husband's caravan returning from Bent's Fort. She jumped up, surprising Fayette who she was reading to. "It's my husband. Come, Fayette, he will be excited to know you are here, safe with us."

They watched the activity as John Rowland directed the unloading of three fully loaded wagons and the unharnessing of a dozen anxious mules.

As the Teamsters led the mules to the stables, John Rowland came toward Maria and Fayette. He smiled and held out his arms. Maria rushed to her husband. Fayette followed. They embraced for what seemed to Fayette a long time. Mr. Rowland looked down, "This must be Fayette Smith. Everyone in the territory has been searching for you." He offered his hand and Fayette shook it.

"It's a pleasure to meet you, Mr. Rowland," Fayette said.

"You're how old, Fayette?" John Rowland asked, impressed with his manners.

"On my next birthday, the twenty-first day of January, I'll be ten years old." Fayette remembered his last birthday and started to cry.

Mr. Rowland realized he'd stirred a bad memory and put a hand on Fayette's shoulder; he quickly changed the subject, "Let's see what Maria has for us to eat."

Mr. Rowland saw Caleb, "What is this?"

"That's Caleb. He's been with me since the mountain slide that killed his owner. Jeremiah was my friend."

Mr. Rowland nodded, not knowing what to say. He put an arm around Maria's waist and the other on Fayette's shoulder. They walked slowly to their quarters. Caleb followed, his short tail wagging.

Fayette thrived on the trading post's energy. It was similar to his courthouse home in Austin, where Fayette had become the ex-officio page-boy for Travis County. He'd learned his manners and diplomacy from meeting and greeting his father's constituents. He delivered documents to the Land Office, often stopping to chat with Mayor Thomas Ward who everyone called "Peg-Leg." General Sam Houston taught Fayette how to whittle on the front porch of the Eberly boarding house. He knew President Mirabeau Lamar, who'd appointed his father Chief Justice.

Fayette transferred those skills to his trading post duties. Grandmother Rebeckah Smith, his only teacher, considered penmanship the most important aspect of a young man's education. Second on her agenda was reading and then math.

John Rowland was worried when he saw the affection in Maria's eyes for Fayette. Saying goodbye would be difficult. Uncertainty and distrust festered in the bosoms of the citizens of Nuevo México. The Mexican Loyalists feared the Texas Compatriots. Everyone dreaded the possibility of war.

Rowland didn't dare chance a letter to Austin, fearful it might implicate him in collaboration with the Texans. Governor Armijo made it clear when he pardoned him and his partner William Workman that he would have their heads for treason should there be any communication with Texas.

If Fayette asked about his family, he was told word had been sent to Austin. A half-truth, as Will was on his way to Austin unaware Fayette had been ransomed.

They warned Fayette not to talk about Texas to anyone, which was a difficult task as everyone knew about the red-headed boy from Texas. When asked, Fayette said he didn't want to talk about it.

As days passed, things became more strained in the Rowland casa. Fayette heard them arguing in the sanctity of their bedroom. Maria spoke rapidly in Spanish when angry. John spoke in English when he couldn't recall his thoughts in Spanish. These frequent language slips from Spanish to English gave Fayette clues to some of their secrecy. Concerned that he was the cause, he listened intently to their bedtime arguments. Usually, their disagreements ended in fierce lovemaking. Fayette came to realize the situation had little to do with him; it was about Governor Manuel Armijo, who hated and distrusted Americans, Texans, and all Anglos, regardless of their nationality.

Estevan Martinez became ill in the middle of May and was bedridden for a week. John Rowland and Fayette opened the store in his absence. Management of the store had been Estevan's responsibility since finishing his studies at Padre Martinez' School for Boys. He had done a remarkable job and the Rowlands were proud of him. Mr. Rowland opened the store's ledger. He didn't recognize the neat and precise hand of the most recent entries. Estevan had many qualities, penmanship wasn't one of them.

"You did this?" Mr. Rowland asked.

Fayette nodded. "Did I...do something wrong?"

"Your penmanship is remarkable. You write as a scribe many years your senior. The daily entries are as perfect as I have ever seen," Mr. Rowland turned the page.

"Does that mean I can keep doing it?"

"Yes, please do." Mr. Rowland turned the large ledger book towards Fayette, "Would you start today's business page in the journal?"

"It would be my pleasure, Mr. Rowland." Fayette dipped the pen in the inkwell and wrote Friday, twenty-first day of May, 1841. His enthusiasm suddenly waned when he realized four months ago his father was murdered.

Rowland saw Fayette's mood change and asked, "Are you alright?"

Fayette nodded. "What's going to happen to me?"

John Rowland looked around the store, making sure they were alone. He realized that Fayette knew something was amiss. He wasn't the typical nine-year-old child. He decided to explain the complicated political situation that Fayette had been cast into. He explained why the natives of Nuevo México were fearful of the Anglos and wary of President Lamar's pending invasion. "The *St. Louis Gazette* described it as much larger and broader in scope than President Jefferson's Lewis and Clark Expedition. Governor Armijo has everyone on edge, saying it is a military takeover."

Mr. Rowland sat on a keg and continued, "Armijo knows that our family and friends are supportive of Texas. He considers us traitors, we only want what is best for the territory. Our citizens should have the opportunity to decide which Government they support."

"That sounds fair," Fayette said.

"It is Fayette, but my brother and brother-in-law were arrested for supporting the Texans. Had your Uncle Will been captured, he would have been shot." Mr. Rowland sighed, "That is why I insisted he return to Austin."

"They would've killed him?"

"Maybe worse," Mr. Rowland said just as Maria entered with their noon meal.

"What are you telling Fayette?" Maria asked, annoyed.

"Fayette is concerned about his future. We owe it to Fayette to tell him what we know."

Maria nodded in agreement, "Then you tell him!"

Maria left their food, gave them both a kiss, and went on about her business. As they ate, the wind began to blow. Tumbleweeds rolled over the adobe walls into the compound. The wind howled from the mountains through the Taos Valley. Small cracks around the window sills and doors whistled. It would be a slow day at the store today.

Fayette listened as Mr. Rowland explained the danger he and Maria feared for him. "Governor Armijo knows you are here, Fayette. He also knows you are from Texas, and that your grandfather is a government official."

"What does that have to do with me?" Fayette asked.

"Governor Armijo has taken children captive before to get what he wants from their parents. He may try to capture you for his purposes. Do you understand?" Mr. Rowland waited for a response.

"Sounds like the Indians that captured me," Fayette said.

"Exactly what I mean." It was obvious Mr. Rowland had more to say, but a business associate arrived. Fayette could tell by the warm greeting that he was a special friend.

"Welcome to Taos, Ceran. Thank you for coming." Mr. Rowland gave his guest a manly hug, "It is such a windy day to travel."

"One of Maria's meals makes the trip worthwhile. Even if we don't make a deal," Ceran St. Vrain said.

Ceran was born forty years ago in St. Louis to French parents. He came west as a young man to trap beaver. With hard work and frugality, Ceran prospered. He and the Bent Brothers, Charles and William, built a trading post on the Arkansas River in 1836. They named it Bent's Fort. Ceran was the money man and silent partner of the successful partnership.

John Rowland's recent trip to Bent's Fort was to find a buyer for his business—not to trade buffalo robes. Time had come for the Compatriots of Texas to leave Nuevo México for California. They needed money. Ceran was their only hope to raise sufficient cash for the exodus.

Thousands of sheep, hundreds of cattle, pigs, and work animals would have to be driven across the barren desert. The nucleus of the caravan included American and European born Anglos and their wives who were natives. Many, like Maria Encarnación Martinez-Rowland, were descendants of the earliest Spanish settlers and didn't want to leave. Now, with their husbands' lives at risk, they began to reconsider their options.

The Conestoga-style wagons used on the well-traced Santa Fe Trail would be of little use on the mountainous Old Spanish Trail. Carts for bulky cargo and oxen and mules to pull them had to be purchased.

Partners Workman and Rowland also needed money to purchase the land grant of San Gabriel Missions, land that Padre Martinez told them about. William Workman left land negotiations to John Rowland as he and his vaqueros rounded up thousands of sheep to be sheared and herded to Abiquiú west of Santa Fe. There, the Rowland and Workman caravan would be joined by others fleeing to California.

Maria Encarnación Martinez-Rowland would not be with them. The men would drive the livestock and mule train to California. The women would remain, carrying on as usual. Should anyone ask, the men were off herding sheep.

From a knoll above the Arkansas River, Will saw Bent's Fort. Its red, white, and blue American Flag of twenty-six stars flapped in the breeze. He dismounted, unbuckled, and stowed the revolvers. Although once across the river he was no longer subject to Mexican law, here Bent's law ruled. The capitals of Mexico, Texas, and the U.S. governments had little influence on law and order in its remote location.

Will admired the mammoth structure as he walked to the low water crossing of the Arkansas River. There he mounted George for the last time, fording the river into U.S. territory.

The walls of Bent's Fort rose thirty-feet high and were fifteen-feet at their lowest height. The adobe walls were two feet thick with two round thirty-foot bastions, each housing a six-pound cannon on top. The nearby river provided water for the fort. The fort employed one-hundred-fifty tradesmen, wheelwrights, blacksmiths, gunsmiths, and carpenters. The total population of about one-hundred-eighty on any given day swelled to double that when a caravan arrived.

Trappers brought buffalo robes and beaver hides to trade. The fort was a gathering place for all the Indian tribes and many nationalities of frontiersmen. William Bent welcomed all and he seldom had problems with anyone. Whether a buyer or a seller, all were treated fairly. The Bent Brothers were respected by Indian and Anglo but despised by the Mexicans for their loyalty to the United States.

The large cypress gates of Bent's Fort had been opened wide for Will. An armed sentinel on the wall waved him in. Chickens ran about the courtyard, and a Newfoundland dog barked its welcome.

A Negro man offered to take his horse and burro saying, "Go on over and let Black Charlotte fix you some vittles. She closes her kitchen soon. I'll take your gear upstairs, if you aim to stay here."

Will nodded.

"What's your name, mister?" the spry but aging black man asked.

"That'll do," Will tried to ignore his question.

"All right, I'll…just call you Mister, then," the black man said. "'That'll Do' is too long a name for me to remember."

"I'll take that," Will pointed at the haversack with his revolvers.

"Don't worry, your stuff be safe in the bunkhouse." He picked up the other bags, "You'll be bunking alone until Mr. Carson gets back from Santa Fe?"

Will stammered, "Who is this man from Santa Fe?"

"Kit Carson. He works for the Bent's. Don't worry. He can be trusted."

"When did you say he was returning?" Will asked, concerned Carson could cause him trouble.

"I didn't say. Cause I don't know."

"What's your name?" Will asked.

"My name is Dick Green. Black Charlotte I told you about is my wife. We the only black folks named Green around these parts." He shook his head, "Matter fact, we be the only black people."

Will laughed.

"Look Mister, you and I going to be black and blue if you don't get your ass over to Black Charlotte's." Dick's arms were full, so he motioned with his head, "Cross the way, to the right. The door be open. You'll smell them frijoles cooking."

"Thanks for your help," Will said.

"You can thank me by not pissing her off!" Dick trudged toward the upstairs bunk room muttering, "I got to live with that woman."

Will smelled the aromas of the kitchen. The dining room had four tables with pine benches. Each could accommodate four to six folks. A fine oak dining table with twelve matching Windsor chairs provided fine dining for family and friends of the owners. A Mexican in peasant clothes ate his beans alone at the small table in the corner; all he wore was a coarse burlap sack with 'Mexican Coffee' stenciled on the front and back in bold black letters.

Will chose to sit at the table near the open door. He watched Dick carry his gear up the outside staircase. A tabby gray cat jumped on Will's table, startling him, and then distracting him.

"What be your pleasure?" Black Charlotte stood waiting for an answer. "Excuse me...Mister...I ain't got all day. The kitchen be closed already...I am just here to feed you...and this poor sick Mexican," Black Charlotte said.

"What's cooking that smells so good?" Will ask politely.

"Pork and Beans, which is all I got."

"If I don't have a choice, why do you ask?"

"You got a choice. Cornbread or tortillas with your beans?"

"Can...I have both?"

She nodded and headed for the kitchen. The Mexican laughed, which made Will laugh. They tried to stifle their laughter but couldn't. When they looked at each other, they started laughing again. Will hadn't laughed in a long time. He and the Mexican enjoyed the short diversion Charlotte had created.

Charlotte came back to the dining room, "Yawl enjoying each other's company so much. I'll put your beans here by Juan. First time I ever seen him laugh."

She set beans, bread, and tortillas down across from Juan and motioned for Will to join him.

Will sat down cautiously across from the Mexican. Black Charlotte eased Will's concerns by explaining that whatever made Juan sick was no threat to anyone now. All his clothes were burned as a precaution. He had a high fever and chills when he was brought in on a stretcher last October. After five months of Charlotte's cooking, he was well and fit as a fiddle. Juan had been doing odd jobs around the fort to pay his room and board. His team of ox, the caravan, its cargo, and eight teamsters were long overdue. Juan paced in front of the gate daily, watching for their return.

Juan spoke some English but said, "Hola." Will said, "Hola." They sat across from each other. While neither could carry on a conversation in the other's language, they enjoyed Charlotte's banter. Each time she came into the dining room from the kitchen they started laughing like school children.

Charlotte explained to Will that Juan became ill while driving a team of ox from Chihuahua north to Independence. His fellow teamsters left Juan in Charlotte's care. The teamsters most likely were waiting out the winter in Independence or St. Louis. Juan was anxious to get back to his family in Chihuahua.

Despite the language barrier, the men kept the conversation going with hand motions and drawings on paper.

"Juan how many days to Independence?"

Juan shrugged his shoulder and said, "Maybe veinte, maybe treinta dias."

Charlotte interpreted for Juan, "Twenty to thirty days with fresh horses."

Will knew his horse and burro would never make the trip without weeks of rest. He dreaded leaving George and Sam behind. Juan suggested two horses each and a Missouri Mule, which would give each horse a break from being ridden every day. Gear could be divided between the mule and extra horse.

Will asked, "How many times," pointing east, "to Independence?"

Juan held up five fingers and said, "Cinco. "

"Five times...down and back?" Will pointed east then west. Juan nodded.

"Dias times." Will motioned back and forth.

"Sí, ten times," Juan said.

Will thought Juan knew the trail and where there was water. The Mexican would make a good guide. Will asked him. Juan said yes and was anxious to go. All he wanted was grub, two horses, and a Spanish saddle. Once they met up with his caravan, he would return the horses and saddle and then drive his wagon and team home to Mexico.

Will traded his horse and the burro and twenty pesos in silver for four fresh horses and a Missouri Mule. He bought Juan a saddle, gun, and bowie knife. Then Will asked the fort's tailor to fit Juan for suitable winter trail wear. Juan was small but looked like a tough hombre in his new clothes. Will purchased tailored buffalo robes for each of them as winter was far from over.

Chapter Fourteen

Provisions for twenty-one days were neatly packed then put into larger burlap bags. Based on Juan's information and others at Bent's Fort, Will planned three weeks travel to Independence, which would take most of the month of March. Passage by boat down the Missouri two-hundred-fifty miles to St. Louis, then down the Mississippi to New Orleans, another month. If all went well, Will could make it back to Austin in time to stop the Santa Fe Expedition.

After two days out of the saddle and three nights of rest in a bed, Will was anxious to head east. Juan led the way as Will watched for Indians. Will wasn't sure of Juan's mettle or his new team of horses' temperament. In time he would know.

Near the Caches on the Arkansas River, five days east of Bent's Fort, Juan signaled that Indians were approaching from the south. A small band of warriors could be seen for miles on the open prairie. Will spotted several small Islands protruding from the middle of the river. He and Juan rode into the icy shallows, leading the tethered horses and pack mule. The untested animals didn't resist. Will was impressed with their easy-going disposition. The water didn't reach the belly of the shortest horse. Will chose the smallest Island that had the most cover to make his stand.

Red Willow trees lay horizontally, victims of raging flood waters. Will and Juan took advantage of the lush undergrowth to hide their animals. They watched the prairie dust of six horses approaching. Will laid out his percussion caps and a handful of shot balls on the horizontal trunk of a large Willow tree. He spun the cylinder of each colt, making sure they were properly loaded.

Juan said, "Your guns have no trigger?"

Will pulled the hammer back, revealing the pistols hidden trigger. "It does now!"

"Very nice gun." Juan smiled, revealing a shiny gold tooth.

Will watched the Indians coming. He whispered, "Juan...they aren't Comanche. What are they?"

"They are Kiowa. The shields, they make from buffalo skull. Only the Kiowa make such shields for battle."

"You've encountered them before then?" Will asked.

"Sí.... Many times."

"I don't see any guns. Do Kiowa use short bows like the Comanche when they attack?"

Juan shrugged his shoulders "I never see Kiowa attack."

The leader dismounted to find where horses entered the river. The mule sensed the Indians presence and started braying. The Indian looked straight at where they were and then climbed on his spotted horse and yelled to his tribesmen. The Indians rode off quickly the way they came.

"They'll be back." Will looked at Juan.

"You think so?" Juan sounded scared.

"Juan, have you ever killed a man?" Will asked as he watched the trail dust of where the Indians went.

"No, I never kill anyone."

"I've shown you how to load and fire that rifle." Will looked sternly at Juan and said, "I want you to concentrate on getting one good shot. Call your shot so I won't waste ammunition on the same Indian. Then reload. You should be able to get a second shot off before they're on top of us." Will looked sternly at Juan and asked, "Can you do that?"

Juan nodded his head nervously. They waited patiently as the sun moved behind them.

Suddenly, they heard sounds of pounding hooves approaching. The Kiowa were back; no reinforcements had been added. They took positions along the riverbank, each warrior fifteen steps from the other, faces freshly painted for war. A brave on each end held their lances high. The others with quivers on their backs, held their short bows of war. They remained in formation, waiting as the scalps of previous battles waved from their lances.

Juan asked, "What are they doing?"

"Trying to make us flinch," Will said.

"I do not...understand the word flinch," Juan uttered.

"They are trying to scare us," Will said.

"It is working, Señor Will."

The Kiowa waited for a flag of surrender or for the white man to fire. It usually happened with this show of intimidation. The Indians began to look at one another, as it wasn't working this time.

"They're getting restless Juan, hold your fire until I tell you."

"I wait for you."

The Indians in position stood like statues one hundred yards from the island. They moved forward, slowly about ten steps and stopped, and then another ten steps to the water's edge, which made the horses anxious, seeing where they were headed.

The leader tired of waiting and let out a war hoop, which led the others forward into the water. One horse spooked at the river's edge and threw its rider. Five horses now in knee-high water splashed the scantily clad warriors with near-freezing water. Their war whoops sounded more like yelps of a dog.

"Call yours," Will said.

"White horse! My side."

"Fire!" Will said.

Both high powered buffalo guns fired at the same moment, sounding like cannon fire. Two Indians hit the water, but three kept coming. Will opened fire with the first revolver, hitting a horse and an Indian. The small island was now covered in a fog of thick blue smoke. When Will started firing the second revolver, the surviving Kiowa Indians headed south into the flatlands.

"You did good." Will pulled out the cylinder pin of each Colt Paterson.

Juan scratched the ground with the heel of his boot. A tear ran down his cheek. Juan wiped it, and the gunpowder on his hands smudged his face.

"Juan, you said you have met the Kiowa before. But never fought them." Will looked at Juan, "Indians have never attacked you?"

"Never…have Indians attacked my wagon," Juan said.

"I don't understand." Will spun the newly loaded cylinder and holstered his pistol.

"It is different…I am Mexican." He paused, "We never fight… Indians."

"They couldn't have known who we were—Mexican or not!"

"When Indians come, we wave white flag. They know…we never fight."

"They never harm you?" Will asked.

"Only… if we don't pay," Juan said.

"How much would we pay to pass through?"

"Maybe one peso per person, or sometimes one peso for the animals," Juan said.

"You mean to tell me if I had paid them seven pesos, they would've let us pass through without a fight?"

Juan nodded.

"Dammit to hell, Juan! Why didn't you tell me that?"

"You didn't ask," Juan shrugged his shoulders.

"Hellfire. We burned more than that in gunpowder."

Juan didn't answer.

"Let's go before they come back with the Kiowa Nation. I don't think their chief will be in the mood to barter when he learns we killed three of his braves and a good horse."

Twenty miles east of the Caches, they came upon a natural low water crossing of the upper Arkansas River. It was the fifteenth day of March; they'd left Bent's Fort five days ago. Juan wanted to camp there. Will wanted to push on. He didn't like riding in darkness but knew they must outdistance the fast-moving Kiowa.

They found nourishment chewing on jerky and hardtack. Juan was still distraught about killing the Kiowa Indian. Will understood. At eighteen, on the trail to Texas, he was forced to shoot his first man—a white man hell-bent on stealing his horse. It took a second killing to get over the first. Will felt guilty for assuming Juan had fought Indians before. Ten trips and no Indian scrapes. Who would have ever thought that?

Will had survived many battles where it was kill or be killed. His brother's scalp in his saddlebag was a constant reminder of the dangers of the trail.

Josiah Wilbarger, Will's Austin neighbor, was scalped and lived to tell about it. Will remembered the last time he saw Josiah, standing at attention, as the search party left Austin. His head wound was visible, as if he was saying, "Kill the bastards that done this to me." The vision of Matilda Lockhart raced through his mind: captured by Indians, her little nose burned off her face. Will thought, *If they did that to Fayette, I'll kill every damn Indian on earth.* Then he remembered Captain Hayes' disciples and how they helped him get to Santa Fe. It was Tonkawa Indians that risked their lives for him. He regretted his harsh thoughts toward Indians.

When Will felt comfortable with the distance traveled, they camped on the north side of the river. Protected from the Kiowa by the Arkansas River. Juan sat on his bedroll with his back against a Sycamore tree, praying the Rosary beads.

"Juan, you did a good thing killing that Kiowa. No reason to ask for forgiveness."

"No, it is not right to kill. I broke the commandment of God. I must repent for my sins."

"Then say a prayer for me. I killed a few and I intend to kill a bunch more."

"Sí...I already say a prayer for you."
"Thank you, Juan. Now I can sleep."

The next morning, Will and Juan ate a hearty breakfast of pork and beans. Will said, "Good beans, Juan. Thanks for putting the bean pot on the coals last night."
"No more pork. From here, just beans," Juan said.
"I'll try to shoot something for your skillet today."

Juan coaxed his horse into the shallow, frigid waters of the Arkansas at the next bend in the river. Will followed, leading the mule and the relief horses. They headed into the sun. Neither mentioned the fight with the Kiowa again.

On the twenty-ninth day of March, they reached Council Grove. This wooded area, one-hundred-forty-five miles west of Independence, was the staging area for all trails west. Twenty large Pennsylvania freight wagons and three small Mexican wagons were there, being outfitted for the eight hundred mile trip to Santa Fe. Hundreds of mules and a vast assortment of domesticated animals grazed about—some hobbled, while others were tethered along Council Grove Creek.

One Mexican wagon belonged to Juan, the other two were his brothers. The Mexicans numbered eight. His brothers, a brother-in-law, and five fellow teamsters embraced in excited jubilation. They spoke Spanish simultaneously. All had assumed the worst. When they last saw Juan at Bent's Fort, he was on death's door. The Mexicans were thankful for Juan's recovery, convinced Black Charlotte saved his life.

They made camp below the others, keeping a distance from the Anglo teamsters who resented them. They celebrated their reunion huddled around their campfire, close to their oxen. Mexicans preferred oxen because an ox cost less than a Missouri Mule. Muleskinners didn't appreciate the beasts because they were slower and had a tendency to stampede, which often caused delays.

Will moved among the campfires of the men who drove the brightly painted Conestoga and Dearborn Freight wagons. The Conestoga was built in Lancaster while the Dearborn came from Pittsburgh. With a six-to-ten mule team, they could haul up to six tons of freight. The five hundred dollar import tax per American wagon added to the animosity the Anglos already had toward their Mexican counterparts.

Will felt the coolness of the Muleskinners' reception, which he assumed was due to his association with the Mexican teamsters. It didn't matter to him—he was heading for Independence the next day. However, Will was concerned about Juan's acceptance and treatment after he was gone. The grueling journey through eight-hundred miles of prairie would take eight to ten weeks. A wagon train was organized like a town. Its leaders were elected based on experience and qualifications. Sometimes a candidate's charisma and kinship overrode their ability.

At each camp, Will told the story of his abducted nephew, including a description of Fayette and an offer of a reward for his return. At the last camp, Will noticed a man standing back from the group as he spoke. It seemed he wanted to participate but didn't wish to rub elbows with the muleskinners. The well-dressed gentleman had also been present when he spoke to the first group. He wore a long wool coat over a well-tailored suit of clothes. The beaver top-hat and clean-shaven face set him apart from the others. The mysterious middle-aged man kept his distance but listened intently to what Will said. The man approached Will as he was leaving. "Mr. Smith, my name is Alfred V. du Pont and I am saddened to hear of the loss of your brother and capture of your nephew."

"Thank you."

"I am honored to meet a man who wears not one, but two Colt Patersons," The man spoke English with a French accent.

"Glad to meet you, Mr. du Pont. My name's William Smith, my friends just call me Will."

"My friends call me du Pont. May I call you Will?" he extended his hand.

Will shook his hand, "Certainly. Isn't du Pont your last name?"

"Yes, it is. Something that my late father started. No one could say or remember his difficult first name; they just called him du Pont. The name seems to have stuck with me."

"You going to Santa Fe with the caravan?"

"That remains to be seen. Perhaps we could discuss my plans over dinner...at my camp?" Du Pont pointed.

Will looked toward the camp and saw two men lingering under a large oak. *Have they been following me?* Will wondered. Both men were well-armed, and Will had noticed that du Pont had a bulge in his cummerbund. Will's protective instincts kicked in. His mind and heart raced.

Du Pont recognized Will's concern and quickly reacted. "Will, they work for me. It is their job to be concerned about my safety." Du Pont motioned them over.

The men weren't the usual hired guns; each spoke French, English and Spanish. Like du Pont, they wore fine European clothing. Du Pont introduced them as Mr. Bidermann and Mr. Lammot. They were courteous. Neither entered into conversation unless asked. They appeared more interested in the side arms that Will wore than him.

"You will join me for dinner, won't you?" du Pont asked.

"I would be honored," Will said, embarrassed his fear was detected.

Du Pont said, "This way, Will. While Francois prepares dinner, we can enjoy some cognac."

"Cog...nac?" Will raised his eyebrows.

"It's French Brandy: made only from the finest grapes around the Village of Cognac."

The security men followed at a distance, carrying on their own conversation in French, obviously talking about Will's unusual guns. Du Pont told Will of being born in Paris and coming to America with his parents when he was only two.

Will was impressed with du Pont's camp. His host was obviously a man of means. The tent was made of heavy duck cloth, erected with strong decorative poles hand carved and painted with vignettes of French nobility. Brightly colored Persian rugs covered the damp earth. The tent was furnished with a small writing desk, a dining table, and four chairs. Hidden from view by a decorative screen was a four-poster bed. The twenty-by-thirty-foot tent was larger than most Austin homes. His servants and bodyguards had their own tents. Francois the chef had his kitchen just outside under a tent, with sides that could be rolled up. The du Pont teamsters and muleskinners camped underneath three custom-built wagons. Each wagon had two teamsters and two mule skinners. Sixteen men made up du Pont's entourage. Each had a specific job and carried out their duties in an orderly fashion.

Will sat in a captain's chair. Uncharacteristically, his back to the tent's entrance, while his host faced him and the entrance. Du Pont's guards took stations in front of the tent. A man servant took Will's dusty buffalo robe. He showed his chagrin at touching what once had been on a bison's back.

The valet approached and waited patiently for a few moments and then extended his arms toward Will. Will looked back at the man perplexed, and then at du Pont.

Du Pont cleared his throat. "Charles, perhaps Mr. Smith prefers eating with his armaments on."

Will realized that Charles wanted to disarm him. He shook his head. "No way in hell am I handing over my guns!" Will looked at du Pont and said, "My brother was killed by Indians the first time he ever left home without his."

"No problem," said du Pont. He nodded and turned to the valet, "Charles please pour us each a dram of brandy, after you put away our guest's coat."

"As you wish Mr. du Pont." Charles laid the robe in a vacant chair and then picked up a decanter of cognac.

Will put a hand over his glass, "None for me."

Du Pont leaned forward, "You're aware—this is the brandy of Napoleon."

Will would've liked to try cognac, but not with two professional trigger men at his back, a host with a derringer tucked in his cummerbund, and a French waiter trying to disarm him.

Du Pont smiled, "Perhaps another time. When we become better acquainted. Then we can toast to our friendship." He handed his brandy glass to Charles.

"It was not my intent to offend you, du Pont. My mission is too important to let my guard down. Even for a glass of fine cognac." Will managed a tense smile.

"I like your commitment to your ultimate goal, whatever that may be. Would you like some green tea from China?" du Pont looked at Charles.

"I would like that. I don't think I've ever had green tea."

"You're a Texas Ranger, I see." du Pont leaned toward Will as Charles poured their tea.

Will tilted his head back, "After eighteen months of service in the Texas Army. I ranged South Texas fighting Indians 'til last summer." Will paused and raised his eyebrows, "Just how would you know that I was ever a Texas Ranger?"

"Your guns! Made by my friend Samuel Colt in Paterson, New Jersey. Sam and I corresponded regularly until recently. His last letter mentioned sending the entire production of Paterson revolvers to the Texas Navy. When President Sam Houston disbanded the navy, the guns ended up going to the Rangers."

"That's exactly how we got them. So, you know Samuel Colt?" Will took a sip of tea.

"We're business associates. We've not been in contact recently."

"Business associates?" Will tried to disengage his finger from the teacup.

"I developed the percussion caps for his first repeating revolver: the Colt Paterson you're wearing." Du Pont rested his chin on fingers that formed a steeple.

Will shifted in a chair too small for his frame. They heard the familiar click of a gun hammer cocking. Will started to jump up.

Du Pont reached forward and placed his hands on Will's. "Listen carefully to me Will. The arm of your chair cocked the hammer of one of your guns. I'm not sure which. A trigger is exposed without the protection of a trigger guard. I think it is the gun on your right."

"How would you know that?"

"I heard the hammer click. That click is the only safety feature the Colt Paterson has. Please listen to me.... Slowly reach for the hammer of the gun on your right. If the hammer is back, gently thumb it forward into the safety position." du Pont leaned back slowly.

Charles had also heard the Colt's click and knew what was happening. He took cover behind the room divider and put his hands over both ears.

Will nodded, acknowledging the hammer was cocked. His forehead glistened with perspiration as he thumbed the hammer down slowly. Then he checked the other gun, which was in a safe position.

"How'd you know?" Will looked wide-eyed at du Pont.

"From experience. If you look at the rug under our table, there, about where your right foot is, there's a large bullet hole discharged by Mr. Colt's prototype of your guns."

"I see the hole," Will ducked his head out from under the table.

"That's how this magnificent Persian rug became part of my camp furnishing. Samuel Colt, after a few snifters of brandy, nearly blew his leg off. I heard the same click when you moved against the chair's arm. Until now, I didn't know how the misfire happened. Now I have proof how dangerous this new gun is. My wife Margaretta insisted I buy her a new rug. I took the damaged one for my tent."

Du Pont explained that he was impressed with the revolver mechanism until it went off in his dining room—in the presence of his wife and children. He advised Samuel Colt that his gun was not safe without a trigger guard. "We argued about it. He left in a huff. I haven't heard from him since."

Charles approached the table with a platter of roasted bison and potatoes. "I was ladling the soup when the gun discharged, I spilled soup all over the table." Charles placed the platter on the table, "That's why Lady Margaretta doesn't allow guns at her family table."

Du Pont gave Charles a hard stare as his entreé was served, but he remained silent until Charles was out of the tent.

"Please eat, Will," du Pont leaned forward, "you must be famished."

Will looked at his plate. "This looks good."

"Please excuse Charles. He's overly protective of my family and me, having served my father Éleuthère in his last days. Charles lost his home and family during an explosion of our powder plant. He has served me well for over twenty years. We consider Charles a member of the du Pont family."

Will leaned his head back, "You're the du Pont...the manufacturer of gunpowder?"

"Yes, but it was my father Eleuthère Irénée du Pont who started the company. I studied chemistry at Dickinson College, joining the company in 1818. The stockholders voted me president in 1837. However, I prefer the dirty work of a powder man. I enjoy working with explosive materials and weaponry. Bidermann, whom you've met, is a partner and tends to the business aspects of the du Pont Company, which affords me time to experiment with blowing things up."

Will's host explained that the du Pont partners had attended President Harrison's Inauguration on the fourth day of March in Washington D.C. and then traveled to Council Grove. The journey took three weeks in the heavy munitions wagons.

Will had never met anyone who'd attended a presidential inauguration, and du Pont had never met anyone from Texas. Will, who was everything du Pont had ever heard about Texans, intrigued him. He also learned that Will's late brother, James W. Smith, was the first Supreme Court Justice of Travis County. The conversation got lively when it turned to politics as Will and du Pont were from political families.

Will explained, "In Texas, the judicial sounding title has little to do with judicial courts. The position is along the stature of a governor of a U.S. Territory."

"So Will, Austin is now the capital of the Republic of Texas?" asked du Pont.

"For now it is. President Lamar chose the spot. Houston detests it because Lamar chose it. I figure if Houston is elected again, he'll move the capital back to Houston: the town named for him."

"Do you know President Lamar?"

"My brother and father, both officials of Texas' largest county, had frequent meetings with Lamar. I have met him several times."

"Will, I would very much like to meet him. Could you introduce me to President Lamar?" asked du Pont, wide-eyed.

"I can. But his term is over at the end of the year."

"But for now, he is still the President. I want to meet him. Also Sam Houston. Could you introduce me to him?"

Will was caught off guard and nearly choked on a tough piece of bison. It gave Will time to think. *I'm in a hurry; this greenhorn could slow me down. Lives depend on me reaching Austin.* Charles gave him a sip of water, and he slowly recovered from his bout of choking.

"Would you take me to Austin?" asked du Pont.

"I must leave first thing in the morning. I have no time to waste."

"What if I can speed your journey rather than hinder it?" du Pont gripped the arms of his chair.

Will leaned towards du Pont, "I'm listening; tell me how you could do that."

"Once you reach Independence, how do you plan to get to St. Louis? Are you going to Texas by land or sea? I have resources at my disposal to get you home in the most expeditious manner."

"Please tell me, how would you get us to Texas?" Will asked.

Du Pont explained he had a keelboat and crew docked at Independence. It could leave at once for St. Louis, arriving the next day. Then they would board a vessel in St. Louis for New Orleans.

"How do we get from New Orleans to Texas?" Will asked.

"We would sail by package ship to Matagorda, from there you could guide us up the Colorado River Valley by horseback to Austin." du Pont shifted in his chair.

"You said us. Who is the other person?" Will asked.

"My brother-in-law, James Bidermann, whom you've met."

"Where in the hell are we going now?" a voice from outside said.

"Come in James," du Pont said.

"What are you up to now du Pont?" James asked.

"We're going to Texas!"

Will listened as du Pont and his brother-in-law argued in French about their trip to Texas. Both his patience and his body were exhausted. "Thank you for a fine meal, du Pont. I am going to get some sleep." He reached for his buffalo robe, "I am heading east to Independence come sun up. If you and Bidermann can stay with me to the Missouri River, I'll take you up on that boat ride."

"See you in the morning," du Pont waved.

Will nodded and said, "Goodnight."

The Frenchmen stopped their bantering to say "Bonne nuit."

Will assumed it meant goodnight, waving as he walked away.

Chapter Fifteen

Juan made breakfast while Will saddled his best horse. What he couldn't tie on his horse, he left with Juan.

Four riders came down the hill at full gallop, stopping at the Mexican camp.

"We're ready if you are," a breathless du Pont managed to say.

"Good looking horses. Can they make it to Independence?" Will asked.

"They got us here from Wilmington. These horses can make it to Independence in two days."

"You think?" Will asked. He tightened the girth belt on his horse.

"I've been there and back a few times," du Pont stretched forward.

Will looked at a third man. "Who are you?"

"My name is Pierre Rabedeux. They call me Pete."

Du Pont explained, "Pete's our wagon master and captain of the caravan to Santa Fe. He and Lammot will follow us out a ways, then circle back, looking for any bushwhackers following us."

Will handed Juan a sealed envelope. "This is for the girl I told you about in Santa Fe. No one is to know who sent it. Do you understand?"

"Sí. I will take it to her: Bella the daughter of Miguel Miranda, owner of La Posada Inn on the plaza."

"Adios, mi amigo." Will placed his right hand on Juan's shoulder, "Until we meet again."

Juan said, "Hasta que nos encontremos de nuevo, amigo."

Will smiled. He did not fully understand the words, but he knew they came from Juan's heart. He turned and looked the wagon master in the eye. "Pete, these Mexican teamsters are my friends. They are from Chihuahua and are good, honest people. I've detected in camp some ill-will towards them. Most likely it has something to do with the import tax you pay. I doubt Juan even knows about that tax, but he knows the trail to Santa Fe better than anyone in your caravan. If I were you, I would seek his guidance."

Will put one leg in the stirrup and pulled himself up and onto his horse.

Pete looked at Juan and said, "If it's alright Juan, I'll place your wagons at the head of the train."

"That would be a smart move. If the Indians stop you, best let Juan… negotiate." Will turned his horse towards Independence, and the others followed. Will took comfort in knowing Juan would be respected and not abandoned on the Santa Fe Trail.

Will was impressed with the Frenchmen's horsemanship on the trail to Independence, Missouri. When they reached Ten Mile Point, Pete and Lammot said their goodbyes. They turned and worked their way back to the wagon train, riding slowly, looking for anyone trying to follow du Pont. A man of his wealth, knowledge, and power, was always vulnerable to robbery or being captured and held for ransom.

They made it to Independence on Thursday afternoon the first day of April 1841. The keelboat captain, George Herbert, was caught off guard by du Pont because he'd arrived a week earlier than expected. The St. Louis Creole lived on the boat when it was out of its St. Louis port. It would take days to gather the du Pont crew now on leave. Advised of the sense of urgency, George scurried about the wharf in search of a crew. He recruited nineteen men. Melting snow from the Rockies above the upper Missouri and the Big Sioux Rivers accelerated the flow of both rivers. It made the trip down easy, but increased the difficulty on the return.

George's familiarity with the rivermen helped eliminate the most dangerous of mariners, those who smoked, which was most of the men of the river. Smoking was forbidden on or around any property of the du Pont Company. Those violating the no smoking mandate were immediately terminated.

Strong young men were needed to handle the heavy ropes and man the oversized oars. The makeshift crew claimed to be knowledgeable of the river. The swift currents could shift a sandbar's position in a day, creating a navigational hazard.

George said, "Mr. du Pont, I select the best men I can find in short time and pray they don't overstate their river experience. Men sometimes have a mouth of an alligator, but tail of a tadpole."

Du Pont chuckled. "Gather your men. I'll talk to them. We'll find the tadpoles."

The boatmen, called voyageurs, were gathered on the open deck of the bow. Du Pont advised the recruits of the sense of urgency of the journey. He said that they should consider this trip a shakedown cruise of their keelboat competency. The du Pont Company had ordered more keelboats for the fleet. Additional river pilots and crew would be needed. If they fared well to St. Louis and back safely, each would be considered for permanent crews on the new boats.

Du Pont asked, "If you have no experience on the river, speak now. If it is discovered you can't pull your weight on the line, you'll be left in St. Louis to fend for yourself. Is that understood?"

No one spoke.

"Good, then…I assume we have an experienced crew." Du Pont gave George a look of confidence.

George nodded in appreciation.

The *Margaretta,* named for du Pont's wife, was painted black with red lettering and a small crest: the family shield. Its ten-foot sail bore a larger family crest. The boat's beam was eighteen feet, with a length of sixty feet, and a cargo-hold four-foot deep. The length and breadth of the vessel could hold thirty tons. The *Margaretta* never carried more than ten tons of highly explosive powder. The powder was packed tightly in small but sturdy waterproof kegs, each one held five pounds of powder.

Freight companies concerned about risk raised du Pont's shipping rates to four dollars a hundred weight. Freight charges became higher than the cost to manufacture black powder, so Bidermann suggested in jest that their company transport its explosives. Du Pont took his brother-in-law seriously, thinking it was a brilliant idea. Freight was back-hauled when it was available for prevailing rates. The du Pont Company became a competitor of the freight companies. The freight business proved to be as profitable as the munitions they shipped. The *Margaretta* was the first keelboat in the fleet. The second was working its way down the two thousand mile back-haul from Fort Union, loaded with beaver pelts destined for St. Louis.

Will enjoyed drifting down the Missouri at the speed of a fast horse canter. When the boat drifted beyond the channel, the crew instinctively grabbed the poles if the water was shallow or the oars if it was deep. Once they worked the boat back into the current of the river, George masterfully guided her with the long arm of the rudder. In the foaming swirl of white water, he fought the long handle of the rudder like he was wrestling a bear.

George asked, "Mr. du Pont, dark come soon. Should we tie up or carry on?"

Du Pont smiled. "You're the Captain, George. Only you can make that decision. I am merely a chemist. I'm trained to blow things to shit!"

Will and Bidermann had a good laugh.

George ignored them. "I don't often ride the river in the dark with a boatload of powder." The seasoned river pilot stared at the moon already showing its face. "No clouds, light be good! River flow fast, but not too fast. I think we keep going," George muttered.

Attempts at sleeping failed Will. When he dozed, the bow would lurch, splashing cold water over him and the deck. When daylight came, the river had changed color. The large chunks of ice that floated with them were gone. The muddy water of the Missouri began to take on a greenish tint while white froth, like dog slobber, formed in large floating pools.

"George, the water has changed. What happened? "Will looked toward shore.

"We be soon at the confluence of the Mississippi. Maybe by noon... less than twenty-four hours. We make record time to St. Louie," he yelled. "Yippee!" George screeched like a banshee.

Du Pont came out of the pilothouse he shared with his brother-in-law, "What's all the excitement about George?"

"We be tying up soon," George said.

Du Pont yelled for all to hear, "We'll be sipping champagne by dark."

"Thanks for the ride," Will hollered over the roar of the river.

"The pleasure is mine. It's still a long way from Texas." Du Pont stepped back inside the pilothouse.

It was a short buggy ride from the wharf to downtown St. Louis. Will wanted to walk off his sea legs, but his hosts insisted they hire a carriage. It was a festive occasion for St. Louis. Results of the 1840 census reported its population at just over sixteen thousand residents. The carriage driver mentioned the Planters Hotel had opened the day before.

"Sounds like a good place for us, don't you think Mr. Bidermann?" du Pont teased his brother-in-law.

The second Planters Hotel in St. Louis had been under construction for years. Disagreements among its partners along with financial and legal issues led many to think it would never open.

The driver said, "Doubt you could get a room with the grand opening celebration and all. Best I take you to the National."

"Take us to the new Planters. I know the manager. He'll find us a room." Du Pont slapped his knees.

Carriages lined the side street of the hotel. A small band played at the entrance. Well-dressed patrons strutted about like peacocks, sipping mint juleps and munching on fancy appetizers. Will had never seen a four-story building before—something he didn't share with his companions.

"Newspaper said every room was sold out," the driver said, pulling up to the curb directly in front of the Planters.

A constable came running up, "You can't wait here in front of the hotel. Those hay burners will be shitting all over the new cobblestone!"

"No problem, constable. Let us get our gear and we'll be gone." Du Pont grabbed his bag.

Will and Bidermann grabbed their gear while du Pont paid the driver. The driver took his leave with a nice tip in hand.

Four hundred miles of trail dust marked them as travelers. The constable wasn't about to let them walk on the new marble floors of the hotel lobby. He warily looked at Will's guns and then at Bidermann's and du Pont's ornate percussion pistols.

A young man stepped out of the crowd and pointed a finger toward du Pont. "I saw you in Washington…at the inauguration…you two were with the President!" He looked at Bidermann, then at du Pont.

The constable attempted to hold the reporter back. More members of the press pushed forward, looking for a story. Will instinctively moved between the reporters who tried to intrude into du Pont's space. When he placed his hands on the large guns he wore, they backed off. Thinking the situation was getting out of hand, the constable blew his whistle. They were suddenly surrounded by other lawmen and quickly ushered in a side door.

"You with the President?" the constable asked.

Du Pont looked around at the officers then at his traveling companions, "I don't see him, so I must not be with the President."

"Then what is your business here at the Planters?"

"I have business with the manager, which does not concern you."

"Mr. Stickney?" the constable asked.

Du Pont nodded and said, "I have my own security, Constable. I am sure your people must be needed elsewhere."

"Back to your post," the constable ordered the security men. "I'll take care of Mr....what did you say your name was?"

"I didn't say. Now where is Mr. Stickney?"

"I'll take you to his office," the constable said. He escorted them up a flight of stairs and down a narrow hallway to a door at the end. A sign read: "Manager's Office".

Du Pont stopped at the door, "Thank you for your assistance, I'm sure you need to get back to policing the crowd out front."

The constable walked down the hallway, his head down in dejection.

When du Pont entered the manager's carpeted office, the reporter that started the commotion in front of the hotel was trying to talk to Mr. Stickney. Out of breath from running up the inside mezzanine stairs, he could only say, "The President's men are here!"

Mr. Stickney immediately recognized du Pont and Bidermann, frequent guests of the National Hotel, which he previously managed. His attention turned away from the reporter to his waiting guests.

"Welcome, gentlemen, to the new Planters Hotel," Mr. Stickney said, careful not to divulge their identity.

Du Pont whispered, "Mr. Stickney...may we have some privacy... please?"

"Certainly." Mr. Stickney turned toward the reporter, "Mr. Kendall, I have important business with these gentlemen. Perhaps we can continue this later. "

George Kendall, an experienced reporter from the *New Orleans Picayune,* pretended not to understand that they wanted him out of the office. He looked out the window like he had no interest in their conversation. Will saw du Pont was agitated. He moved toward the eager reporter and said, "Please excuse us."

Kendall hastily exited the office.

Will's effective way of handling the reporter and his unusual guns impressed Stickney. He assumed that Will was du Pont's bodyguard. He waited for du Pont to introduce him.

Du Pont said, "This is Will Smith."

"Glad to make your acquaintance, Mr. Smith. I appreciate your handling that pesky reporter. Now what can I do for you, Mr. du Pont?" Stickney asked.

"We need rooms and baths. We're taking the next steamer to New Orleans," du Pont sat his bag down.

"That will be the *Queen of St. Louis*. She arrives Saturday evening and departs Sunday morning at ten."

"We are overbooked, Mr. du Pont. What with the President and his people coming, every room in town is booked. I wish I had known you were coming—," he paused, "I'll find you accommodations somewhere."

Du Pont smiled, "Tippy is coming to St. Louis? The President didn't mention coming to St. Louis when I saw him last," du Pont said.

A white-gloved bellhop barged into the room.

"Have you no manners, Robert?" Stickney glared at his protégé.

"But sir, it's from Washington. The Office of the President." Robert excitedly held a silver tray in front of Mr. Stickney.

Stickney looked at his guests. "Please excuse me for a moment." He took the envelope from the tray. He opened it eagerly, breaking the wax seal in the process. His long face revealed his disappointment. Stickney attempted to hide his feelings from his guests. "How was this letter sent?" Stickney asked his assistant.

"By government courier on horseback. He'll head back first thing in the morning. Do you intend to send a reply?"

"Yes, I must send my regards. Please see that the courier is fed, then take him to the couriers' quarters. I will have my reply ready by morning," Stickney said.

"Yes, sir," the assistant said.

"Keep the courier away from the reporters," Stickney warned.

Robert nodded and exited the room.

"Something wrong?" du Pont asked.

"Yes, Mr. du Pont." Stickney sat down in his chair. "President Harrison is gravely ill. This letter was penned by Vice President Tyler. He gives his condolences and asks us to pray for the President."

"Sounds serious," du Pont said, "What about the Vice President?"

Stickney shook his head. "I am afraid no one from Washington is coming to our grand opening."

Du Pont leaned over, "I am sorry Mr. Stickney. These things happen. We mortals have no control over them."

"Thank you, Mr. du Pont! I must look at my predicament positively. I now have rooms for you and your associates. If you will take the Presidential Suite."

Du Pont looked at Bidermann, then at Will.

"All I need is a bed," Will said.

Stickney said, "The grand salon of the Presidential Suite has three adjoining bedrooms, each with a four-poster feather bed and private bath."

"Say no more; we will take it," du Pont said.

"Good. I will take you up to the top floor. Follow me, gentlemen."

They followed Stickney up two flights of stairs to the Presidential Suite. The large double-entry door opened into the impressive suite of rooms. Will had never seen such elegant furnishings. He began to appreciate the advantages of traveling with du Pont and company.

Two attractive dark-skinned girls with silky black hair that dangled in their faces entered Will's private bathroom. He watched the young chambermaids pour hot water into the copper tub. They motioned his bath was ready, and he closed the door behind them. Their presence had kindled his yearning for Bella.

Will looked forward to a bath but had never expected anything like this. Once in the tub, he laid his head back and enjoyed the sweet smell of lavender scented soap flakes. His thoughts turned toward Bella, he imagined her in the tub with him. Someday they would have the opportunity to enjoy such luxury together.

As the bathwater cooled so did Will's spirit, as negative thoughts and self-doubts about his failed attempt to find Fayette filled his mind.

He shook the negative notions from his mind and made a positive affirmation. Once his message was delivered to President Lamar, he would head back to Santa Fe and return with Bella and Fayette.

Will put on his last set of clean clothes. The chambermaids took his dirty laundry to wash and then dry on the hotel's roof.

Chapter Sixteen

Will found du Pont and Bidermann in the living room of their suite, sipping champagne from hand-cut glassware.

Du Pont said, "Will, I told you this morning that we would be drinking champagne tonight." He looked at a man server. "Please pour our friend from Texas a glass of champagne."

The waiter poured and offered the glass of champagne to Will on a silver tray.

Du Pont lifted his glass, "A toast to Texas! And the men who fought for Independence!"

"Here here," Bidermann said.

They heard a knock on the door.

Bidermann said, "Must be the tailor. I'll get the door." Bidermann peered through the peephole. It was the constable. Bidermann said, "Yes, what is it?"

The constable had a new attitude. "I beg your pardon, sir. I have a Mr. Busch and two of his sons waiting in the lobby. They are local tailors known to me. Mr. Busch says you sent for them."

"Yes, we sent for them," Bidermann said.

"Mr. Stickney has asked me to check out all who might want to disturb you. I will bring them up right away."

"Thank you, Constable," Bidermann said.

Frederick Busch, his sons Benjamin and Frederick Jr., had made clothes for the du Pont family for years. They had du Pont and Bidermann's measurements on file but needed Will's, which is why they were at the hotel. Will liked the idea of a smart looking suit, but didn't want to be obligated to Mr. du Pont, so he protested when Frederick Busch pulled out his tape measure.

Bidermann and du Pont explained the importance of making a good impression. They had ordered suits on their way to Independence, so their garments were ready. Will was measured. The tailors promised they would work through the night so that the hand stitched suit of clothes would be ready by morning, and then left.

Waiters arrived with two carts of food and wine. "Compliments of the manager," the waiter said. It was timely, as they hadn't eaten all day. Will enjoyed his first oysters, but he refused to try the escargot.

As the waiters rolled out remnants of their meal, Mr. Stickney arrived with a folded newspaper in his hand. "I hope you enjoyed your dinner," he said.

"We did indeed, thank you," du Pont said, motioning for Stickney to sit down in the high backed chair facing the settee where he lounged.

"I hope your accommodations are adequate?" Stickney said.

"Yes, we are quite comfortable," du Pont said. Will and Bidermann nodded in agreement.

"Good." Stickney cleared his throat, and said, "I have a problem and need your help, Mr. du Pont."

Stickney unfolded the special edition of the *Gazette*. On the front page, a bold headline read: "President Harrison to Speak." The story told of the president's security team arriving earlier in the day and how the Presidential Suite of the new Planters Hotel has been under heavy guard since their arrival. "One armed guard wore two revolvers," the article claimed. The printed program in the paper said the newly elected president would speak on the steps of Planters at noon Saturday, April 3, 1841. It mentioned that Harrison would be the first president to visit St. Louis.

Stickney said, "Everyone will come expecting to see the president. But he isn't coming." He stood. "I don't know what to do."

"I don't understand your concern," Bidermann said. He stood. "You have thousands of people coming to your front door tomorrow. They'll see your beautiful hotel for the first time."

Stickney looked at Bidermann. "You don't think they will be disappointed?"

Bidermann shook his head, "No one will be disappointed."

Du Pont watched his business partner intently, knowing what the marketing genius was up to. Will listened as Bidermann laid out his plan. "Mr. Stickney, there is no way to get the word out that the President is not coming. The front page coverage in the *Gazette* is a gift that couldn't be bought for any amount of money."

Stickney said, "But they will be disappointed."

Bidermann spread his arms. "Don't let them be! You'll have an audience. Entertain them."

Stickney's eyes began to sparkle, and his demure demeanor began to change.

Bidermann said, "If the President were here, then he would be the center of attention and not your hotel."

"You're right, the owners would like that." Stickney thought for a moment then said, "You haven't said anything to anyone...have you... about the President's illness or him not coming?"

They looked at one another; everyone shook their head.

Stickney took over the plan, "No one knows he is not coming. When it's time for the President to speak, then we'll make the announcement that he is gravely ill."

The program would remain as published except Mayor Daggett would open the ceremony by introducing Mr. du Pont as a longtime friend and confidant of the President. He would read the regrets sent by Vice President Tyler. A moment of silent prayer would be observed for the sixty-eight-year-old President's recovery. Then Mr. Stickney would introduce the hotel's owners, special guests, and dignitaries. All would be invited to tour the hotel and enjoy food and beverage as the local orchestra performed on the mezzanine.

As promised, two suits were delivered to the suite in the morning. "Why two suits?" Will asked, "I just need one for today's festivities."

"Every man should have at least two good suits," Bidermann advised. He looked approvingly at the suits. "Which one are you going to wear today?"

Will chose the brown plaid over the solid gray suit and went into his room to change. He smiled when he saw himself in the mirror. He joined Bidermann in the sitting room. "Tell me how much they cost," Will said to Bidermann, "I'll repay you."

"It's a business expense. Du Pont's Texas agent needs to be properly attired," Bidermann picked at a piece of thread on Will's coat.

"Texas... agent?" Will asked.

"Since Texas declared Independence from Mexico, du Pont and I have wanted an agent in Texas representing our interest. We think you're that man. If you accept our offer you would report directly to me." Bidermann handed him a string tie.

"What would I do for you?" Will asked.

Bidermann heard du Pont calling from the next room, "I need to check on du Pont. We'll have seven days on the *Queen* to talk about it."

He went to the window and watched people arriving. Carriages were parked helter-skelter along the cobblestone streets. It was a clear but windy morning. He opened his window and listened to the hustle and bustle below. A dozen workers set up folding chairs reserved for special guests.

Two newspaper boys hawked papers: "President coming! READ ALL ABOUT IT!" The noise was too much. Will closed the window. He went over to the mirror once more for another look and liked what he saw. He decided against wearing his dusty felt hat.

Bidermann returned to Will's room. "The suit looks good on you."

Will turned to him and said, "Thank you, I appreciate everything you and Mr. du Pont have done for me."

"Now, as I was saying, du Pont has wanted to go to Texas for years, but I discouraged it...that is until we met you at Council Grove." Bidermann sat down in a chair. "Do you fully understand who we are and what we do?"

"I know you make black powder out of bat shit." Will grinned.

Bidermann explained that du Pont furnished the United States Government enough explosives to drive the British off its shores during the War of 1812. "There were others who made black powder, but we were the ones the army depended on. The Secretary of War even asked the du Pont Company to make uniforms for the troops. Our stockpiles of war materials are the largest in the world. This is why meeting President Lamar is so important to us. Texas will be at war again with Mexico, and the Indian battles will continue. Texas needs us, and we want to help." Bidermann stood, walked over to Will, and straightened his collar.

"You understand Texas no longer has an army. The Rangers and the militia are the only protection Texas has," Will said as he tugged at the string tie.

Bidermann nodded. "Speaking of protection, when du Pont and I travel, we usually have Lammot and Pete for security backup. Today, you and I are the only ones to keep an eye on things. I am worried about du Pont being exposed to such a large crowd."

"Why is that?" Will asked.

"There are people who would harm du Pont if the opportunity presented itself." Bidermann straightened his own tie.

"He is such a pleasant man. Why would anyone want to hurt him?" Will strapped on his guns.

"It's not about him. It's about what he represents. The explosion that killed thirty-three employees and Charles' family was not an accident."

"Just tell me what to do," Will tightened his gun belt.

"We'll walk him down; I'll be in front. You'll have our backs. Du Pont likes to talk to people he doesn't know: curiosity of a chemist,

I guess. Keep him moving. We'll stand on each side of the podium. Watch for people who appear anxious. Give them lots of eye contact." Bidermann checked his gun.

Du Pont knocked on the door, "Gentlemen are you ready?" Will opened the door. "Yes, we are."

Du Pont wore a black top-hat, a frock coat, and matching waistcoat with heavy linen pants. He looked very presidential for his part of the program. Stickney was waiting to introduce du Pont to Mayor Daggett, who would introduce him. The mayor was gracious but disappointed that he wasn't introducing President Harrison. Will and Bidermann took their positions and started observing the growing crowd. People stood behind the filled chairs several rows deep into the closed street.

Family carriages and farm wagons were used to give height to those the farthest away. They could see, but it was doubtful they could hear. A military color guard raised the twenty-six star U.S. Flag up the hotel flagpole. Everyone stood at attention. Men removed their hats. The band played patriotic music as the excitement intensified. Stickney introduced the mayor, who welcomed honored guests and introduced du Pont.

Du Pont read the letter from Vice President Tyler, not knowing that his friend William Henry Harrison had slipped into a coma and would die twelve hours later, having served only thirty-two days as president.

The crowd's mood turned somber. They were disappointed but understood why the president couldn't travel to St. Louis. Some openly wept as others prayed. President Harrison was popular in the West, having been a hero of the Indian Wars.

When Stickney announced the hotel was providing free food and beverage in the lobby, a stampede of spectators rushed for the doors. The band started playing and the grandest party ever held in St. Louis, Missouri began without their guest of honor.

Three well-dressed men boarded the *Queen of St. Louis*. Mr. Stickney personally made reservations for the best accommodations on the sternwheeler for the seven-night passage to New Orleans. It was the least he could do for the men who had made the Grand Opening of the Planters Hotel a success.

The captain greeted them warmly, "Welcome aboard the *Queen of St. Louis* Mr. du Pont, Mr. Bidermann, and Mr. Smith. We are honored to have you on board." He shook their hands and introduced them to the head steward who took them to their quarters.

Will sat on the end of a small sleeping berth and peered through a portal the size of his head. The flowing river mesmerized him. His mind drifted back over all the rivers and creeks he had forged to get here. He was almost home, without Fayette, but with two Frenchmen instead. Would his family understand?

Bidermann's job offer caught him by surprise. Will looked at his passenger voucher dated Sunday, April 4, 1841, and suddenly realized that today was his twenty-third birthday. Will thought about his options. All he knew was farming and fighting Indians. *Maybe the offer is something to seriously consider.* He looked at the furnishings of his stateroom. He thought, *I could get used to this.*

Will changed, hung his suit in a small armoire, and then took a walk around the upper deck to the landing side. Will leaned on the rail and watched passengers waving at friends and family on shore. The last of the baggage and provisions were loaded. The ship's bell indicated they would soon depart.

The *Queen* would tie up in Cairo tonight where the Ohio River flowed into the Mississippi. Passengers coming down the Ohio would board in the morning. Will was anxious to get underway.

"The elusive Mr. Smith, we meet again."

Will recognized the pesky reporter from the hotel on Friday. "I don't recall us ever meeting."

"We weren't introduced, but I know who you are," he said and extended a hand. Will ignored it. "My name is George W. Kendall, a reporter for the *New Orleans Picayune*."

"Damn, you're like a Texas tick—when you bite someone, you don't let go!" Will continued to ignore Kendall.

"Coming from you Will Smith, I consider that a compliment," Kendall said.

"It wasn't meant to be." Will watched as longshoremen furled the heavy hemp lines into the water while deckhands tugged and pulled them on deck.

"Mr. Smith, I am in a position to help you find your nephew."

"Tell me how you can help me." Will turned towards Kendall.

"The eastern papers like stories about Texas and Texans. I could do a story about you and your nephew. Once the *Picayune* runs it, the *St. Louis Gazette* will pick it up. They are the most read newspapers in the west."

"What's in it for you?" Will looked down at the busy dock.

"A good story. That's what I'm paid to do—write good stories!" Kendall pulled out his reporter's pad and pencil.

Will told the story as Kendall scribbled his notes. He described the Comanche mutilation of his brother James and abduction of Fayette in detail.

"That's horrible, Will!"

"Savage bastards! I want to kill every damn Comanche on Earth."

"Can I quote you on that?" Kendall asked.

"If I said it, you can."

It was the first time Will talked about his brother's murder and Fayette's capture. It seemed to help him by telling Kendall the story. He didn't mention the Texas Commissioners or the thousand peso reward on his head.

Will thought, *This reporter is not a bad fellow. He's just doing his job, telling folks what needs telling.*

"What's your connection to du Pont?" Kendall asked.

Will's attitude changed, "This interview, as you call it, was supposed to be about Fayette and my search for him."

"I didn't mean to offend you. Just curious how someone from Texas meets up with the richest man in the world." Kendall smiled like a possum.

Having heard the confrontation, Bidermann walked up behind them. "It is our intention to help the Smith family find Fayette."

"May I quote you... Mr.—"

"James Bidermann, Operations Manager of the du Pont Company."

"I thought you were with President Harrison and his security detail?" Kendall shook his head.

"So, you're the person that jumped the story to the *Gazette?*" Bidermann chuckled.

Kendall's face flushed, "Guilty as charged."

"We all, from time to time, assume things that aren't so." Bidermann leaned on the railing "You're a perfect example of that, Mr. Kendall."

"How is that Mr. Bidermann?"

"I assumed you were an ass confronting us as you did, right there in front of others that we didn't want knowing our business," Bidermann said.

"I apologize for the scene I caused," Kendall said.

"I accept your apology, Mr. Kendall." Bidermann shook his hand.

"Please, both of you just call me George."

Bidermann invited them to du Pont's stateroom for food and drinks. They found du Pont and the ship's captain engaging in conversation about transporting explosives safely by water. The captain assured du Pont should he ever encounter a du Pont vessel on the river, it would have the right of way. All had a good laugh, making light of the dangers of shipping black powder.

"Remember George Kendall, the reporter for the *New Orleans Daily Picayune?* He's writing a story about Will's search for his nephew," Bidermann said.

Du Pont's face turned red, "Mr. Kendall, how dare you come to my stateroom after accosting us in front of the Planters Hotel."

"I'm sorry Mr. du Pont. The reporter in me took over in the excitement of the moment. I have apologized to Mr. Bidermann and Mr. Smith. I hope you'll forgive me?"

"If you are sincere in your efforts to find Fayette, I might be able to find it in my heart to forgive you." du Pont leaned back in his chair.

Kendall said, "With a front-page story in the *Picayune* and *Gazette,* everyone in the West will be looking for him."

Du Pont nodded his approval. He shuffled a deck of cards and asked, "Do you play poker, Mr. Kendall?"

"On occasion, I've been known to play a game of chance," Kendall smiled.

Du Pont motioned for Kendall to sit at the card table. He looked at Will and Bidermann. "We have a foursome. Let's play."

They played poker until the ship's bell announced their arrival at Cairo. Du Pont had a run of luck, which put him in a mood to celebrate. Kendall and Bidermann were not as jubilant as du Pont and Will.

"You played some good hands, Will. Where did you learn to play like that?" du Pont raised an eyebrow.

"Birthday luck, I guess," Will said.

"Today's your birthday?"

"Yes."

Du Pont raised his arms, "Then we must celebrate!"

Du Pont toasted Will's birthday with French brandy followed by French champagne and a Cuban cigar. Word of a lively party in the du Pont stateroom reached a bevy of ladies on board.

"Looking for a good time?" they asked Bidermann, who opened the door.

"Always!" Bidermann opened the door wider.

"Who sent you?" Bidermann tried to ask over the men's rowdy catcalls. He never received an answer.

The prettiest of the three Creole girls rubbed her voluptuous body against his and whispered, "We're looking for a good time too."

The girls sang and danced for the men. The three sisters—each in their twenties—said they were born just years apart from the same mother, but each had different fathers. The talkative one said they were bound for New Orleans, having learned the tricks of their trade in St. Louis. Tricks their mother had taught them.

Will watched closely as two of the girls snuggled close to du Pont on the settee, while the leader made a move on Bidermann. Will asked the captain, "Where did you get these girls?"

"I didn't get them! I assumed one of you procured them." The captain was offended by the insinuation.

"I didn't mean to offend, Captain but I need to find out who sent them."

Will knew du Pont or Bidermann couldn't have arranged for them. Bidermann never received an answer when he'd asked who sent them. Kendall had no way of knowing he would be joining their celebration. *Mr. Stickney certainly wouldn't have jeopardized his hotel's reputation by pandering,* Will thought.

Alarmed, Will remembered Bidermann's words. There were people that wanted to harm du Pont. He watched their every move, convinced they were up to no good. The shortest of the three girls rubbed du Pont's waist. Will saw her gently unhook his gold pocketwatch chain from the small fob pocket of his vest. She already had his wallet.

"Damn, she is good." Will looked at the captain, "Whatever happens, don't let them out the door."

The captain nodded and moved to the door. Will moved near the settee, intending to grab the girls' wrist and pull her away from du Pont before she could harm him. She saw Will coming and intentionally spilled her wine glass on a surprised du Pont. All three girls headed for the cabin door, but they were blocked by the burly captain.

"Let us out, you big bastard!" They shouted and beat on the captain's chest.

Will came up behind the short one who had du Pont's watch. He grabbed her at the waist, but she broke loose, turned, and kicked him in the groin. Will bent over in pain and saw a small pearl-handled Derringer pulled out from a pocket on her skirt. She cocked it and pulled the trigger. Will placed his hand on the short barrel, preventing the cap from firing. He held onto the gun, sending her to the floor. The pocket watch tumbled out of one of many pockets on her skirt.

"My watch...the watch my father gave me! You no good whore! You bring shame to your profession," du Pont shook his fist.

Will held on to her as she continued to kick and scream. "You give it up now—everything you've taken or I'll—"

"You'll do what? You, sorry son-of-a-bitch—" She kicked at Will.

He'd never heard such a vile woman before. Will wondered what could fill a person's heart with so much anger. She was the one who had picked du Pont's pockets, but she was now angry with him for catching her in the act. Objects that fell from her pockets indicated that she had picked other passengers pockets of valuable items. Bidermann discovered his wallet and pistol missing. They were returned.

Had they have gotten away with the loot, it would've been a successful heist. Instead, the sheriff came for the wayward girls.

Chapter Seventeen

The *Queen of St. Louis* left Cairo the next morning. It arrived in New Orleans six days later on Easter Sunday. A ship to Matagorda would depart the following Tuesday. The packet ship, the *Columbia,* was not as luxurious as the *Queen of St. Louis,* but traveling through the Gulf of Mexico under steam it was on time. It averaged ten-knots-per-hour and would make Texas in two days. Under a sailing vessel, the trip might take a week.

Word reached New Orleans that President William Henry Harrison had died. People cried openly as word spread. He was the first U.S. President to die while in office.

Du Pont took the news of his father's friend exceptionally hard. He grew up hearing the war stories of "Tippecanoe"—the president's nickname. His father met secretly with General Harrison during the War of 1812 and as a child, du Pont had sat on Harrison's knee.

Du Pont looked sadly at Bidermann. "We must go home. Gather our family." Du Pont sobbed, "Pay our respects to Anna. Everything we have is because of 'Tip.' "

"I know. I'll make the arrangements." Bidermann touched du Pont's arm.

They would take the next steamer north to Pittsburgh, and then hire a carriage from there to Delaware. Du Pont was disappointed about not going to Texas, but Bidermann was relieved.

On land, Will could make better time to Austin alone—two to three days on a good horse.

Mr. Bidermann gave Will a year's salary of twelve hundred U.S. dollars in advance, three times the pay of a Ranger. Will signed on as du Pont's Texas agent. He was also given eight hundred U.S. dollars for incidental expenses, more than enough to buy a good horse in Texas. He signed an employment contract for a year's service and would receive a commission for all sales shipped to Texas.

"You're paying me well, Mr. Bidermann. What exactly is my job?" Will asked.

"You represent the du Pont Company. We expect you to represent us in a professional manner at all times. Your job is calling on those that need our products. Texas will need powder and munitions to defend its borders. With your help, we can be their supplier."

"Texas has no money. What there is, is worth only sixteen cents on a dollar."

"We know that. For now, Texas is in dire straits." He stood to leave. "When du Pont's father came to The Colonies they were financially strapped, but then they formed a Federation of States and conquered the strongest army in the world."

Will nodded in agreement.

"The back door of Texas leads to the Pacific Ocean. Texas may be temporarily short of cash, but not broke. Let us worry about getting paid."

"Where do I start? I've never done anything like this."

"Neither have we. For now, call on Lamar and give him our regrets. Be our eyes and ears in Texas. Write often about what you see and hear. We want to be prepared for whatever happens in Texas."

"Like war?" Will asked.

"Exactly."

They'd become friends and confidants during the fast three-week journey. They said their goodbyes on the wharf as passengers boarded. Will carried his saddle and harness to the *Columbia* and stowed his gear in the lock-up. Tonight and tomorrow he would sleep in a hotel—the

Mason Dupuy— a nice two-story structure, not as elaborate as the Planters, but sufficient for Will's needs.

Will agreed to meet George Kendall for dinner in the French Quarter at a place he couldn't pronounce. They agreed to meet in the hotel lobby at six.

They were the only diners in the usually busy dining room. It was Easter—the holiday along with word of the president's death left the streets of the French Quarter barren. Will wore his gray suit; its long coat covered his guns. The wool cloth was perfect for St. Louis weather, but it turned clingy in the sultry humidity of New Orleans.

Kendall was intrigued by Will and his stories of Texas, and over dinner he questioned Will about Austin and its people. He wanted details of the buffalo stampeding down Pecan Street. Kendall had read about the incident in the *Austin Gazette* but didn't believe it.

Will leaned forward and said, "Buffalo are shy. They wouldn't on their own ever stampede toward town or down the main street of Austin."

Kendall looked wide-eyed at Will, "Are you saying someone drove the buffalo through Austin on purpose?"

"I didn't say that," Will shook his head, "you just don't listen, Kendall!" Will pushed back from the table. "You're trying to get me to say things I don't know for sure."

"Who would know for sure?" Kendall asked.

Will finished chewing his steak and said, "Maybe the buffalo. I bet they know."

"You feed me bullshit information like this buffalo thing and don't have any idea who would do such a thing," Kendall gripped the table.

"I have an idea—it was someone who didn't want Austin as the capital," Will said.

"Sam Hou—"

Will interrupted, "There you go again, Kendall. I can't talk to you man-to-man. You're always trying to make up a damn story to print in your paper. I didn't say 'cause I don't know. You damn reporters make your own assumptions. Don't quote or involve me in accusing Sam Houston of anything."

Kendall changed the subject to the president's passing and how it might affect the nation, as the United States had no precedence for selecting a successor. After dinner, they sat outside in the Dupuys' courtyard, sipped brandy, and smoked cigars at a small round table.

Will told Kendall about the thirty-two men killed by Indians in Austin prior to his brother's death. And how a like a number had left home to tend their livestock, or run traps, never to return. "Ten percent of the male population gone the first year of the town's existence."

Kendall blew a puff of smoke and then asked, "So why go back there?"

"It's my home. Three generations of my family are there." Will blew a large puff of cigar smoke and watched it dissipate in a whiff of breeze.

Kendall turned serious and handed Will an envelope. "I would like you to personally deliver this letter to President Lamar. Would you do that?"

"What's this?" Will admired the fancy envelope.

"I am accepting his invitation to join the Santa Fe Expedition," Kendall pushed back in his chair.

"After what I just told you," Will shook his head, "you want to go to Texas?"

"Wanderlust I suppose...or maybe it's the writer in me." Kendall paused, "I may write a book about the adventure."

"Are you serious?" Will asked.

"It will be a great opportunity for me. This expedition is on a much grander scale than Lewis and Clark's Corps of Discovery Expedition." Kendall looked at Will. "Besides, I might be able to find your nephew and bring him home."

"That would be good...if you could," Will said.

"I can tell you're not excited about the Santa Fe Expedition," Kendall said.

"No, I am not. I hope you'll reconsider. It's too dangerous," Will said.

"It's an opportunity of a lifetime. The owners of the *Picayune* are as excited as I am."

"Is there anything I can say or do to change your mind?" Will placed his hand on the envelope.

Kendall shook his head.

"Then I'll be glad to deliver your letter."

"Thank you Will. I appreciate your concern for my well-being, but three hundred soldiers and a Howitzer should be able to protect me." Kendall smiled.

Will shrugged his shoulders, "Time will tell."

They parted friends. They argued, but each respected the other one's point of view. Kendall promised to find Will when he got to Austin the first week in May. Will wanted to tell Kendall what he knew about the ill-conceived military expedition to Santa Fe, but this reporter was the last person on Earth that he could or would tell. Hopefully, given the information and resignation letters of his commissioners, President Lamar would cancel the invasion. Will went to bed—his burden now heavier than before.

Horse and carriage noise woke Will from a deep sleep. Kitchen aromas below kindled his hunger. He washed and shaved and was ready for breakfast.

The dining room host asked, "Would you like to check your guns?"

"No thank you, hammers down on both of them, but thanks for asking."

The host didn't understand the answer any more than Will understood his question.

He found the chicory coffee strong but to his liking, Will consumed six eggs, a half-pound of bacon, and a funny looking biscuit the waiter called a croissant. An uneaten beignet still lay in the bread basket.

A young boy stuck his head in the open window and said, *"Picayune?"*

"What did you say?" Will asked.

"Do you want a *Picayune?*" The newspaper boy held the paper up for Will to see. The headline read: "Picayune Editor To Travel With The Santa Fe Expedition."

Will motioned for the boy to bring in a paper. The doorman tried to stop the boy from entering the hotel. "Leave me be, I got a customer—ordered a *Picayune.*" He pointed at Will seated by the open window that faced the street.

Will signaled to the doorman that he wanted the paper and to allow the boy in.

"*Picayune* is two cents." The boy eyed the freshly-baked beignet.

Will gave him five cents for the paper. "You hungry?" he asked.

"I sure am mister—"

"Sit down and I'll buy you breakfast."

As the boy sat down, the waiter rushed over stuttering, "He can't sit... in...in the dining room."

"Why not?" Will raised his eyebrows.

"He's a...a street urchin." The waiter turned up his nose.

"He is my guest and I would appreciate you treating him as such. Now bring us a finger bowl with warm water and several towels so he can clean up," Will said.

"What did you have...to eat?"

"Bacon and Eggs," Will said.

"I'll have what you had."

The waiter returned with finger bowl and towels and asked for the order.

"He wants what I had."

"Six eggs—"

Will interrupted the waiter. "Exactly what I had."

"You want coffee?" Will leaned toward the boy.

"Yes, please."

The boy said his name was James Thomas. Born in the French Quarter, his Irish mother married a Frenchman who was killed in a barroom brawl when James was an infant. He sold papers; his mother kept house for a family near Girard Park. James and his mother, Agnes, lived over the carriage house on the estate of her employer.

While James ate breakfast, Will read the story of George W. Kendall, now the editor of the *New Orleans Daily Picayune*. The story read: "Kendall has been selected by President Lamar to travel with three-hundred volunteer soldiers and fifty Texas merchants to Santa Fe. Kendall will write the story of the pioneers of the Santa Fe Expedition."

"Why do you wear two guns?" James asked.

"Two guns is better than one, don't you think?" Will smiled.

"I guess so," James shrugged his shoulders.

Will asked, "Would you know where I can buy some clothes? Nothing fancy, just everyday wear."

"Rawlings Mercantile on Canal. It's not far. I'll take you if you like," James said.

Will nodded. "I would appreciate that."

"Least I can do for the breakfast. What's your name mister?"

"My name is William Smith." Will extended his hand, James shook it, "Everyone calls me Will."

After breakfast, they walked down Bourbon to Canal Street and found Rawlings Mercantile in the middle of the block. The owner was just opening and held the door open for them.

"Can I help you?" Mr. Rawlings eyed Will and the boy.

"I am sailing to Texas in the morning. I'll need something lighter than wool pants." Will picked up a pair of ready-made cotton trousers.

"These will do, if you have my size?" Will handed the pants to the merchant.

"Try these on." The merchant motioned toward a fitting room but kept a watchful eye on the boy.

"They fit well for ready-made. You got another color?" Will asked from behind the curtain.

"I have the buff that you have on and indigo."

Will selected a pair of each color and two loose fitting shirts. He bought boots, a big brim straw hat, and summer weight cotton undergarments.

Will noticed James eyeing a pair of linen britches. What he wore was two sizes too small and threadbare. "Can you fix my friend James up with a fresh suit of clothes?" Will asked.

"Let me put something together for him." The merchant laid out a young boy's playsuit.

James puffed up, "That's a sissy suit. You got my size in what Will bought?"

Mr. Rawlings nodded. "I have everyday wear for boys."

"Well then. That's what I need—clothes I can wear every day." James rolled his eyes.

Will enjoyed watching the banter between the gray-haired merchant and a boy who wasn't afraid to stand up for what he wanted. Will paid Mr. Rawlings and they left. James wore the first new clothes he could remember. He liked the smell of his new shirt and sniffed at the sleeve often as they walked down Bourbon Street.

James thanked Will for the clothes, "I never had new store-bought clothes before."

"You're welcome." Will looked at James, "where do you usually get your clothes?"

"Different places. Sometimes the church has hand-me-downs. If I get desperate, I make a clothesline run." James lifted the old clothes wrapped in brown paper, "That's where these came from."

Will asked, "Does clothesline run mean what I think it does?"

"Stealing. That's what it is, but clothesline run sounds better," James said.

Will noticed a ring of dirt around the collar of James' new shirt. "When did you last bathe?"

James squinted, "You mean like with soap and water?"

"Of course I meant soap and water that's warm."

"I never had soap and warm water at the same time. Just cold water and soap that's the best I ever had," James said.

"Where does your mother bathe?" Will asked.

James didn't answer, he just looked down at the cobblestone walk to the end of the short cross-street. The sun in his eyes made him squint.

"You want to see, where I really live? I'll show you. You can't tell anyone. You promise!"

"I promise. What about your mother?"

"I don't have a mother! I tell people I do. If I don't, they'll put me in an orphan's home. I've been there, and I don't like it." James led Will to the next block.

"Here's where I live." James pointed toward a large Cathedral.

"You live in a church?"

James held the heavy cypress door open with his backside and pushed against it. "Come in, it's always open." James pointed at the baptismal, "That's where I wash up when I get really dirty." They climbed to the choir loft. "This is where I sleep." James pointed at a padded pew in the loft.

"No one knows you live here?" Will whispered.

James whispered, "Just the cat. We share the loft." He pointed toward the back stairs and said, "Let's go. Confessions be starting soon." James stopped at a box and reached his small hand in. "Nothing today. Sometimes they leave me money."

"James the box says donations for the poor."

"That's me; I'm poor."

Will didn't know what to say, so he didn't. He thought about Fayette alone in a foreign land held captive by savages. *Here in the center of a large city lives a homeless child with no parents. How can this be?*

The two went and sat on a park bench. Will asked, "What really happened to your parents?"

"I don't rightly know. The first thing I ever remember was waking up in an orphanage with lots of other children. I thought all children came from a place like that." He turned toward Will. "Couples come in, buy you from the nuns, and you go home with your new owners." James shook his head, "That's how I thought it worked."

"There is no Agnes Thomas or a room over the Carriage House. You just made that up?"

"It sounds real, don't you think?" Thomas grinned.

"Why would you make up such a story?"

"I had to if I wanted to stay out of the orphanage. Good people like you come along and they'll give me some coins to buy a meal. If I told them I was a homeless orphan, they would turn me in to the authorities, thinking they was doing me a favor." James started to cry, "Please... don't report me. I take care of myself. I've been living in the choir loft for two Christmases now."

"You don't have any family? Grandparents, an uncle?"

"Nope," James shook his head.

Will just sat quietly as James looked up at the belfry and said, "Cover your ears. Father Giraud is fixing to ring the church bells." James covered his ears.

The bells rang with such intensity that birds fluttered in all directions. Squirrels froze in place, fearing to move. Local carriage horses shook and nickered, knowing the bells would soon stop. Horses not accustomed to the bells panicked, and one threw its rider.

Will looked at James and asked, "How did you know the bells were about to toll?"

"Birds fly out of the belfry when Father Giraud moves the ropes attached to the bell. They always do."

"They're loud. How do you stand it?"

"You get used to it. Besides, I can sneak out while he's busy ringing them."

James seemed to have everything figured out. He had a roof over his head and a source of food. He made a few pennies selling the *Picayune*. He fended for himself and had for some time. Will thought, *I must do something. I promised I wouldn't turn him in. What would my brother Mitchell Smith, a man of the cloth, do in a situation like this?*

James looked at Will and asked, "What you thinking about?"

"I was thinking about what I should do with you."

"That's what I thought!" James jumped up and ran away from Will and around the corner. Will chased after him. James was fast and knew his way around the Quarter. Will searched frantically for James, but the boy was nowhere to be found.

Exhausted after hours of searching, Will went back to his room and ordered warm bathwater brought to his room. After bathing, Will washed his clothes in the bathwater, placed them out on the balcony railing to dry. It was his last chance to bathe and wash clothes before reaching Texas. Then he went to bed.

Will couldn't sleep. He tossed and turned, worrying about James Thomas. He thought, *I have enough to worry about. James will survive as I know Fayette will. They are so much alike.* He remembered a sermon his Brother Mitchell Smith gave in St. Augustine about God caring for the little children of the world. It gave him comfort. He fell into a deep sleep.

Chapter Eighteen

The sounds of horse hooves on cobblestone woke Will. Early morning venders chattered loudly as they unloaded their provisions. Will folded his clothes and packed them and his gear in a canvas haversack.

He ate breakfast at the same table as yesterday, hoping to see James again. Will wanted to give him some money and say goodbye. Hopefully the guilt he felt would go away. Will didn't understand his feelings. He thought, *Guilt for what? I didn't cause James Thomas to be an orphan. His frightful situation was not my doing. Why should I be so concerned with his plight?*

James didn't show. Will left the hotel with saddlebags on one shoulder and a haversack over the other. With the broad-brim straw hat on his head and shiny new boots on his feet, Will was ready to head for Texas—and his first sea voyage. Still, hoping to see James one last time, Will stopped and looked down every cross street for a boy hawking newspapers.

He took one last glance along the wharf looking for a boy that wasn't there and then boarded the steam ship *Columbia*. He purchased steerage space for fifteen dollars. A cabin was twice as much. The trip from New Orleans to Matagorda was two nights. Anxious to get home, he couldn't sleep, even in a feather bed.

As the *Columbia* churned her way toward the Gulf, Will watched from the open steerage deck. The Mississippi River meandered through the Lower Delta for over a hundred miles. It would be near midnight when the *Columbia* steered into the azure-blue water of the Gulf. For now, Will studied the eerie swamps and saw mammoth cypress trees along the riverbank. Large long-legged birds fished in the lagoons, their sounds barely heard over the engine. Twin smoke stacks thirty feet high protected the boat and passengers from hot embers. The *Columbia* was two-hundred feet long and twenty-two feet wide. It carried passengers, cargo, and mail to Texas weekly from New Orleans.

A man's voice called out: "Mr. Will Smith! Is there a Will Smith in steerage?"

"That's me; I am William Smith."

"Come with me, Mr. Smith. Captain Morgan needs to talk to you."

"Is everything alright?" Will asked.

"I've only been asked to bring you to the captain's quarters, Mr. Smith."

Will knew it must be important to be summoned by the captain. It must be du Pont business. *Only Mr. Bidermann, du Pont, and Kendall know I am on the Columbia.* The stoic crewman knocked on the captain's door.

"Who is it?" a deep voice asked.

"Dinkins here, Captain, with Mr. Smith."

The captain, a short balding man with a wide girth, opened the door.

The crewman said, "This is William Smith, Captain. I found him aft in steerage."

"Thank you, Dinkins. That will be all." Captain Morgan shut the door, turned towards Will, and extended a hand. "Glad to make your acquaintance, Mr. Smith. I am sorry for your recent loss."

"Thank you, Captain." Will shook his hand.

"The boy you have been searching for has been found."

Will was elated. Then he got emotional. "He's alive?"

"Yes...very much so." The captain smiled.

"Thank you, Captain that's wonderful news." Will asked, "Who found him? Where is he?"

"My quartermaster, Mr. Dinkins, who brought you to me found him in the kitchen stealing food." The captain raised his eyebrows.

"He is on this boat!" Will looked surprised. "He stole food?"

"You assume responsibility then for the boy?"

"Yes! Now please, I want to see him." Will placed his hand on his chest.

"There is the matter of his fare and pilferage in the galley, Mr. Smith."

Will handed the Captain a U.S. twenty-dollar bill, "That should cover everything?"

"More than enough, Mr. Smith." The captain opened the adjoining door.

Will expected to see Fayette. Instead, James Thomas sat at the captain's table. James rushed to Will and wrapped his skinny arms around Will's waist. "You found me," James smiled.

"Yes, I did James Thomas." Will looked at the smiling captain.

"Thank you, Captain. I'll see that James causes you no further trouble."

Neither said a word as Will and James walked to the forward deck away from passengers. Water splashed onto the deck as the river turned west directly into a setting sun. Will pointed toward a storage box where they could sit and talk.

"What are you doing on this boat?"

"Same as you. I'm going to Texas."

Will said "What about—"

"I got nothing to 'what about,'" James interrupted.

If everything James told him was true, he left nothing in New Orleans. He had a worn out haversack with all his worldly possessions over his shoulder. Will saw something move in the haversack. It was a small black kitten.

"It was the only one of the litter that lived," James said, "I couldn't leave it."

"James, we're together now. When you ran off yesterday it was because I expressed concern for you. You heard Captain Morgan— I am responsible for your safety and actions. He assumes that I'm your father. If I assume that responsibility, you must obey me. Is that understood?"

James answered with a nod.

Will put a hand on the boy's arm. "You'll always tell me the truth. No more taking what isn't yours."

James looked at Will, "I only stole because I was hungry."

"Honest people don't steal. If you're hungry tell someone you'll work for something to eat. Then do a good job for them." Will looked at James, "You understand?"

James nodded, and then blurted out, "When will we be in Texas?"

"On Friday morning we'll be getting off in Matagorda. I'll find us some horses. We'll be on the trail by noon."

"What's 'noon?' " James asked.

Will explained the meaning of the word for midday as they walked to the steerage deck. Will realized James knew nothing about time. Most likely he couldn't read or write.

"How did you know the name of the ship I was on?" Will tilted his head.

"I didn't. I followed you, knowing you was heading to Texas." James Thomas looked aft, "What's the name of this ship?"

"It's the *Columbia*. Just what did you tell the captain about us?"

"That you were my Pa. We be going to Texas to start a new life after losing Ma." James grinned. "Good story, ain't it!"

"No, because it's a lie! From now on everything you say must be the truth. You understand?"

"Yes, sir." James Thomas looked out to sea.

"How did you get on alone without a boarding pass?" Will raised his eyebrows.

James eagerly told how he got behind a portly woman with six children. "I got behind her close enough, she couldn't see me. Her size and petticoats hid me. She told the agent we were all there together. I followed right behind her onto the boat, and then headed for the kitchen."

"You can't be doing things like that," Will sighed.

James grinned again. "Well I did and here I am."

Will realized he had his work cut out for him. *A boy who thinks he knows everything, but knows nothing,* Will thought, *God help me.*

The *Columbia* made it into Matagorda Bay Friday morning the sixteenth day of April 1841. The bulky steamer worked its way to the wharf of Texas' second busiest port. Will and James patiently watched as the ship's crew tied up alongside the dock.

"Have you ever ridden a horse?" Will asked.

"Never been on a horse." James stuttered, revealing his fear.

"You're in Texas now—best you learn to like horses." Will put his hand on James' shoulder.

"I don't know—"

Will interrupted James, "Don't worry. I'll teach you to ride as soon as I buy a couple of good horses."

Will hung the saddlebags over his left shoulder, and then his saddle. Haversack, ropes, and a harness hung on the other. James slung his sack over his shoulder, mimicking Will. His free hand held the kitten. They passed the smiling captain who said, "I pray God be with you and the boy. Texas is a great place to start a new life."

"Thank you, Captain." Will sauntered down the ship's gangway, relieved to be on land again. Two weeks on the water was enough for him.

The wharf was a beehive of activity. Workers unloaded bales of cotton from farm wagons. Fancy European furniture was being lifted off the boat, along with bolts of fabric, barrels of whiskey, molasses, salt, and sugar. They were stacked on the wharf, awaiting ground transportation.

Will heard a nervous horse nicker and stomp its feet. It was anxious to get off the boat but refused to step on the loading ramp that led down to the wharf. Each wave that hit the bay side of the *Columbia* moved the ramp just a few inches, but enough to spook the chestnut stallion. Two black boys in their teens, slightly older than James, struggled with the horse, trying to force it onto the ramp. Fear showed in their eyes as they tried to make this horse do something it didn't want to do.

"Wait a minute. Someone is going to get hurt." Will laid his gear down and walked up the gentle incline of the loading ramp.

Will extended his hand to the boy holding the reins, "Let me have 'em." He looked at the other boy and said, "Stand aside." He turned the horse away from the creaking ramp. "Where's the stall?" The boys warily pointed to an open stall. Will led the horse into the small compartment and asked for a bucket of corn. He stroked the horse's neck and talked low, like they had been friends forever. The boys handed Will a bucket of corn. "Everyone, stay calm and quiet. Don't make any sudden moves." Will fed the horse a handful of corn and then made a blindfold out of his red bandanna. He gently tied the blindfold over the horse's eyes, and then continued the hand feeding.

Holding the reins in one hand and the feed bucket in the other, Will walked the stallion slowly out to the ramp. Coaxing it with gentle talk and cracked corn, the horse ambled onto the ramp and Will walked it down to the wharf.

"Well done," a well-dressed but rather homely looking man said. Will had seen him on the *Columbia*. He presumed he was a first class passenger. The man was traveling with an attractive young lady.

"Your horse?" Will patted its neck, "Good looking animal."

"Thank you. I bought him and two fillies in New Orleans as breeding stock for my ranch in Jackson County." He extended his hand, "Name's James Kerr. You a Texas Ranger?"

"My name's William Smith, they call me Will. No longer a Ranger. I stopped fighting Indians after the Battle of Plum Creek."

"Some battle, I was told." James Kerr shook his head.

"Yes, it was." Will picked up his gear.

"To have a pair of Colt Paterson's, you must've been mighty good at Ranging."

"I was issued one and inherited the other from my brother. Comanche's killed him last January."

"Judge James Smith...was your brother?"

"Yes, he was."

"I knew him well. Sorry for your loss." Mr. Kerr looked at the boy and his kitten, "I see you found your nephew."

"No, sir. Fayette is yet to be found. This is James Thomas who took up with me in New Orleans. He's got no family—just me as a friend. We're headed to Austin as soon as I can buy a couple of horses and a saddle for him."

James Kerr came to Texas from Missouri years before Texas Independence. He was one of Stephen F. Austin's "Ole' Three Hundred" and had received a league of land west of Houston in Jackson County on a creek that would be named for him. Representing Jackson County in the Third Congress of the Republic, Congressman Kerr introduced the bill to relocate the Capitol. He suggested Thomas W. Smith to President Lamar for the appointment of Supreme Court Justice of the new county that would be created for the Capital City.

"Let's get these horses off the wharf and I'll tell you a story about your father."

"I never heard him speak of you," Will shook his head.

"That's because all the old Indian fighters like Thomas called me Major Kerr."

"That's a name I recall hearing often: Major Kerr."

Will led the stallion, and Major Kerr led the two fillies along the wharf. James Thomas followed at a distance, taking in this new land, not sure what to think of it.

Major Kerr said, "When President Lamar asked your father to be the Supreme Court Justice of Travis County, Thomas turned it down and suggested James be appointed instead. Lamar agreed, providing Thomas would accept the appointment of County Treasurer."

Will said, "I always wondered how they both got appointed."

"When I heard of James' murder and Fayette's abduction, my daughter and I headed to Austin. We visited your ma and pa, paid our respects to them and James' widow. I was afraid they might have hard feelings toward me," Kerr's voice cracked. "I know how it is losing a loved one. I lost my first wife and two oldest children years ago to cholera."

"Why would you think my family would have hard feelings toward you?"

"I persuaded President Lamar to appoint your father."

They walked in silence. The only sounds were horse hooves and an occasional nicker.

Major Kerr broke the silence, "Had I not recommended your father, James might still be alive."

"You can't blame yourself for his death. It was Comanches that killed him. It was fate that put him in the wrong place at the wrong time."

"Fate, you say?" Major Kerr stopped in his tracks and faced Will to make sure he understood what he said.

Major Kerr started walking again. "Power and politics sometimes makes for strange bedfellows. I quit politics to become a doctor because I didn't like the politicians I had to sleep with."

Will stopped and turned to face Major Kerr. The seed of doubt the major planted had germinated, "I want to hear more about your thoughts on James' murder."

Will saw a large black man drop his apron and come running towards them from the stables. The man had a farriers' knife in his hand. Will instinctively reacted by putting a hand on his revolver.

Major Kerr said, "Don't worry, Will. Shoe's a good friend. That knife's just a tool of his trade."

Breathing hard, Shoe said, "Welcome home Major Kerr, or should I say, Doctor Kerr."

James Kerr had just completed two years of medical studies at the New Orleans School of Medicine, having earned a degree in medicine.

"How are you, Shoe?"

"Be good now that you're home." Shoe hugged Major Kerr and asked, "Where is Ms. Minnie?"

"Your boys be bringing Minnie shortly, with her trousseau."

"Can't believe our Minnie going to be married," Shoe shook his head.

"Will Smith, meet the best blacksmith in all of Texas. Everyone calls him Shoe because he shoes horses. He won't give us his last name." Major Kerr laughed.

"I didn't have no pedigree like you Major. I don't know who my momma was, much less who my daddy be. I go by Shoe. That's the name I give myself."

"Then you're an orphan just like me," James Thomas looked up at Shoe.

Shoe bent down on one knee and gently placed a hand on James' shoulder. "If you don't have no momma or papa, we be alike in that kind of way." Shoe turned away so James couldn't see the tear he was about to shed. "I'll let Beth know you're here. She'll fix you a good meal."

One rainy night, Shoe showed up at Major Kerr's ranch, hungry and cold. He said he was looking for work. Major Kerr took him in and discovered Shoe possessed the skills of a farrier. Major Kerr assumed Shoe was a runaway slave, but never asked, not wanting to know his past. Shoe took a liking to Beth, the eldest of two black sisters born on the ranch. Shoe and Beth married seventeen years ago and had twin sons. Expecting only one child, Shoe decided if the baby was a boy to name him Andrew Jackson. When Beth gave birth to twins, Shoe named the first born Andrew and the other Jackson. Major Kerr gave Beth and Shoe legal papers proving their family was free, even though he never owned Shoe as a slave.

The twins arrived with the load of provisions and medical supplies Major Kerr purchased in New Orleans. Doctor Kerr would be setting up practice in his home.

Minnie was an attractive nineteen-year-old girl exquisitely dressed. Fortunately, she didn't have the ears or the nose of her father.

"This is my daughter Minnie," her father said and helped her down from the carriage, "Say hello to Will Smith. His parents are Thomas and Rebeckah Smith. You met them on our last trip to Austin."

"Yes, I remember. I'm sorry for your loss," Minnie said politely.

"Thank you, Minnie."

Her tone changed abruptly as she said, "Only family and friends call me Minnie. My proper name is Mary Margaret Kerr: Pronounced Caar as it's a French name."

"Excuse me for being so presumptuous," Will removed his hat and bowed gracefully, "Ms. Mary Margaret...Caar. My name is William Witherspoon Smith—the name my father gave me back in Tennessee where I was born. My friends just call me Will! You may call me anything you like...but Will."

Will turned away from her and continued, "Now that we've been properly introduced and know each other's proper names and pedigree, excuse me. I need to buy a horse."

Mary Margaret had never been put in her place like that. Her father enjoyed watching Will bring her down a notch or two. She was impressed with Will's wit and good looks but didn't let it show.

"Come Will, I'll show you where Shoe keeps his horses that are for sale," Major Kerr pointed to the stable door.

Will looked over the horses and didn't see a horse to his liking. He wanted Major Kerr's horse and offered him five-hundred U.S. dollars.

"Will, that's a very good offer. Let me think about it."
Will looked at the sun. "It's getting late, I need to be going. Daylight's a burning, Major Caar."

"You call me Kerr. That Caar bullshit is something Minnie brought home from that damn boarding school."

"I am sorry, I shouldn't—"

"Don't you fret about hurting Minnie's feelings. She tries to impress people with her Eastern ways, but that girl is tough. She can outride any man around these parts. Minnie can shoot the balls off a running squirrel at twenty paces."

"Thanks for the warning." They shared a laugh.

Beth's dinner bell rang for the midday meal. Major said, "Let's eat! This old man is ready for some of Beth's cooking."

Beth made bits and pieces of yesterday's meat with cream gravy over toast—something her mother taught her in Major Kerr's kitchen. It was one of those meal stretchers for when unexpected company came.

Shoe told Beth that James Thomas was an orphan and her maternal instincts kicked in. She wanted to know more about the boy.

"You want some more gravy and biscuits, Mr. Thomas?"

James Thomas didn't answer her question. Beth looked at Will, "Why doesn't he answer me?"

"Most likely because he's never been called Mr. Thomas before." Will looked at James Thomas disapprovingly; the boy was licking his plate. "Beth asked you a question."

"She was asking me if I wanted more biscuits and gravy. I sure do," James Thomas handed his plate to Beth.

As Beth made James Thomas a third plate of biscuits and cream gravy, Mary Margaret asked, "When did you last eat a good meal, James Thomas?"

"My last good meal?" He thought for a moment. "The last good meal I stole from the ship's galley in New Orleans. I almost had my fill when they caught me."

Will spoke, "James Thomas, I believe we shared my bread and smoked ham."

Will marveled at how James Thomas could garner sympathy from anyone. He knew just when to say or do the right thing. Will knew the boy could make it on his own by using his unique skills for finding people who wanted to help.

Mary Margaret noticed how dirty his clothes were. "Do you have any clothes other than what you have on?"

"No ma'am, these all I got."

Beth said, "James Thomas, the twins have outgrown some of their clothes. I've been looking to give them to someone that could wear them. You're the first boy I seen that could wear them."

Shoe went into a room and came out with a large denim bag full of clothes the twins had outgrown.

"I've never seen so many clothes, and they fit me!" James held a pair of dungarees against his legs. He found a shirt made of linsey-woolsey and chose to change into them. Beth made sure he cleaned up first.

While they waited for James to bathe and change, Major Kerr said to Will, "Why don't you ride the stallion to my place? It'll give you time to decide if he's worth the money. It's on your way. We'll be there by dark. Have a good dinner. You and James Thomas will have a feather bed to sleep in tonight."

James came back into the room in his new clothes and said, "I've never slept in a feather bed before," he looked at Will, "please?"

"Alright then, we'll ride to Major Kerr's," Will said.

It was for the best. James wasn't ready to get on a horse. They had no provisions ready for the three-day journey to Austin. It was late in the day. It would be dangerous traveling in daylight much less in the dark of night.

Major Kerr looked toward the stallion, "That horse is jest green-broke. He needs some good training. I can tell you know about horses and can handle him. I am too damned old to be on a horse with his spirit."

"Major Kerr, I'd be honored to ride your horse."

Chapter Nineteen

*J*ames enjoyed his first carriage ride, sitting beside Mary Margaret and across from Major Kerr. Andrew and Jackson followed with a wagon load of cargo and the fillies tied to the tailgate. The stallion performed well on the rocky road, despite being born and raised on a Louisiana Plantation, kept in manicured paddocks, and never exposed to cactus or mesquite thorns. It was startled at the sight of an armadillo, and Will tried to assure the stallion that the armor-laden critter would do him no harm.

Mary Margaret pointed out the bluebonnets blooming, making the rolling prairie an ocean of blue. She was the only surviving sibling and therefore unaccustomed to children, but she seemed to enjoy James' companionship.

James told the Kerrs how Will found him, fed him, and bought him clothes. He failed to tell them about stowing away on the *Columbia,* leaving Mary Margaret to believe Will knowingly and willingly brought James to Texas.

After dinner, Mary Margaret played her new piano and sang for them in the parlor. Will learned from Major Kerr that Mary Margaret was to marry Isaac Newton Mitchell. Once she moved to Mitchell's plantation in Lavaca County, Major Kerr would be alone.

While Mary Margaret got James Thomas ready for bed, Major Kerr invited Will to join him on the front porch. The "dog trot" style house was the typical home of a Texas Rancher: bedrooms on one side, living and dining area on the other, joined together by roof and floor, creating an open breezeway that Kerr's dogs claimed for their own. Major Kerr had it built facing west toward Kerr Creek. From here, he had watched many a day come to an end. Now alone, they sat in high-back rockers, puffing cigars and sipping French brandy as sounds of cicadas and frogs echoed in the night.

Will rocked back and blew a large smoke ring. He watched it disappear in the evening breeze, thinking about their conversation earlier in the day.

"Why did you say my brother's death wasn't the result of fate?"

"Too many coincidences in his death. I'm not the only one that thinks so." Major Kerr took a sip of brandy.

"Who else shares your view?" Will rolled his head to look at Major Kerr.

Will rocked forward, trying to see the eyes of his host. "I saw the arrow that penetrated my brother's arm. It had markings of the Comanche on it: the red band around its shaft. My brother Fenwick was an eyewitness to his scalping and the abduction of Fayette."

"No doubt about it, Will. The Comanche carried out the deadly deed, but I don't believe Buffalo Hump would've taken such a risk for a couple of horses and the boy," Major Kerr looked intently at Will. "There had to be more to it!"

Will asked, "Then you believe the attack was premeditated murder, carried out by Buffalo Hump on someone else's orders. Like a bounty for his scalp?"

Major Kerr picked up the decanter and poured them each another glass of brandy.

"Why, Major Kerr, would anyone do that? My brother James was a good man!"

"Yes, your brother was a good man. But he made mistakes and enemies along the way. Whoever planned your brother's murder was trying to destroy Austin. News of the Supreme Court Justice of Texas' largest county being murdered in broad daylight," Major Kerr shook his head. "That got everyone's attention, even in Washington."

"Really?" Will said.

"If Austin wasn't safe for its leaders to live there, then It wasn't safe for anyone." Major Kerr finished his brandy. "My last official act as a legislator was the introduction of the bill that would move the center of government away from Houston. I succeeded but dug my own grave as a politician in the process."

Will finished his brandy. "I don't understand how moving the capital city could make anyone mad enough to kill my brother."

Major Kerr explained that the Allen Brothers and others had heavily invested money in Houston, buying land to develop it. They named the Capitol of Texas for its first elected President and popular hero of Texas Independence. Sam Houston had little if any financial interest in the town that bore his name. The tribute of having the Capitol City bear his name meant more to Sam than all the riches in the world. His political enemies disliked Houston and the town that bore his name. Lamar selected the new site to build his empire. He made James Smith acting Chief Justice nearly a year before Travis County was established by Congress.

"Will, another group of investors were perpetrating the same land scheme in Austin as the Allen Brothers did in Houston." Major Kerr said.

"I didn't know that."

"I did, and I confronted Lamar and Burnet. They denied any knowledge of a plan for making Montopolis the new Capital of Texas. I knew they were lying. The reason I fought for moving the capital was the generation of much needed revenue for the treasury. I thought the government should be the sole beneficiary of land sales rather than a consortium of private land speculators hand-picked by President Lamar." Major Kerr stood.

"I bet that made you an enemy of both Houston and Lamar, didn't it?"

"I was never Sam Houston's friend, even though I served under him at the Battle of San Jacinto. I didn't like his style then and I don't like it now. He is a flamboyant and obnoxious bastard. I supported Lamar in moving the Capitol from Houston—"

Will interrupted, "What happened with the Montopolis plan?"

Major Kerr stretched. "When I threatened to expose the plan, they backed away from developing Montopolis, selecting the current site—selling lots for the purpose of financing the new center of government, as my legislation intended."

Will looked up at Major Kerr and asked, "You sure stirred up a hornet's nest, didn't you?"

Major Kerr nodded. "Politically, I was ruined. But it was the best damn thing that ever happened to me. I had no stomach for politics. I busied myself studying medicine and tending the ranch."

"Looks like you've done pretty well for yourself ranching."

Major Kerr sat back down. "Will, I have all the material things a man could want." His lower lip quivered, "When Minnie moves out, it'll be lonely here. That's my only regret, being alone."

Will sat quietly and looked out into the darkness. He thought about what Major Kerr had said about being alone. That was a situation he'd never given much thought to—never had to. Neither spoke. Each sat in their own thoughts, rocking on the porch. Stimulated by brandy and Major Kerr's revelations, Will's mind raced.

"Will, you're awfully quiet."

"Sorry, I was thinking about what you said."

"You're not going to recognize Austin." Major Kerr shook his head and said, "The day Minnie and I arrived to pay our condolences, large groups of Austin's first settlers were moving out." His voice cracked, remembering, "It was like San Antonio after the Alamo fell. They called it the Run-Away Scrape. Families with what few possessions they could carry scurried east, away from the turmoil. Now Sam Houston says the Mexican Army is headed north again."

"Major, the Mexican Army is headed north, but not to attack Austin. They're planning to ambush the Santa Fe Expedition when it arrives."

Will revealed to Major Kerr his mission and message to President Lamar from Commissioners Dryden, Workman, and Rowland.

Will said, "The expedition must be stopped." He stood and looked at Major Kerr, "Can you help me?"

Major Kerr looked up at Will. "You know President Lamar is in New Orleans in a hospital?"

"No, I didn't. What's wrong with him?"

"Don't know, just that he's suffering from some type of digestive disorder. Vice President Burnet is acting President until he returns. The expedition would've already left had Lamar not taken ill. I reckon they're just waiting for him to return."

"Then there's still time to stop the expedition," Will exclaimed.

"If you hurry. First you have to convince Burnet to cancel the Expedition, which he won't want to do. There's been so much press back East." Major Kerr shook his head, "Canceling it now would be a terrible embarrassment for the current administration."

"If they go into New Mexico, thinking they're going to be welcomed with open arms, they're in for one hell of a surprise. I'm lucky I got away when I did."

"Yes, you are, Will."

"Major Kerr, thanks for what you've done for me and the boy. I must get some rest before sunup. It's a hard ride to Austin. Could take three days with James."

"Will, why don't you leave James with us? I'll teach him to ride. Minnie can school him. He'll be taken good care of, I'll promise you that."

"I know you would. I need to discuss it with James Thomas. I'll let you know, come morning."

Will found James asleep with the kitten cradled in his arms. "Goodnight, James Thomas."

Will blew out the candle and slid under sheets that smelled like spring flowers. He enjoyed the feel of a feather bed.

James was awake. "I like it here," he said.

"Would you like to stay here with the Major and Mary Margaret?" Will asked.

James sat up in bed. "Minnie said I could...please?"

"Let's discuss it in the morning. Right now, I need sleep."

Will knew it was best to leave James with the Kerrs. Austin wasn't safe for adults, much less children. Besides, he couldn't take him to Santa Fe.

Activity in the kitchen, just steps from the backdoor, woke Will. Ranch hands and house servants ate in the large kitchen. The Major sat at the end of the long table listening to their stories. From the breakfast table, he ran the ranch. When guests were at the ranch, Major Kerr ate with them in the dining room. Most of his vaqueros were descendants of early Spanish settlers who arrived in Texas one-hundred-years before the first Anglo colony was established. His black servants were slaves brought from Missouri.

Will washed his whiskered face in a large ceramic wash basin. Water from a matching vase sat on the wash stand. Neatly laid out was an array of matching men's grooming items.

Will saw Mary Margaret's reflection in the mirror. She stood behind the hall door that was slightly open. He only saw her face. She stood looking at Will's backside—naked except for a towel wrapped around his narrow waist.

His shave finished, Will brushed his long thick head of hair. She watched intently. Will wasn't embarrassed, rather aroused by her gaze. He was afraid to turn around.

"Can I help you, Mary Margaret?"

"If you would uh…wake James Thomas, I'll see that he gets dressed for breakfast. Father is waiting for you in the dining room."

"Thank you," Will smiled into the looking glass.

Major Kerr sat alone at the end of an ornate dining table. A male servant poured coffee. "Welcome home, Major Kerr. We missed you and Miss Minnie."

"Thank you, Sam. I'm glad to be back in Texas. How's your family?"

"They be good. Thank you for asking, Major."

Will looked into the dining room, trying not to interrupt. Major Kerr motioned him in.

"Sam, this is Will Smith from Austin. He's on his way back to the capital." Sam pulled out a chair for him to sit.

"Thank you," Will said.

Sam tilted the serving pot, "Coffee, Mr. Smith?"

"Yes, please. Coffee smells good."

"Fresh chicory from New Orleans." Major Kerr looked over his reading glasses.

"I thought about your offer, Major. James Thomas and I talked last night, and he would like—"

Suddenly, they were interrupted when Mary Margaret came bustling into the dining room with James Thomas following. "Good morning Father, Mr. Smith. A beautiful morning, isn't it," she said.

Major Kerr and Will stood as Sam pulled chairs out for Minnie and the boy at the far end of the table. "Welcome home, Miss Minnie." Sam pushed in her chair.

"Thank you, Sam. It's good to be home again. This is our guest, James Thomas from New Orleans."

"Glad to meet you, Mr. Thomas. You want your usual breakfast, Miss Minnie?"

"Sam, I'm impressed you remember. I've been gone so long. Remember, lots of pepper."

Sam looked at James Thomas, "What will you have for breakfast?"

"I'm having what Minnie ordered."

Everyone laughed as only Sam and Minnie knew her favorite meal. Will and the Major gave Sam their order as he poured them more coffee.

Mary Margaret wore dungarees and a cotton blouse that fit her well. Will had only seen her in a long dress. The petticoats and satin material of a Southern belle had obscured her voluptuous body. The nineteen-year-old maiden studied under the Catholic Sisters of St.

Genevieve in Missouri. Well-read and knowledgeable of world affairs, her demeanor was that of a woman twice her age. Her fiancé, Isaac Newton Mitchell, was thirteen years her senior. The marriage had been arranged by her father while she was at St. Genevieve. She met Mr. Mitchell once at his home on Mitchell's Point during a visit with her father. It was a marriage of convenience. The wealthy plantation owner wanted children—Mary Margaret would make him a proper bride and mother to their children.

Sam brought breakfast in on a large silver platter. They ate, enjoying pleasant conversation. When everyone had finished breakfast, the dishes were cleared, and Sam left.

Mary Margaret took a deep breath and said, "So, Mr. Smith you're planning to put James Thomas on a horse and drag him off to that savage infested town of Austin?"

Major Kerr said, "Minnie, Will and I've—"

Will interrupted, "Please, Major, I want to hear what she has to say."

"You're aware James is afraid of horses and hasn't been on one…ever!"

"Yes, but—"

"He's never seen an Indian and fears the savage beasts that abducted your nephew will capture him."

"Mary Margaret, what do you recommend I do with this young stowaway that followed me to Texas?"

"Followed you? You didn't willingly bring him with you?" She gave James Thomas a stern look.

"No, I did not. When I offered to find him a home, he ran away. After searching the French Quarter for hours, I gave up hope of ever seeing him again. The next morning James Thomas followed me and boarded the *Columbia* hidden behind petticoats of a woman he pretended was his mother."

"Then what happened?" Mary Margaret looked at James Thomas.

Will said, "When we were out of port, crew members caught him stealing food from the galley."

"How did that involve you?" Margaret leaned forward.

"James Thomas lied to the captain and told him I was his Father."

James Thomas squirmed in his chair and said, "But...."

Major Kerr looked sternly at the towheaded boy, sliding lower in his chair. "I remember hearing talk of a young stowaway on board."

"I remember hearing that, too. Was it you they were talking about?" Mary Margaret pointed at James Thomas.

"I had no choice but to take him in." Will looked at his host.

"You did the honorable thing, Mr. Smith." Mary Margaret placed her palms down on the table. She looked long and hard at her father and she read his thoughts, as only she could do. "We think it best that you leave him with us. I'll educate him. Father will teach him to ride. Together we will raise James Thomas in the Catholic faith."

"I'm concerned about something. Major Kerr tells me you're soon to be wed. After you marry and start a family of your own, would your new husband want another man's child?" Will looked toward Major Kerr for assurance.

Major Kerr said, "I appreciate your concern. He has a home with me regardless." Major Kerr looked at the boy, beaming with happiness.

"Then it's settled, Mary Margaret Caar." Will tried the French pronunciation of Kerr but failed miserably.

She smiled approvingly. "Please, just call me Minnie."

"Very well, Minnie, but there is more about James Thomas you should know."

A rider from a neighboring ranch near Goliad, some fifty miles away, interrupted their conversation. There had been a shooting and a doctor was needed. Major Kerr had often helped his neighbors in medical situations. This would be his first official call as a doctor.

"I'll help you pack your medical supplies." Minnie pushed back in her chair.

"No need, I loaded my medical bag the day I graduated from medical school. You take care of our guests."

James Thomas pleaded "I want to go with you."

"I'm going in the carriage. I don't see why he shouldn't. I would enjoy your company James Thomas." Doctor Kerr looked at Will and Minnie for approval.

Minnie said, "Please be careful, Father."

"James Thomas is now your responsibility, Dr. Kerr." Will looked at James Thomas, making sure he understood.

James Thomas followed Dr. Kerr, grabbing the remaining biscuit from a platter on the side table.

Will and Minnie laughed at how quickly James Thomas slipped the biscuit into his pants pocket. Sadly, they witnessed a learned trait of his survival—a skill he would never need again.

Chapter Twenty

*W*ill knew that Kerr's horse gaited and cantered well, but wondered, *How well would it fare in a running gunfight?* A good run would tell him a lot about the horse's temperament. Will looked across the table at Minnie. "I'd like to take your father's horse for a run. Would you care to join me?"

"I haven't been on a horse in months." Minnie looked out the window, "It's a beautiful day for a ride. I would love to join you."

"I'll get the horses saddled. Which horse do you ride?"

"The red dun with stocking feet. Call for Peaches and she'll come to you."

Will saddled the horses and tied them to a hitching post. Minnie came out of the ranch house with a haversack over one shoulder and a carbine over the other. She walked around Peaches and asked, "Will, where'd you find that side-saddle that's on Peaches?"

"It was the only side-saddle in the tack room. I assumed it was yours."

"I've never ridden side-saddle in my life. A girl can't outrun Indians sitting like a sack of corn."

She untied Peaches, walked her to the stables, and unsaddled the horse. She went into the tack room and returned saying, "This is my saddle."

"I know that saddle! My brother Fenwick made it."

"Fenwick Smith is your brother?"

Will took the shiny new saddle from her. "He's my youngest brother." Will secured the saddle on Peaches.

"Major says he's the best saddle maker there is." Minnie pulled herself gracefully up onto her horse.

"I'll tell Fenwick that when I see him."

Will mounted up and the two headed out.

They rode slowly, allowing the horses to warm up. Minnie pointed out a grove of cypress trees along the banks of the Lavaca several miles distant.

Will put Kerr's stallion through the paces, including a mad run with Minnie chasing in pursuit, making all the noise she could muster as Will fired several shots from the saddle. The horse was initially startled by the gunfire but didn't flinch after subsequent shots.

After the test, they let the horses graze. Minnie picked a spot under the canopy of a tall cypress tree. The river made a wide bend, which created a fertile grassy knoll. Wildlife and cattle grazing kept it well-groomed down to the water's edge. Minnie spread a quilt and laid out the hastily prepared vittles. They munched on a medley of turkey, fresh blackberries, and native pecans in a creamy honey sauce.

Minnie reclined on her elbows and watched a red-tailed hawk soaring overhead. "Wouldn't it be fun to fly like a bird?"

Will looked up and said, "I've tried it. It didn't work so well for me."

"You flew?"

"Only for a moment. When I was about James Thomas' age. I jumped from a sycamore tree and spread my arms like a bird—nearly broke my leg."

"I bet that hurt."

"Yeah, I got bruised up pretty bad."

"From hitting the ground?"

"No, from the whipping I got for trying to fly like a bird."

Minnie laughed. Suddenly, she turned serious. "What's it like growing up in a big family like yours?"

"I've never thought about it. I suppose I took my family for granted. I figured they'd always be there for me. Now my oldest brother is dead; Indians took Fayette; Fenwick, Angelina, her girls, and Mother will never be the same." Will looked toward the river, "My brother Mitchell is a preacher. He stayed in St. Augustine. I doubt he knows about all this."

"What about your mother—Rebeckah, right? It was obvious when I met her that she loves you dearly and is quite worried about your going after the Indians alone."

"Do you remember your mother?"

Minnie shook her head. "I was told she was pretty, only twenty-three when she died. I was three, the oldest of three children. Father was away. He came home and found us with Mrs. Pettus, a neighbor who took us in. My brothers died on the way to our new home in Gonzales. The slaves took good care of me." She looked up at the sky, "Father married Sarah Fulton, thinking she would be a mother to me. But Sarah had little time for me once her children were born. We fought often. That's how I ended up at St. Genevieve. The nuns taught me the little I know about life."

"Well, you certainly lived virtuously," Will's attempt at humor failed.

"It's not funny." Minnie rose to a sitting position, "I'm getting married soon and I've never been kissed!"

"You've never had a boyfriend before?"

"This is the first time I've been alone with a man other than Father. I'm surprised he left me in your company."

"You've never—?"

"No, I've never had sex. Every time I asked the nuns about it they would say, 'In good time Minnie; in good time.' Now I'm nineteen years old and I know nothing about sex."

Uncomfortable with the conversation, Will sat up on the quilt and wrapped his long arms around his knees. "Minnie…, you'll know when the time is right."

"You sound like the nuns at St. Genevieve," Minnie smiled.

Will stuttered, "I don't know…what you want…me to say."

"I want you to kiss me." Minnie puckered her lips and closed her eyes.

Will hesitated, then moved toward her, searching for a comfortable position to kiss a girl who had never been kissed. He wanted it to be the perfect kiss.

Minnie opened her eyes. "I'm waiting…"

"A kiss, especially your first, shouldn't be hurried," Will mumbled.

They kissed. She instinctively lay back on the quilt. After several minutes of kissing, Minnie gasped, "You're right."

"What do you…mean?"

"That I would know when I was ready." She turned away, "We must stop!"

Totally confused, Will stopped.

Minnie, still breathing hard, straightened her blouse, looked at Will, and said, "Thank you."

"For what?" he gasped.

"Teaching me to kiss."

Confused and lightheaded, Will mistook the symptoms of oxygen deprivation for love. Having caught his breath, he leaned towards Minnie for another kiss.

Minnie put a hand up between their mouths. "We must stop," she said, "you've stirred a passion in me I didn't know I had. I now know that I'll be ready for my wedding night." Minnie smiled at Will, "I'll always be grateful to you."

"You're welcome… I guess." Will picked up his hat and put it on. "We best head to the house?"

"I suppose we should." Minnie looked up at Will, and he extended his hand to help her up. They rode in silence, each in their own thoughts. Will was confused. *How can I yearn for a gal I didn't even like yesterday?* Once back at the ranch house they dined together, never mentioning their afternoon on the river. Will realized she was a woman he could never have and accepted they would be no more than friends.

Minnie requested the kitchen staff prepare and pack provisions for Will's journey the next day.

Will had determined that the stallion was worth the price and waited for the major to return home so he could complete the transaction. Kerr and James Thomas arrived just in time for the noon meal. Anxious to be on his way, Will declined an invitation to eat with them.

Will saddled the chestnut horse he would name Major as James Thomas, Minnie, and Major Kerr watched. Will knelt to say goodbye to James Thomas and reminded him to always tell the truth. "When you learn how to write, send a letter to me in Austin."

Tears streamed down his face as he hugged Will. "I'm going to miss you," he said. James Thomas wiped away his tears with his sleeve. "Thanks for bringing me to Texas."

Will shook Kerr's hand firmly and thanked him and Minnie for their hospitality and taking in James Thomas. Will handed Major Kerr five-hundred dollars, "This is for your horse. He's worth every dollar."

Major pushed Will's hand away and said, "I will not take your money." He placed one arm around Minnie the other on James' shoulder. "We're family now and you're part of it."

Minnie kissed Will on the cheek like a sister, "Thank you for everything!"

Will placed his boot in the stirrup, put both hands on the saddle horn, and pulled his lanky body up into the creaking saddle.

Tipping his broad-brimmed hat, Will turned the horse towards Kerr Creek. Kerr suggested he follow the creek to the Lavaca. When it forked with the Guadalupe, he would follow the trail east to the Colorado. The river would take him north through Bastrop and into Austin.

Will's confusion mounted as he rode. He had yearnings for Minnie but was still in love with Bella. He knew leaving James Thomas with the Kerrs was the right thing to do, but he would miss the boy. His greatest concern was his failure to find Fayette or bring Buffalo Hump to justice for the murder of his brother.

On the twentieth day of April, Will rode into Austin. He stopped on a hill overlooking the town—it was the site selected for burying the town's dead. The graves now outnumbered the living.

He knelt at his brother's grave. "I'm sorry James." He bit his lip, "I didn't find Fayette. I'm going back for him. Soon as I can put a stop to this Santa Fe Expedition."

He picked up a fallen tree limb and with its sharp end dug at the grave with furor. Once the madness driving him was over, he removed the scalp from his saddlebag and placed the last of his brother's remains carefully in the hat size hole, and then gently covered it with dirt.

Along the road overlooking the Colorado, Will encountered only deer and turkey on the once busy trail. Buffalo grazed across the river, unconcerned about his presence.

Will's horse carefully waded the shallow water of Waller Creek. The creek named for the architect of Austin was the eastern border of the town's limit. Most of the homes and government buildings were now vacant. Jacob Harrell had boarded up his home and moved the family to Brushy Creek near the protection of Kenney's Fort. The Harrell's were the first white settlers to arrive.

Crossing in front of the Eberly Boarding House, Will saw Mrs. Eberly sweeping her porch. She looked at Will as if asking, *"Where's Fayette?"* Will shook his head slightly. Mrs. Eberly said nothing. Thinking the worst, she put a hand on her heart to show that she understood and cared.

Will's sister Margaret and brother-in-law Lorenzo Van Cleve lived at the end of the long block. Their week old baby girl Elnora slept in her bassinet. Margaret heard a rider; a seldom occurrence of late. She stood in the doorway, wondering and hoping, *Could the rider be my brother?* She wasn't aware Fayette's mother and sisters stood behind her thinking the same thing.

Margaret, still weak from the birth of her first child, squinted and shielded her hazel eyes from the afternoon sun. She didn't recognize the horse or its gaunt rider. Slumped in the saddle, he rode like a defeated soldier returning from war. Margaret thought, *It can't be Will,* but the horse kept moving straight towards her open door.

Angelina and Rebeckah joined Margaret, filling the expanse of the front door. Angelina hollered, startling everyone near, "It's Will!"

Lorenzo and Thomas rushed out the back door. Neighbors came running to see what all the commotion was about.

They helped Will off his worn-out horse. They asked no questions, but it was obvious that Will hadn't found Fayette.

Mrs. Eberly came and suggested they take Will next door to her boarding house so he could rest in the peace and quiet of a private room. Family and friends were disappointed Fayette hadn't been found, but thankful Will was home. He slept undisturbed until noon the next day.

A crowd gathered at the capitol just blocks away from the boarding house. "Peg-Leg" Ward, Austin's Mayor prior to being appointed Land Commissioner, stood behind the cannon and lit the fuse. Everyone covered their ears and waited. Nothing happened until Peg-Leg moved to look into the cannon's barrel.

"KABOOM!" the cannon exploded.

The explosion shook the walls of Will's room. He sat up in bed, unsure if it was a dream. He heard women and children screaming—a man hollered for a doctor. He instinctively pulled on his pants and shirt. Before he could put on his boots, a bloody and burnt Thomas Peg-Leg Ward was carried into the room next to him.

Ward had lost a leg five years earlier during artillery fire at the Siege of Bexar in San Antonio. The nickname Peg-Leg was a reference to his wooden leg. Now another cannon mishap had taken an arm.

Will finished dressing and stepped into the crowded hallway. He gasped when he saw his father covered in blood and gunpowder.

"Father, you're hurt?"

Thomas grabbed his son's arms with both hands, keeping him from touching his bloody clothes. "No Will, this blood and black powder is from Peg-Leg. I'm fine, but he's in a bad way."

"What happened? The explosion, Commissioner Ward being hurt?"

"I warned him not to use that old black powder. It's been wet—not fit to cauterize a wound let alone fire a cannon."

"Why was he firing a cannon?"

"Don't you know what day it is?"

"Not exactly. I know its April."

"It's April twenty-first—San Jacinto Day! Five-years-ago today, we stopped Santa Anna's army down on the bayou. We're celebrating the best we can with what we've got."

"Father, we've got to talk," he looked at the throng in the hallway, "...in private."

"I know. We've got much to discuss. Get cleaned up and meet me at Bullocks'. Mrs. Bullocks is putting on a feed for San Jacinto Day."

Mrs. Eberly had taken Will's clothes to wash. Her husband, Jacob, had died peacefully in his sleep a few months after Will left Austin; now she placed some of his clothes on Will's dresser. Will cleaned up as best he could and began to put on what Mrs. Eberly had provided. The struggling boarding house was clean and simple, so different from his stays in St. Louis at the opulent Planters Hotel and in New Orleans at the Mason Dupuy.

Things continued to deteriorate in Austin since he left in January. Austin real estate was worthless. Residents that remained couldn't pay their debts, much less the taxes on their homes. Government expenses exceeded revenues by a four-to-one ratio.

Abundant game and fish provided meat. Thankfully, pecans, grapes, persimmons, and blackberries grew wild. Everyone had chickens and pigs. No one went hungry. Austin's population had dwindled from eight-hundred-thirty to just under a hundred. It now consisted of about fifteen family clusters and twelve single men. All six of the town's maidens had married.

Peg-Leg's horrific accident failed to dampen the celebration. Corn whiskey, which was in ample supply, combined with the reminisces of victory, brought loud laughs and huzzahs from the crowd. Joseph Lee, the newly appointed Supreme Court Justice of Travis County, assumed the ceremonial duties for the injured land commissioner. The young attorney led them in a prayer for Peg-Leg's recovery.

After making an appearance at Bullocks' and grazing on the smorgasbord of food, Thomas and Will retired to the back of Fenwick's saddle shop only steps away from Bullocks' Hotel. They sat on a log bench under the shade of a large oak tree where the men of the Smith Family and friends often gathered to tell stories and talk politics.

Will told his father about most of his three-month journey. *The details of Bella and Minnie can wait,* he decided.

"You think we'll ever find Fayette?" Thomas stared toward the trail where he last saw his grandson.

"If he is alive, I'll find him!" Will saw tears in his father's eye.

"You sound pretty certain of that…" Thomas wrapped his arms around his shoulders and rocked back and forth.

Will spoke softly, "In Santa Cruz there is this Catholic Priest—Padre Martinez. He is a friend of William Dryden and a cousin of John Rowland's wife. They have enlisted his help in finding Fayette. The padre is well known and respected by his followers. The padre, other friends, and I made in Nuevo México will find him."

"Time may be running out," Thomas said.

"I'm heading back to Santa Fe and on to Taos, but first I have to deliver a message to the president." Will furrowed his brow, "Is Vice President Burnet still acting president?"

"Yes, but Burnet's back in Galveston trying to make a crop and save his farm."

"What about President Lamar? When's he coming back to Austin?" Will asked.

"I received a letter last week. President Lamar sent his regrets for missing today's celebration but mentioned that his health had improved. He's planning to be here to send the Santa Fe Pioneers off."

Thomas shook his head and laughed, "Pioneers…that's what he calls them?"

"Father, do you think Lamar plans an invasion of Santa Fe?"

"Lamar may have illusions of grandeur, and may envision himself as the creator of a vast empire from here to California," Thomas gestured west with both arms, "but, we've got no army or ammunition," he cried out. "Hell, the damn Indians come into Austin, kill our kin, take our children, and we can't stop them."

Will was surprised. He had never heard his father curse before.

"We'll have plenty of ammunition soon; I can promise you that." Will told his father of befriending du Pont and being made his Texas agent.

Thomas' dour mood changed. He stood and looked toward the Bullocks' Hotel, "I can't wait to tell the sheriff we're finally getting some lead shot and gunpowder."

They rejoined their comrades in celebration of the Battle of San Jacinto and Texas Independence.

Chapter Twenty-one

Fayette helped Maria Rowland and Estevan Martinez at the trading post. John Rowland was away preparing for their exodus from New Mexico. The sheep were sheared of their winter fleece and the wool carted to the wool house.

Peter Duncan, the bookkeeper, taught Fayette to weigh and grade the large burlap bags of wool. The wool was consigned to Rowland and Company and awaited the next wagon train east. The sheepherders received store credit against the value of their wool for merchandise.

Only Maria knew where John and his partner William Workman were. Everyone assumed they were away on business. Fayette knew something was amiss. He often saw Maria looking out the window crying. Maria held Fayette and rocked him like a baby. She treated him like a man in the store, but as a child when they were alone.

"Momma Maria, when will I be going home?" Fayette looked into Maria's eyes.

"Soon, Fayette." Maria stroked his forehead, "Soon, we will say our goodbyes."

"Goodnight, Momma Maria." Fayette shuffled his moccasin feet toward his bedroom. His wounds healed, but he would forever bear the affliction of his abduction.

"You say your prayers, Fayette. Use the Rosary I gave you—It is blessed by Padre Martinez. Your prayers will be answered," Maria said.

Bella Miranda came to live at the Taos trading post with her Aunt Maria. Fayette recognized her from the Plaza in Santa Fe because she looked like Momma Maria. He remembered her trying to help him and how concerned she was about his welfare.

Bella was with child. Fayette recognized the familiar bump in the abdomen. He remembered when Aunt Margaret placed his hand on her abdomen and he felt the faint kick of her unborn child. He would never forget that sensation. Bella often visited Fayette as he worked in the general store. She asked about his family and Texas. The questions always included his Uncle Will; he didn't know why. They became friends. Talking to Bella about family gave Fayette hope.

Bella brought lunch to the general store for Fayette and Estevan. She sat on an empty keg with folded deer-skin for padding and enjoyed watching Fayette eat. Through him, she could visualize how her child might look.

Now into her fifteenth week of pregnancy, the baby kicked. Bella grabbed her side, but instead of grimacing, she smiled and said, "The baby...wants out."

"Can I feel?" Fayette asked.

Bella took his hand and placed it where the baby had kicked. The baby kicked again.

"That's the baby?" he asked.

Bella smiled. "Fayette, this child you feel inside me is your cousin." She held him close. "Your Grandmother Rebeckah is also my baby's grandmother."

"...I don't understand."

"Your Uncle Will is my child's Father." Bella hugged him and asked, "Do you understand?"

"That makes you my aunt just like Lorenzo is my uncle," Fayette smiled, "...because he married Aunt Margaret." He looked up at Bella, "Then you and Uncle Will are married?"

Bella held Fayette close as tears streamed down her face. She didn't answer his question.

Fayette knew the answer, but in his mind, she was his Aunt Bella. That's all that mattered for the moment; he was happy.

Will sat on the front porch of Mrs. Eberly's boarding house reading the *Austin Gazette*. The newspaper was one of the few amenities Mrs. Eberly offered. She kept the latest editions on a wooden water barrel between two high-backed rocking chairs. The headline of the June 2, 1841 edition read: "Mexican Invasion Pending."

Wagons and riders could be heard crossing Waller Creek. Will took a protected position behind the large water barrel where he waited and listened. Mrs. Eberly came to the open door, rifle in hand. Fenwick Smith hurried from the stables, followed by Harvey, his brother and business partner. Both carried rifles and wore pistols. Will's brothers, Fenwick and Harvey, were both active members of the local militia known as the Travis Guards. They took defensive positions along Pecan Street where several other men joined them. Women and children hunkered down in their homes, accustomed to taking cover during Indian raids. Dogs barked incessantly as the chickens clucked about in their coops. They waited.

Is this the invasion from Mexico Sam Houston warned about? Will wondered.

The first rider appeared, having turned the corner at Congress Avenue and Pecan Street. Fenwick recognized the horse he'd raised from a colt. He stepped boldly into the street. Fenwick had sold the horse and custom-made saddle to President Lamar last year.

Six riders and three freight-wagons, each pulled by six oxen, followed President Lamar. The wagons' contents were securely covered in canvas. The caravan stopped in front of Mrs. Eberly's Boarding house. When the teamsters set their brakes, the oxen felt their burden lifted and instinctively shook their muscular bodies. Eighteen broad-shouldered oxen bellowed in excitement, knowing that today's work was done. The teamsters gently coaxed them to the lush forage of the river bottom where the beasts would graze, awaiting what would be their last journey.

"Hello, Will…it's your friend George Kendall." The editor of the *New Orleans Picayune* climbed down from the first wagon.

"I see you made it to Austin." Will stepped off the dusty wooden porch, "How are you?"

George extended his hand, "My ass is sore from riding that damn wagon all the way from Houston."

"Good to see you again George," Will chuckled.

President Lamar dismounted. Mrs. Eberly stood her gun upright in the corner by the door and rushed out to greet the President. She called out, "Fenwick! The president is here; can you please take care of his horse?"

Fenwick went over and took the reins from Lamar who smiled and said, "Thank you, Fenwick."

"You're welcome." Fenwick said.

Harvey and Fenwick helped the other riders. As the owners of the only stable in town, they'd be busy for the next few weeks as hundreds of Santa Fe Pioneers began to arrive.

Mrs. Eberly took President Lamar's arm and escorted him into her boarding house, followed by the president's entourage.

George Kendall and Will stood in the Eberly's dining room. "Will, I told President Lamar about your association with du Pont. He is most anxious to talk with you," George said.

"I'm sorry George, but I haven't delivered your letter to President Lamar," Will said.

"That's alright. I met George Howard, McLeod's aide-de-camp, in New Orleans shortly after you left." Kendall beamed, "I sailed with him to Galveston. The president and his men escorted me to Austin with their convoy."

"Good for you, Kendall."

As President Lamar descended the stairs, Kendall said, "Here comes the president now."

They waited at the bottom of the stairs. Kendall said, "Mr. President this is my friend, Will Smith, I told you about."

"Will and I met when I swore in his father and brother as Travis County officials," Lamar gave Will the handshake of a Freemason.

"I'm sorry for your loss. James was a member of my lodge and a good friend. He'll be missed."

"Thank you, Mr. President."

"Please, call me Lamar," he said, releasing Will's hand with the secret Masonic signal for help.

The President introduced Commander Hugh McLeod who would lead the three-hundred-twenty-man expedition to Santa Fe. The other horsemen were William Cooke, Richard Brenham, and Jose Antonio Navarro. George Van Ness was the lead teamster. George Howard drove the supply wagon that George Kendall rode in.

"Let's go to my room upstairs," Lamar started up the narrow staircase as Will, McLeod, and Kendall followed. When Kendall started to enter Lamar's room, McLeod blocked him and said, "We'll see you and the others at dinner, Mr. Kendall. This is a private meeting."

Lamar sat in a high-back cowhide chair and motioned for Will and McLeod to sit on a settee facing him. Will excused himself to get his saddlebag from his room two doors down the hall. When he returned, the President and McLeod were looking over a map. Will sat down on the settee. McLeod folded the map and looked at Lamar.

Lamar leaned toward Will, "I understand from your friend George Kendall that you're employed by du Pont and Company. Is that correct?"

"Mr. Kendall is not a friend, but an annoying acquaintance who I can't help but like. We met at the opening of the new Planters Hotel in St. Louis. That meeting didn't go well."

President Lamar raised his thick eyebrows and said, "Kendall certainly speaks highly of you."

Will leaned in and said, "That's good to hear, sir. Kendall is a fine man. Sometimes, in his eagerness for a story, he has been known to stretch the truth," Will leaned back, "but Kendall is correct. I've been appointed the Texas agent for du Pont and Company. Due to the nature of du Pont's business, I would appreciate confidentiality in our dealings. Especially around Mr. Kendall."

Lamar glanced at McLeod and said, "We understand."

Hugh McLeod nodded in agreement.

Will placed his saddlebag on his lap. "Mr. du Pont and Mr. Bidermann were traveling with me from Council Grove to call on you personally. Word of President Harrison's death reached us in New Orleans. It curtailed their travel plans to Texas to meet you." Will opened his saddlebag. "I have a letter from Mr. Bidermann, the Managing Director of du Pont and Company, addressed to you." He handed the sealed envelope to President Lamar.

Lamar opened the envelope and methodically read the letter. He then handed it to McLeod, who read it, nodded approval, and then handed it back to the President.

President Lamar tucked the letter in his saddlebag, "Will, the future of Texas appears to be in your hands."

"How is that?" Will leaned back on the cowhide settee.

Lamar spoke softly, "The expedition to Santa Fe is provisioned. The Pioneers and their military escorts are arriving daily. Two-hundred-thousand dollars in merchandise has been secured to trade." Lamar pointed at McLeod.

McLeod, on cue, took over the conversation, "It's like this, Will. Our military escort, made up of volunteers, has guns and a cannon." He shook his head, "but we have no lead to shoot or powder to fire them."

Will raised his eyebrows and said, "Then the expedition is an invasion of New Mexico."

"Where in the hell did you get that idea?" Lamar snarled.

"From the papers in St. Louis, Independence and…"

Lamar interrupted, "Poppycock!" He then stammered, "Those eastern papers don't know what they're talking about. That's why I've invited George Kendall, editor of the *New Orleans Picayune,* and Thomas Falconer, a London journalist, to come along and document the journey. What I anticipate will be the greatest expedition known to man," The President grimaced in pain.

"Are you alright, Lamar?" McLeod leaned toward him.

"I'm fine. These damn stomach pains come and go," President Lamar leaned back in his chair.

Will asked, "What do you need for this expedition?"

Lamar motioned feebly for McLeod to answer.

"We need a hundred pounds of lead and two-hundred pounds of black powder, preferably in small wooden kegs." McLeod, a West Point graduate and Indian fighter, had meticulously calculated his needs for munitions.

"Can you supply that?" Lamar leaned his head back.

"Yes, but it's on a boat. Most likely in the Port of New Orleans," Will answered.

"How long would it take to get the munitions here?" Lamar grimaced, holding his right side.

Will stroked his chin and thought for a moment, "Two weeks if the *Margaretta* is still in New Orleans. Four weeks if she is in St. Louis."

Lamar looked at McLeod, "You should send Major Bennett; he's the quartermaster."

"I'll have Bennett put together a detachment for the detail." McLeod excused himself, leaving Will and Lamar alone.

Will cleared his throat, "You should know, sir. I've just returned from Santa Fe and Taos. Things are hostile toward Anglos. Especially those who support Texas."

"You're wrong. I have commissioners there now and four more going on the Santa Fe expedition. One is Jose Antonio Navarro, a Catholic who speaks Spanish and knows the customs and traditions of the people. Commissioner Dryden who lives in Santa Fe has assured me the people of New Mexico are most anxious to become a part of Texas."

Will slowly opened his leather saddlebag, "Mr. President, I have letters from all three of the Texas Commissioners." He handed them to him one at a time, "Mr. John Rowland and his business partner William Workman of Taos and William Dryden of Santa Fe."

"How did you...?"

"You need to read them while I get a glass of water."

Lamar motioned for Will to help himself. Will brought his glass back to the settee and waited until Lamar finished reading the correspondence.

"Damn it to hell, Will—you bring me the good news about the munitions and then hand me the resignations of my commission? I had depended on their local support for our cause," President Lamar put his hand on his head and closed his eyes.

"I'm sorry to be the bearer of bad news," Will placed his glass on a side table.

The President opened his eyes, "Why now? Just weeks before the expedition is to leave." Lamar shook his head.

"They couldn't correspond with you. Lives were at stake." Will leaned forward, "Governor Manuel Armijo was watching their every move. The commissioners took a big chance helping me escape."

"You escaped from the Mexicans?" Lamar raised his eyebrows.

Will told Lamar about Armijo posting a reward for his head. He explained how Commissioner Dryden agreed to surrender to Armijo in hopes that Commissioners Rowland and Workman would be spared. "I assure you, the majority of New Mexicans are not interested in becoming a part of Texas."

President Lamar leaned forward and asked, "Have you discussed this with anyone else?"

"No, sir. I haven't."

"Good, let's keep it that way." Lamar stood, "I appreciate your help with acquiring the munitions," He abruptly stood and showed Will to the door.

Will asked, "What about the shipment?"

Lamar stood and said, "You and McLeod work out the details." He opened the door and said, "Good day," and closed it behind him.

Will wandered slowly down the hall to his room, confused and disappointed with their meeting.

Will opened both windows in his room, hoping for a breeze. The air was still, but he heard the familiar bawling of calves and the moo of their protective mothers. He leaned out the corner window and saw a herd of Longhorns headed toward the river. The sweet smell of running water lured them down Congress Avenue. Their journey would end on the grassy banks of the Colorado.

"Hello, Will," a familiar voice called from across the street. George Kendall was waving.

Will waved back.

"Come on down," Kendall hollered.

Will motioned that he would be right down. *Maybe Kendall could shed light on Lamar's strange behavior,* he thought. He met Kendall on the porch. They moved the rockers into the afternoon shade.

"That was some stampede. Hundreds of wild longhorns running through Austin. What a story," George tilted his head back.

"Wasn't a stampede and it wasn't hundreds of Longhorns—maybe a hundred at most." Will looked at the dust still settling.

George shook his head, "You wouldn't call that a stampede?"

"No—a stampede is when a herd of animals gets spooked by something. These beeves had been on the trail and were thirsty. When they smelt the water, they headed toward it," Will rocked back in his chair.

George raised his eyebrows, "I don't understand; what's the difference?"

"It's simple. When a herd stampedes, they're running away from something that scared them. Like thunder or fire." Will put his elbows on the armrest and looked at George, "When they head for something they want like water or grass, that isn't stampeding."

George popped out of his rocker, "Then what the hell do you call what I just saw?"

Will looked up at George and smiled, "Beeves for the expedition, lured to water."

George shook his head and flailed his arms. He turned and walked to the end of the porch talking to himself, "They were lured…one hundred damn cows were lured to the river."

Will was amused at Georges' antics, but his stoic disposition never let it show.

George turned and walked back to Will, who was gently rocking back and forth. "Say I was to send this headline to my paper: 'One Hundred Longhorns Lured to Water,' You think they would publish it?" George leaned down into Will's face. Will kept on rocking, trying not to laugh at the agitated newspaperman.

"What the hell! It doesn't matter what I say, you always have to correct me," George walked to the end of the porch again. He looked up at the sky and stretched out his arms.

"I didn't mean to upset you, George," Will rocked, "You being the big city newspaper man. I wouldn't want you to embarrass yourself… again."

George turned. The tight jaw of his red face and his clenched fist conveyed his ire. George lunged at Will, who came out of the rocker just in time to deflect a hard blow to his head. He grabbed George's wrist and wrestled it behind his back.

"Let go of me," George hollered.

"Not until you settle down." Will pushed George into the rocker. When he tried to get up, Will pushed him back and said, "Stay put George, I don't want to hurt you."

"You better not hurt Mr. Kendall," Mrs. Eberly hollered as she stepped onto the porch. "What are you two squabbling about?"

"Nothing, Mrs. Eberly. Nothing at all," George looked down.

"It better be nothing or both of you'll be sleeping in Fenwick's stable tonight," The innkeeper looked up at Will and said, "You know my house rules. Shame on you, Will Smith, for roughing up Mr. Kendall. He's a guest of the President." She smiled at the newspaper man, "We hope that he'll write nice things about Austin and this boarding house. Don't we, Will?"

Will smiled at Mrs. Eberly. "Come on, George. I'll buy you a drink," Will helped George out of the rocker.

"I'm sorry," George said.

"Me too."

They walked across Congress, stepping around fresh cow paddies on the way to Swishers Saloon. Swishers was the only saloon that remained out of the eleven that had opened two years earlier. The owner, John Milton Swisher, had fought at the Battle of San Jacinto. He came to Austin at the urging of his friend Judge James Smith. John Swisher dressed Judge Smith for burial and shoveled the last spade of dirt on his coffin. The next day, Swisher gave the saloon to his bartender and rode out of Austin.

Major George Thomas Howard, aide-de-camp to Commander Hugh McLeod, stood at the bar. He'd met Kendall in New Orleans, and they traveled together by boat. Will knew Howard from their Ranger days.

"Good to see you again, Will," Major Howard shook Will's hand, "Sorry about your brother and nephew."

"Thank you, Major." Will turned, "So, you know George Kendall?"

"Yes, I've spent some time answering George's questions over the last few weeks."

George nodded, "You helped me better understand the Texas Revolution. I appreciate that."

Will motioned to the bartender, "I'm buying my friends this round."

The conversation quickly turned to the expedition. Howard and a detail of four men would be leaving at daybreak for Galveston. From there, they would board the first ship to New Orleans. Will scribbled a note to the *Margaretta's* captain, along with a sealed note for Mr. Bidermann explaining the situation in Texas. Once all the Santa Fe Pioneers arrived in Austin, they would rendezvous at Camp Cazneau at the springs on Brushy Creek thirteen miles north of Austin. When Howard's detail returned with the ammunition, the caravan would depart for Santa Fe.

Chapter Twenty-two

Hundreds of bawling bovines grazed the banks of Brushy Creek. Trying to protect the water supply, drovers kept the horses, oxen, and longhorns downstream from Camp Cazneau. The goats and sheep wandered wherever they wanted. The noise and excitement of the muster could be heard inside the block walls of nearby Kenney's Fort. George Kendall and Will Smith sat on a flat rock in the middle of Brushy Creek, which was a cool place to sit on a hot June day.

Centuries of flowing water turned their limestone perch into a round rock the size of a wagon bed. The rock looked like a table standing in the water. From it, swimmers could dangle their feet in the cool stream. They shared a crock of Bullocks' Best and listened to the shrill sounds of summer katydids.

George took a sip from his daily ration of whiskey. "What you thinking?" He passed the pint-size jug to Will.

"I was thinking of how to persuade you not to go on this expedition." Will held the crock by the jug hole and took a swig. "I've convinced my brothers not to go."

George interrupted, "I know, and President Lamar is not happy about it."

"You shouldn't go either." Will took another sip.

"Not go? You've got to be kidding." George took the jug. "This is a dream come true. Tom Falconer and I are the only journalists going." He took another sip. "This expedition will be far greater than Lewis and Clark's Corps of Discovery. The whole world will be reading about the Santa Fe Pioneers in the *Picayune*," George paused, "…Hell, I might even write a book about our adventures."

"You may be right, George. This idea of Lamar's may make you famous." Will skipped a rock over the water. "Do you realize where you're going?"

"I spent weeks going over maps and reading everything I could find about Santa Fe. I know very well where we're headed."

Will gazed across the creek, "Do you understand the danger you're going into?"

"If you're talking about Indian raids and Mexican desperados, then I think McLeod's army can handle anything that comes our way." George pointed toward the two-pound cannon on a hill that overlooked the camp. "Will, you should come with us. It'll be fun."

Suddenly, the camp burst into loud hurrahs and cheers of excitement. Will stood for a better view, "Looks like President Lamar has arrived."

"From the men's reactions, it could be a troupe of dancing girls," George laughed.

Will and George waded across the shallow creek, holding their boots and clothes high.

President Lamar and his entourage arrived by horseback from Austin. The President looked fatigued from the thirteen-mile ride, but his volunteers' admiration rejuvenated him. Lamar's popularity was waning; it would be worse by years' end. This was Lamar's last hurrah as President—and he was enjoying it—that is until he saw Will and Kendall together.

Will approached President Lamar and spoke in a low voice, "Can we finish our last conversation?"

Lamar put a hand on Will's shoulder and said for all to hear, "We ordered munitions. You delivered! We owe Will Smith a debt of gratitude. Let's have a hurrah for him!"

The Pioneers cheered.

Will whispered into his ear, "After what I told you, you're still sending these men into harm's way?"

Lamar turned to Commander McLeod and said something. Will was quickly escorted to his horse by the President's men and told to leave and not come back.

When Fayette wrote the Fourth of July, 1841 in the trading post's ledger, he remembered what his grandmother had told him about the Declaration of Independence. Today was Independence Day—the day The Colonies officially declared their Independence from Great Britain.

Excited, Fayette shuffled his way to Maria. She was sitting with Bella in the grand sala. "It's the Fourth of July!" Fayette gasped.

"What is this Fourth of July?" Maria asked.

"The Declaration of Independence was signed in Philadelphia on the Fourth of July 1776," he said with pride. "It's a time of celebration, with fireworks and cannons firing, kaboom!" Fayette exclaimed. "We should put up the American flag."

"Fayette, come and sit with Momma Maria," She patted the space between her and Bella.

"Can we celebrate?" Fayette asked as he wiggled in between them.

"Do you remember, Fayette? What I told you when you first came?" Maria put an arm around him. "I told you, things are different here." She looked deep into his blue eyes. "The people here are afraid of the Texans."

"I don't understand. Why don't they celebrate the Fourth of July? It's America's birthday!"

"If we celebrate your customs the people here will not be happy. We must be careful of what we say and do, for now."

"What do you mean for now?" Fayette looked up at Maria.

"Soon we must leave," Maria's lips quivered, "for California. It is no longer safe here for us." Maria dabbed her eyes. "My husband has bought a rancho in the valley they call San Gabriel." The women embraced and burst into tears.

"What about me?" Fayette asked.

Maria regained her composure and said, "So many decisions I must make. I wish my Juan were here to help me," She sobbed. "I can't leave you and Bella here alone. I don't know what to do, Fayette."

Fayette put an arm around her shoulder. "Don't worry Momma Maria, everything will work out for the best. It always does."

Maria hugged Fayette. Bella embraced them both as tears rolled down Maria's cheek.

It was the seventh day of August, Will had been back in Austin for nearly three months. He was on the roof of his cabin securing cedar shakes that had been loosened by spring storms and a family of raccoons. Some shakes were missing, so after breakfast, Thomas Smith had set out for his shingle yard north of Austin's town limits to get more.

From his vantage point, Will saw Louis Horst slowly leading his horse toward the cabin. A body lay across its saddle. The German-born Louis and his wife Mary were First Footers of Austin. Louis brewed good beer and was Austin's best fiddler. Louis had left Brushy Creek seven weeks earlier with the Santa Fe expedition. He returned on orders of Commander McCloud to report that the Santa Fe expedition was in trouble. Will scrambled down the rickety ladder.

"What happened, Louis?" Will asked, dropping his hammer on the ground.

"I'm so sorry," Louis said in his German accent "I am truly sorrowful."

Will looked at the body and saw his father's stockings—the ones his mother had knitted for his father's last birthday. "Oh no, this can't be."

He ran toward the horse, startling the mare for a moment. He gaped at his father's blood-covered body. "Who did this?" he demanded.

"I find him face down, mallet still in his hand." Louis shook his head. "Looks like Indians did this from behind. They stole his boots."

"Help me get him in the house. I don't want Mother to see him like this." Will untied the body from the saddle horn. They lugged the mutilated body into the cabin and laid him on the table board.

"What can I do...for you...Will?"

"Please find my brothers Fenwick and Harvey."

"I will bring them." Louis headed for Fenwick's stable.

Will placed a cypress bucket of water next to his father's bloody head. The bucket his father had made would be used to cleanse his body. Will cut small slivers of pine-tar soap off a large block. He mixed the soap with his hand and dunked the washrag up and down to make the hard water soapy. The scent of pine helped to mask the stench of death.

Will began the grizzly task by cutting loose what clothes remained. Wringing out the wet rag, he gently washed the body from head to toe. He then wrapped it in clean linen sheets, carefully covering the head where there was once a full head of hair.

Sheriff McFarlane opened the door, stepped inside, and removed his hat. "Will, I'm sorry. Louis told me what happened. I sent him on over to Webber's Prairie to fetch your brothers. They're trying to pen some wild mustangs for Mr. Webber."

"Thank you, Sheriff. Does Mother know?"

"I don't know. I haven't seen her today," Sheriff McFarland scratched at today's whiskers.

"I hope Louis didn't tell her." Will pulled a bundle of leather straps off a shelf and started to secure the sheets around his Father.

Sheriff McFarland touched Will's forearm, "Hold-on there. I'll need to see the body to document Thomas' murder... for the record."

"I don't want him uncovered, Sheriff." Will stood defiantly between the sheriff and the body.

"I'm sorry, Will, but it's my sworn duty to investigate and report my finding."

The door opened. Rebeckah stood ashen-faced in the small doorway. She heard their exchange and her trembling hand went to her lips. Rebeckah looked at her husband's wrapped body on the table, then at the sheriff. Will reached for his mother as she began to sink slowly toward the dirt floor and grabbed her frail body just in time.

Will looked at the sheriff, "Do what you have to do while I tend to Mother." He carried her out to a growing number of concerned neighbors. Someone brought over a milk stool for Rebeckah to sit on.

Reverend Amos Roark arrived to comfort grieving friends and family. Roark attended seminary with Mitchell Smith, Thomas and Rebeckah's second child. Roark came to Austin to assist the Smith family in establishing its first Presbyterian congregation.

A pale-faced Sheriff McFarlane came to the door and clung to the doorframe. Everyone waited for him to say something. Instead, the sheriff hurried around the cabin to a privy. Will left his mother with Mrs. Eberly and went to check on him.

Will heard the sheriff heaving loudly. When the heaving subsided, Will asked, "You all right?"

He didn't answer. Eventually, he stepped out of the small wooden structure and feebly walked towards his horse tied at the hitching post. Will followed and asked again, "Are you all right, sheriff?"

He turned slowly towards Will. "No...I'm not all right...." He took a deep breath. He moved closer and placed a hand on each of Will's shoulders. "Seeing what I just saw, I don't think any man could ever be right again."

"That's why I didn't want—"

"I know Will," the Sheriff nodded. "You finish what you started. I'll guard the door. No one else needs to know...what they did to Thomas."

Neighbors dug a grave for Thomas Witherspoon Smith next to his son James. They hastily placed his body in the ground, not waiting for a coffin to be made. Reverend Roark led a graveside service. Louis Horst, the fiddler—now the violinist—played for his departed friend long after the mourners had left. The sweet melodies of the Rhineland soothed the soul of the musician.

Rebeckah lost her firstborn. Fayette had been captured. No one knew if her grandson was alive or not. Now her husband of thirty-six years had been brutally murdered. Like many in Austin, she wanted to flee. But for now, her family needed her.

Chapter Twenty-three

John Rowland and William Workman met up in Abiquiú an ancient Pueblo town fifty miles northwest of Santa Fe. Abiquiú meant "timber point" in the Tewa language and lay on the west side of the Rio Chama—the start of the Old Spanish Trail.

Rowland had closed the deal with Ceran St. Vrain on their trading post. Workman and his family, with the help of native sheepherders, rounded up and drove herds of livestock to Abiquiú. Maria Rowland would remain in Taos with Fayette and Bella for now.

Two dozen men, four with families, joined Rowland and Workman. The men from Missouri purchased one-hundred-fifty of Workman's culled sheep for meat. With the herders and servants, the party now numbered around fifty. On Tuesday morning the sixteenth day of September 1841, the herders started moving several hundred head of livestock northwest toward Four Corners. They crossed the Western Colorado and Green Rivers and then moved over the Continental Divide before turning southwest through the Arizona and Nevada Desert. The caravan passed just south of what became known as Death Valley.

The first week of November 1841, they reached Puente Hills. William Workman, his wife, and his family stopped to admire the San Gabriel Valley. They saw the mission that gave the valley its name. John Rowland rode up and stopped next to his friend of twenty years. They looked at one another and nodded. Both knew that this valley would be their home forever.

One-thousand-dollars in gold purchased forty-nine-thousand acres in the San Gabriel Valley of California. They named it Rancho Puente. In time, Workman and Rowland would become prominent citizens of Los Angeles County.

At the request of Judge Joseph Lee, Will reluctantly agreed to fulfill his father's unexpired term. Bored with the job of treasurer, Will jumped at the opportunity to ride with his brother-in-law Lorenzo Van Cleve and other Austin militia to aid San Antonio. Mexican General Rafael Vasquez had invaded Texas with seven hundred Mexican troops. They took over San Antonio on the fifth day of March 1842 with little resistance. Vasquez raised the Mexican flag over the bell tower of San Fernando Cathedral, claimed victory, and high-tailed it to the Nueces River, when he learned that three-hundred militia along with Texas Rangers were in route. The invaders were gone by the time the Texas Volunteers arrived.

Lorenzo returned to Austin with the local militia. Will rode into San Antonio alone in hopes of finding Captain Jack Hayes. As he rode along the winding San Antonio River, cattle grazed about freely.

Homes were vacant, shuttered, or boarded up. Most places of business were closed. The residents who remained were Tejanos of Spanish or Mexican ancestry. Their families had lived in San Antonio for decades under flags of both Spain and Mexico. They spoke the language of the invaders from the south. It was the invaders from the north they didn't trust, but they were content to live in peace with either.

Will waded his horse into the river's shallow waters and gave Major rein to drink from it. He heard a voice and turned to see a fancy carriage.

"Willie, is that you?" a well-dressed man called out.

He knew it had to be Captain Jack, the only person who called him Willie.

"You wait right there until Major gets his fill. You and I got to talk."

"You better hurry, I got people to see." Captain Jack replied.

Will slowly walked the stallion out of the water. "I've been looking for you, Captain Jack."

"I know, I ran into Lorenzo on the road to Austin." Captain Jack shifted on the buckboard. "Sorry to hear about your pa." He shook his head, "It's been a bad year for your family."

"Yes, it has." Will looked around. "Captain, we need to talk."

"Best we talk now. I'm headed to the mayor's house for an important meeting. Tie your horse to the carriage and ride with me."

Will tied Major to the rear of the carriage and climbed in, "What's the meeting about?"

"It's about the town's committee for public safety." Captain Jack whistled the horse into a full trot. "We've got to get ready."

"Ready for what?"

"The Mexicans, who do you think?" Captain Jack shook the reins. "Hell, we've had four invasions this month. General Rafael Vasquez took Victoria, Refugio, and Goliad. Then they came to San Antonio and hung their damn Mexican flag like they owned the place. And on the eve of the Fall of the Alamo!" He shook his head. "No one fired a damn shot to stop them. Vasquez high-tailed it to the border, knowing militia was on the way. We don't know who's with us or against us."

"I've never heard you sound so angry," Will held on to the buckboard.

"Your damn right I'm angry." He slowed the carriage as they entered the plaza, "I'm mad at our own citizens that didn't lift a finger to stop them." He pulled the reins, "Whoa, damn it! This is it."

They'd arrived at a house built of cut limestone on the corner of Soledad and Commerce. Captain Jack handed the reins to Will and climbed down. A black servant came out to unload the carriage's storage bin. Then he took the carriage and horses to the stable on the river.

"That black man, I know him from somewhere." Will said.

"Come on, let's get inside." Captain Jack hurried Will into the mayor's house before anyone could see them.

"You made it just in time, Captain." Mayor Maverick looked at Will. "I know you. You're one of the Smith boys from Coosa." The mayor grabbed Will's hand and shook it vigorously, "Which one are you?"

"Glad to see you again, Mr. Maverick. My name is William. Everyone calls me Will."

The mayor was Samuel Augustus Maverick, a signer of the Texas Declaration of Independence. It was Samuel Maverick who had convinced three generations of the Smith family to come to Texas. They traveled in the same convoy from Coosa to St. Augustine. Samuel Maverick married Mary Ann Adams, a schoolmate of Will's. Many in Coosa thought Will and Mary might marry. Maverick, from South Carolina, was fifteen years older and much wealthier, married Mary Ann in Tuscaloosa on the fourth day of August 1836.

"If everyone calls you Will, then that's what I'll call you," the mayor said.

"Everyone except me. I call him Willie." Captain Jack grinned his mischievous grin.

"We're sorry for your loss, Will." Mayor Maverick placed his left hand on Will's shoulder.

"Thank you, Mr. Maverick. Or should I call you Mayor Maverick?"

"I see no introductions are necessary," Captain Jack tried to jest.

"I'm no longer the mayor, but once elected the title stays with you." Mayor Maverick smiled, "Feel free to call me either. Or just call me Sam."

Will looked around, "Is Mary Ann here?"

"No, and she's going to be disappointed she missed the opportunity to see you," Mayor Maverick looked at Captain Jack.

"Mayor, is Mary Ann all right?" Will asked.

"She was when we left her and the children with trusted friends last week," Maverick's voice wavered.

Captain Jack took over the conversation, "My guides spotted General Rafael's army on the border weeks before they invaded San Antonio," the captain said. "We moved the women and children to safety."

243

"I hope they are still safe," Maverick said, choking up as he spoke.

"Mayor, Will brings news from Austin and Santa Fe. You should hear what he has to say before the others arrive."

They moved into Samuel Maverick's office. He was no longer mayor but was an alderman and a lawyer. The other aldermen considered Samuel the authority on public safety. They would soon be at his house for a special meeting. Only those loyal to the Republic of Texas were invited. Mayor Juan Seguin was not invited as the meeting was about his ouster.

Mayor Maverick sat at his desk. Captain Jack and Will sat on brightly painted Mexican chairs with cane bottoms, padded with cowhides.

Mayor Maverick leaned forward, "Will, I'm anxious to hear what news you bring. It must be quick. I expect the other members soon."

"Mayor...I'm sure you know about the Santa Fe Expedition that left Camp Cazneau on the nineteenth of June?"

"We've received sketchy reports but have no details."

"The pioneers who survived the trip surrendered to Governor Armijo without firing a shot. Some were executed; the others are now prisoners of war." Will looked at the mayor.

"What the hell happened?" Captain Jack squirmed in his chair. "It was supposed to be a trade mission."

Will looked at Captain Jack then at Mayor Maverick. "Things were never as President Lamar thought. He was led to believe that the citizenry of New Mexico would be excited about the possibility of being a part of Texas. In reality, only a small group of Anglos supported that notion."

"I would have thought as much." Maverick bit off the end of a cigar. "Who was it that mislead him?"

Will leaned forward and said, "William Dryden, a lawyer in Santa Fe. Lamar appointed him Texas Commissioner. Lamar sent Dryden back to Santa Fe with a proclamation to the people of the territory."

Mayor Maverick lit his cigar, took a puff, and asked, "What happened to this Commissioner Dryden?"

"He and Mr. Rowland and Workman all resigned, trying to avoid imprisonment by Governor Armijo."

Captain Jack raised his eyebrows and asked, "Willie, how would you know that?"

"While I was in Santa Fe looking for my nephew," Will explained, "I met the commissioners. They helped me escape from Armijo's soldiers."

"Escape?" Captain Jack stood. "You escaped?"

"Armijo offered a thousand pesos for my head." Will looked up at Captain Jack.

No one spoke. Maverick offered the other two a cigar. Captain Jack took one, but Will declined. Captain Jack sat down, lit his cigar, and then blew a large puff of smoke that enveloped the room. "Damn, Will, you sure know how to stir shit up," he said.

"The commissioners gave me their letters of resignation." Will looked at Captain Jack, "I delivered the letters on the second day of June, shortly after President Lamar arrived in Austin."

Mayor Maverick looked at his calendar. "That's two weeks before the convoy left from Camp Cazneau?"

Captain Jack jumped up, "You told President Lamar his commissioners resigned for fear of being arrested for supporting Texas?"

"Yes, and I advised Lamar of the citizens' hostilities toward Texans." Will looked from Captain Jack to Mayor Maverick, "I also told him that the Governor of Nuevo México, Manuel Armijo, considered the Santa Fe Expedition an armed invasion of his territory."

"Shit!" Captain Jack plopped down on the chair. "First Juan Seguin turns against us, and then our President knowingly sends the Santa Fe Pioneers into an ambush."

Mayor Maverick turned and looked out the open window. "Juan Seguin begged his friend Antonio Navarro not to go on that expedition. Juan knew…he had to have known."

Captain Jack nodded, "Yes, he did."

"How would he know?" Maverick looked at Captain Jack. "That information could've only come from Mexico." Maverick turned pale and said, his voice quivering, "Seguin swore to me on the oath of a Freemason," he sighed, "…I no longer know who we can trust." He wiped a tear with the back of his hand.

Captain Jack stood, placed an arm on Maverick's shoulder, and said, "I've already confiscated the records and the arsenal that Seguin had, and Griffin stored them in your cellar. Juan hasn't left us much to fight with."

"Did Seguin give you any trouble?" Samuel frowned.

Captain Jack sat down. "He wasn't happy but knows that as long as he's in Texas, he'll need our protection. The family fears for their lives. They're packing as we speak." Captain Jack stood again and moved to the window. "Dam-it-to-hell. Juan was such a good soldier during the Revolution; he served Texas well after Independence... I can't believe he's a traitor." Captain Jack expelled a large puff of cigar smoke out the window.

"What do you mean...what's this about Juan Seguin?" Will asked, surprised.

Maverick pointed at the open window, indicating to Jack to pull the shutters in—he complied. Maverick leaned forward and spoke softly, "The committee and many in San Antonio believe Juan Seguin was the instigator of the recent Vasquez Invasion." He leaned back. "Captain Jack and I don't want to believe Juan's a traitor, but we keep hearing things like this which implies that he is complicit. Some want to hang him."

"Everyone knows Juan's been in dire financial distress. There were some financial shenanigans that don't reflect well on him as a public official," the captain said. "We've asked for Juan's resignation. That's why he isn't joining us for the meeting."

"I'm surprised, but I understand," Will said.

"My men will escort Juan's family out of town tonight," Captain Jack said.

"What about his resignation? It would look better if he resigned." Maverick said.

"Juan promised to give it to Luke, my Tonkawa guide, as soon as Seguin's family gets safely across the Nueces. General Vasquez is probably lingering on the border waiting for them." Captain Jack stood and began to pace the room.

"Jack, what the hell's the matter with you?" Maverick asked.

"I'm upset and got a bad case of the red ass. I just can't believe Juan Seguin is in cahoots with the Mexican Army; or that Lamar sent friends of mine knowingly into an ambush."

"Griffin," Maverick called out, "bring us a pot of coffee before Captain Jack starts frothing at the mouth."

Griffin, Maverick's only servant to remain in San Antonio, carried in a pewter carafe of coffee and five cups on a tray.

Samuel asked, "Griffin, why five cups?"

"Master Guilbeau and Mayor Smith are here, sir. I assumed they'd be joining you." Griffin Bell had been Maverick's favorite slave. When offered his freedom, Griffin chose to come to Texas with the Mavericks.

"Certainly. Send them in." Maverick rose to greet the aldermen who would make the required quorum for a vote.

Former mayor John William Smith and Mayor Pro Tem Francis Guilbeau entered the corner room. Griffin lit lamps as the sun was setting. Maverick introduced Will to Mayor Smith, San Antonio's first Anglo Mayor and the first mayor after Texas Independence. Francois Guilbeau would serve out the remainder of Juan Seguin's term of office.

Will stood. "Gentlemen, I know you have business to conduct and I will be about mine."

"You're going back to Austin?" Maverick asked.

"No…I'm heading to Santa Fe." Will looked at Captain Jack. "I'm going to find my nephew and bring him home."

"You should stay the night. You can bunk in the carriage house with Captain Jack. Come morning Griffin can pack provisions for your journey," Maverick offered.

Will accepted.

Griffin escorted Will to the door. "I remember you, Master Smith, from that long trip from Coosa with your family. Sure sad about what them Indians did." Griffin looked down and shook his head.

"Thank you, Griffin."

Chapter Twenty-four

The nickering of horses woke Will. Someone fumbled in the dark for a candle. The sound of a match struck—followed by the familiar click of a revolver.

"Don't shoot! Willie, it's me." Captain Jack lit the candle, "You asleep?"

"Not anymore." Will thumbed back the hammer of his revolver.

"I should've warned you, but I didn't want to wake you." Captain Jack unfurled his bedroll.

"You did...so let me go back to sleep." Will rolled on his side.

"Can't Willie. I got to talk to you about your going to Santa Fe."

Willie turned over, "Can't it wait till morning?"

"Afraid not." Captain Jack moved a three-legged milk stool close to Will's bunk.

"You're not going to let me sleep, are you?" Will sat up. "What's so damn important it can't wait 'til morning?"

"You can't go to Santa Fe."

"Who's going to stop me?"

"I guess that'll be me. Willie, I need you, your horse, and your guns. The Mexicans are going to attack again...soon...and with a hell of a lot more troops. Vasquez's little raid was just a forerunner of what's to come."

"Are you sure?"

"Hell yes I'm sure!"

"Damn it, I couldn't go after my nephew earlier because I had to finish serving my father's term. Now you're trying to conscript me to fight the Mexicans."

Captain Jack blew out the candle. "Isn't it nice to be needed?"

"It's been fourteen months since Fayette was taken. I promised Angelina I would find him and bring him home."

"If you don't help me, Will, there won't be a home to bring Fayette to. You know they'll destroy Austin along with San Antonio."

"You make it hard to say no."

Will slid back into his bedroll and Captain Jack got into his. They were both silent for a while.

"After we've driven the Mexicans back across the border for good, I'll go with you in search of Fayette," Captain Jack said, "that's a promise."

The crowing of a Rhode Island Red rooster woke them long before daylight.

Captain Jack yawned. "I'm heading to the house…Griffin promised to put the coffee on when the rooster crows."

"I'm hungry." Will pulled on his pants.

Captain Jack buckled on his guns. They walked up the embankment to the plaza. Someone whistled from the bell tower of the San Fernando Cathedral. Captain Jack waved.

"Who's in the tower?" Will squinted, trying to see the whistler in the faint light of morning.

"We've kept a look-out in the tower around the clock since the raid. From there, a sentinel can see south to the Medina River."

They made it to the house and Griffin opened the door for them. "Good morning, Captain Hays and Master Smith. Mr. Maverick is in the dining room. I'll bring coffee and your breakfast shortly." Griffin pointed the way.

Maverick sat at the end of a long pine table. Three Springfield muskets and two flintlock pistols lay on the table. Black powder and lead bars partially filled a wooden ammunition box on the floor beside him. Griffin had carried the arsenal that Captain Jack confiscated from Juan Seguin yesterday up from the cellar.

"This is San Antonio's arsenal?" Maverick was clearly disheartened at the guns and ammunition.

Captain Jack said, "Juan claimed that's all there was."

"How can we stop the Mexican Army with this puny arsenal?" Maverick shook his head. "The worst thing is, Juan knows what little munitions we have. He'll tell General Vasquez for sure."

Will pulled out his chair, "I can get you all the gunpowder and lead you need."

"How?" the other two asked in unison.

"Give me a requisition for your needs. As the agent for du Pont, I'll arrange delivery to the Port of Matagorda. From there it's up to you to get it to San Antonio."

Griffin brought in a large plate of fried eggs, bacon, and biscuits and placed it on the table. Maverick motioned for them to partake of the food.

"You're an agent for du Pont?" Captain Jack asked and took a sip of coffee.

"Why didn't you tell us last night?" Mayor Maverick inquired.

"I never had the opportunity to say," Will responded.

"Will, we have no money to pay for ammunition," Mayor Maverick said apologetically. "Lamar has left Texas in a state of destitution."

"Mr. du Pont knows your situation, and your requisition to me is good enough for him."

"How long would it take to get the powder and lead?" Maverick asked, anxiously.

Will calculated in his mind: *Two days to Matagorda; three days for a packet ship; then two to three days at sea...if a keelboat was in New Orleans....* "Two to four weeks," he said.

"Time is everything," Captain Jack said.

"True," said Maverick, "and we don't have much of it." He went to his desk and wrote out a requisition for a quarter ton of black powder, a like amount of lead bars, and fifty pounds of cartridge paper. He blew on the paper to dry the indigo ink. He handed it to Will, "Here's your requisition."

Will took it and said, "If Griffin can pack provisions for a two-days' ride, I'll be saddling my horse soon as I finish breakfast." Will reached for more bacon.

Captain Jack put a hand on Will's shoulder, "Thank you for what you're doing. If I could spare a man, I would send him with you."

"I know." Will stood. "I need you to send a rider to Austin to warn everyone to get out now."

Mayor Maverick looked at Captain Jack and said, "Have as many men as you can spare escort that munitions wagon. We can't have the Mexicans capturing that arsenal."

"I'll be waiting for you with my men two weeks from today, in Matagorda." Captain Jack looked at Will and asked, "You are coming back?"

"No Captain Jack...I'm not coming back to Texas."

"Where you going?" Captain Jack asked, knowing the answer.

"Thank you, Mayor Maverick, for your hospitality. Please give Mary Ann my regards."

Mayor Maverick nodded. "Be careful Will...there a lot of two-legged critters out there that want your scalp."

Griffin handed him a haversack and said, "This will make do to Matagorda."

"Thank you, Griffin."

Will stood on a high vista overlooking the narrow riverbed of the Guadalupe River. He heard the boom of a musket, saw blue smoke from where the shot was fired, followed by Indian war hoops. He tied his horse a distance from the overlook and lay down to wait and watch. He saw four Indians on foot and one mounted on an old Indian pony. His mind raced, *The Indians killed another settler.*

He scrambled down the steep embankment thinking, *They're not going to mutilate another person.* His rage increased each step of the way down.

Will snuck-up on them hovering over their kill. The young bucks were cutting and pulling at their kill, unaware of his presence until both revolvers emptied ten rounds into their half-naked bodies. The lone Indian on horseback watched the massacre from afar. Will ran toward the Indian waving his now empty revolvers, screaming and hollering obscenities like a madman. He chased after the Indian on foot with empty guns and no cartridges to reload. The Indian, frightened by Will, ran his horse straight up the hill. Exhausted, Will sat on a large rock to catch his breath.

Once the adrenaline rush was gone, he realized what he had done and started laughing uncontrollably at his folly. The climb up the steep incline brought Will back to his senses, and he became upset at his carelessness. He reloaded and mounted up, vowing to never again chase an Indian with empty guns.

Something drew Will toward his kill—maybe morbid curiosity, or was it something else? He pulled the first Indian off the carcass of a deer. He'd never taken a scalp but knew how and made quick work of it. He then took one of the braves' spear and tied the scalps to it. For a moment, Will questioned his euphoric feelings. *The spear will be full when I arrive in Matagorda,* he swore.

Will followed the tracks of the old Indian on horseback and found their camp. What was left of the small tribe grieved in the largest of four teepees, chanting and carrying on over the death of their loved ones. Will emptied his guns into the side of the teepee. Only the rattle of death could be heard inside. Four squaws and three braves lay dead on the dirt floor.

People gawked at Will as he rode into the Port City of Matagorda that March morning. The blood of his victims still looked fresh on the clothes he wore. Will made it to the hotel and rented a room, then boarded Major at Shoe's Stable. Shoe and Beth's twin sons, Andrew and Jackson, recognized the horse but did not recognize the shabbily dressed rider. Will had to remind the twins of their meeting last year. Will gave the twins a fifty-dollar Texas red back along with instructions to deliver the stallion and a letter to Major Kerr.

The *Columbia* was due in at sunset and would depart for Galveston at noon the next day. Will returned to the hotel to get cleaned up. The hotel's laundry maid wasn't excited about washing Will's bloody clothing, but an upfront gratuity overrode her objections.

"Yes sir, Mr. Smith. Your clothes be ready and smelling sweet by sundown." She kissed the ten-dollar note and tucked it in her apron pocket.

"Could I get a tub full of hot water?" Will pointed at the elongated copper tub that sat in the corner of his room.

"My boys be right up," she said as she backed out of the room.

Two young black boys delivered the scalding hot water and poured it into the tub, spilling nary a drop. This gave Will another opportunity to dispose of a ten-dollar note. *Texas money will be of little use in the United States,* he reasoned. Will soaked until the water cooled and became thick with grime.

Using the soft terry cloth towel the hotel provided, Will dried his shoulder-length hair. He trimmed his facial hair with razor and scissors and waxed his moustache. He wore his gray suit to the dining room.

One of the young men who delivered his bath water was in the dining room and seated Will at the only available table. The other lad was waiting tables. The hotel was always busy when the *Columbia* was in port. Carriages brought arriving and departing passengers to and fro. Matagorda was now the second largest port in Texas.

A well-dressed woman approached Will's table. "May I join you?"

Will knew her from somewhere. The pretty Creole woman was about his age. They had met. *But where?* "Yes, please sit down," Will stood and graciously pulled out the other chair.

"Why would a good looking man like you be eating alone?" she asked with a smile.

"Had I been with another, you wouldn't have asked to join me." Will realized who she was and gave her a cold stare.

"Where are you headed Mr. ...err?"

"Smith is the name. I'm heading to Santa Fe. My last night in Texas for a while." Will hailed the waiter, "Please bring us a dozen shelled oysters each and a bottle of your best champagne."

"I've met many men named Smith." She fidgeted, settling her bustled skirt into the small chair.

"I'm sure you have." Will leaned back, enjoying his wit.

He remembered the girl from the *Queen of St. Louis.* He now had long hair and a beard and moustache, which made him unrecognizable. For now, he would not mention their altercation or her arrest. He would just enjoy her presence.

"How did you know I liked oysters and champagne?" She licked her lips as the waiter poured champagne. "I'm from…"

"You're from New Orleans," Will said before she could finish.

She raised a painted eyebrow "Yes…I'm from New Orleans, but how would you know that?"

"Your dress has enough satin to dress five Texas women. But it's a beautiful dress."

"Well… thank you, Mr. Smith." She feigned a sigh of appreciation and a Southern Belle smile.

Will saw only greed in her cold but beautiful brown eyes. He remembered the petite young woman who kicked him in the groin and then tried in vain to shoot him.

"You're most welcome." Will managed a smile, and thought, *You treacherous little whore.*

She assumed Will had taken the bait. Pretty as she was, most men did.

They toasted each other without saying a word. Using her particular skills, she sensually rubbed Will's leg under the table with a bare foot. Will enjoyed the magic that took down many a man, knowing she was only searching for something to steal.

"What do you do Mr. Smith?"

"I kill Indians."

"Not really, you jest." She tried to smile.

He didn't answer but nodded that he did.

"How...many have you killed?" She threw her head back ever so gracefully.

"I've lost count...but I killed seven this morning."

She feigned a look of horror. "Seven! You killed seven people today?"

"They weren't people...they were Indians."

She removed her leg and crossed her arms. "You're not joking, are you?"

The waiter delivered the shelled oysters and poured more champagne.

"I don't joke about such things." Will forked an oyster and swallowed it whole.

She shook her head. "How can you do that?"

"Just dip them in sauce and swallow." Will forked another raw oyster.

"I meant...kill them." She said it loud enough to be heard across the room.

"It's easy...if you hate them enough." Will took a sip of champagne.

"I don't believe you." She smiled and then scarfed down an oyster.

Her foot was now on the other leg, searching something of value.

Will moved his leg and said, "Not tonight. Maybe another time."

He stood, bowed graciously toward her, and gave a red back note to the waiter, sufficient to cover their bill and a good tip. The scarlet lady was left to find another victim.

Will retired to his bayside room where he wrote letters to his siblings, advising them of the pending Mexican invasion and recommending they move away from Austin. Will reminded Fenwick and Harvey of a dugout they found on Mustang Ridge, far enough off the San Antonio Road to avoid invaders from the south. The ridge near Plum Creek offered a defensive view of the open prairie.

He went to bed and slept fitfully.

At breakfast the next morning, Will read a week old *New Orleans Picayune.* The headline read "Ambassador Seeks Freedom for George Kendall." The story described the tireless efforts of U.S. Ambassador to Mexico, Waddy Thompson, to free the *Picayune's* editor. Will thought, *George wanted to be famous, now he is.*

Will checked out of the hotel and went to the dock. There was a stateroom available on the *Columbia;* he took it, paying in U.S. dollars. He boarded the ship and was shown to his room where he wrote a report to du Pont and Bidermann on the sad state of affairs in Texas.

The *Columbia* arrived on Good Friday, the twenty-fifth day of March, 1842. The Holy days of Easter were a special blessing for Texas. The *Columbia* would hold over until next Tuesday instead of the usual departure. Will had three and a half days to find the *Margaretta* and then get the munitions loaded on board the *Columbia.*

Will ambled off the rickety gangway and saw Captain Morgan tending to ship's business. He approached the captain, hoping he didn't recognize him from the last trip."

"Could I have a moment of your time, Captain Morgan?"

Captain Morgan raised an eyebrow. "Do I know you?"

"My name's Will Smith," he offered his hand.

The captain turned without shaking it. "I'm busy, Mr. Smith, but you can talk to me as I check the mooring lines." He walked to the aft of the ship.

"Can I get freight loaded over the weekend?" Will followed the captain as he gave rapid orders to dock workers.

"The stevedores are off for Easter, soon as we're unloaded. They won't be back 'til Monday. The captain turned and asked, "Just what are you shipping Mr. Smith?"

"Munitions," Will spoke low as not to be overheard.

"Just carry your powder horn and shot bag with you when you board." Captain Morgan stood legs spread, hands on hips. "No problem."

"It weighs a ton, sir."

"You're joking?"

"No, sir. I need one hundred five pound kegs of black powder, a half ton of solid lead bars, and cartridge papers shipped to Matagorda."

"Are you planning a war?"

"Trying to stop one, sir."

Captain Morgan took a deep breath. "No way in hell I'll take on a ton of explosives." He shook his head. "No sir, not on my ship."

"Could we talk in private, Captain?" Will motioned away from the ship.

"Nothing you can say will change my mind." Captain Morgan stood, arms folded.

"I represent du Pont and Company, and the Texas Rangers under Captain Jack Hays, the commander of Texas forces. I have a requisition signed by him and Samuel Maverick for munitions. If they don't receive the shipment soon, the Mexican Army will take over, and your weekly runs to Texas will stop."

Morgan shook his head. "I thought the fight between Texas and Mexico had been decided."

"I'm afraid not," Will said.

Captain Morgan raised his bushy eyebrows, "Where are the explosives now?"

"The munitions are on one of du Pont's keelboats...most likely the *Margaretta*."

"Let's check with the wharf master. He'll know who's in port." Captain Morgan pointed toward the small shack that served as the wharf master's office.

They walked over, opened the door, and looked into the small space. A desk and chair took up most of the space, the seated wharf master the rest; his back was to the door.

Captain Morgan stood in the door frame and inquired, "Where is the berth for du Pont's boat?"

The wharf master turned toward the door and said, "They have no berth." He shook his head. "I keep them moored away from the docks."

Will stood next to the captain, looked down at the wharf master, and asked, "Then the *Margaretta* is in port?"

"Afraid so. There's always at least one in port these days—an accident waiting to happen."

Will stuck his head in the doorway, obviously annoyed. "Just tell us, where is she?"

"Who wants to know?" The wharf master squinted through thick round spectacles.

"Will Smith is my name."

The wharf master adjusted the wire frame glasses on his nose and looked at a list on his cluttered desk. "Mr. Smith, where are you from and who do you report to at du Pont?"

"I'm from Texas and I report to Mr. Bidermann, du Pont's brother-in-law." Will responded, tersely.

The wharf master pointed and said, "The *Margaretta* is moored south of here about a mile in Gator Cove on your port side. Tied to a red buoy."

"Thank you." Will turned, and Captain Morgan followed.

Captain Morgan said, "I want to help Texas, but you heard what the wharf master said. He won't allow explosives near the wharf. It wouldn't be safe pulling a sternwheeler in the cove. With boilers burning, one cinder could spark an explosion. I don't own the *Columbia* or make the rules."

"I understand, Captain."

"I'm encouraged by the owners to accommodate passengers the best I can," Captain Morgan said, and then stopped. He thought a moment and said, "On turnarounds, I can sometimes let passengers stay on board."

"I wasn't planning on staying on board."

"If you want my help, you best listen and do what I tell you." The captain glared at Will, "Is that understood?"

Will nodded. The conversation stopped as a wharf worker passed by.

"Sometimes I let turnaround passengers stay on board until the next departure. You have four nights on board, to do what you have to do. Follow me, I'll make arrangements with my first mate."

"Do you know where I can get a rowboat?" Will asked.

Captain Morgan stopped and looked Will in the face. "Inquire around the wharf. From this point on, I know nothing of your activities. You're just another passenger requesting turnaround privileges. Is that understood, Mr. Smith?"

"Yes, and thank you, Captain. How can I repay you?"

"By not getting caught. If you're caught don't implicate me or my crew."

"I understand."

Chapter Twenty-five

Will found a boat lying upside down on the wharf with a "For Hire" sign on it. It had long oars set in cast iron oarlocks. It was owned by a baker. During the week, the boat plied the riverfront delivering food from the bakery. The owner needed it back by Monday morning.

Will rowed the boat down river an hour before sunset and saw landmarks in the light of day, which would make his late night return easier. Will moved into a fast current and was able to float down the river with little effort. He marked the location, not wanting to get pulled into the spot when he returned. He saw the cove on the port side where the *Margaretta* was tied to a buoy. A one-person dingy was tethered to her, *A good sign someone's aboard,* he thought.

Within fifty yards of the *Margaretta*, a large brindle dog appeared on the bow. It paced and became anxious as Will rowed closer. It barked a warning.

"Who goes there?" an armed man called out.

"Is George Hebert aboard?" Will hollered.

The man, who was no more than eighteen, pointed a rifle at Will and demanded, "Identify yourself or turn away from this boat immediately."

Will raised his hands. "I'm Will Smith…du Pont's Texas agent."

"I expected a Texas Navy Ship. Not a rowboat!"

Will lowered his hands, "This is the best Texas can do for now." He swooped the oars.

The man kept his gun pointed at Will and the dog became more disturbed as the boat came closer. "Who do you report to?" the man insisted.

"I report to Mr. Bidermann. Who are you?"

"Do you have a letter from Mr. Bidermann?"

Will stood and pulled the wrinkled letter out of his pocket. The boats were now alongside each other.

"Show me your letter from Bidermann," the man commanded.

Will handed the letter of employment to him.

The man lowered his gun, handed the letter back to Will, lifted a rope, and handed it to Will. "Grab the rope; I'll pull you in."

"Come aboard Mr. Smith." The man tied the dog to the rail and offered a hand up to Will.

"My name is Peter Rabedeux."

"You're kin to…?"

Peter interrupted, "Pierre Rabedeux, du Pont's wagon master—he's my father. He told me about you, the Texas Ranger."

"You the Captain?" Will looked nervously at the dog.

"Learning to be from Captain Hebert. My dog's name is Delta. She's upset because you're in Frenchie's boat." Peter rubbed Delta's ears. "She's never seen anyone else row his boat."

Along with food, the baker brought laundry and the *Picayune* to the Margaretta every weekday, leaving sufficient food and water on Fridays for the weekend. The baker built a brisk business tending the needs of seafarers.

Will handed the requisition to Peter, "I'll need a hundred kegs of powder and a quarter ton of lead bars. Do you have it on the boat?"

"I've got it. But how are you going to take it?" Peter glanced at the small rowboat.

"You tell me; you're the seaman." Will pointed toward the boat. "How much can I row upstream to where the *Columbia* is berthed?"

"Why don't you ship it like Mexico does… on a freighter?" Peter asked.

Will's left eyebrow raised "You telling me Mexico gets their munitions from du Pont?"

"Everyone buys our black powder. That's our business."

Will felt like he'd been punched in his stomach. It never occurred to him that du Pont sold munitions to Mexico.

"Are you all right?" Peter asked.

Will nodded. "I'm fine ...how much can I load?"

"I've seen this boat loaded with provisions. Munitions are heavier." Peter climbed down into the boat. "It's got seats for four people—that equates to about six hundred pounds. What do you weigh?

"One fifty last time I was on a scale." Will climbed in the boat.

They removed the seats, which eliminated some weight and made room for the kegs to stand. Will could sit on kegs to row. The bottom of the kegs were designed to keep the powder dry. They estimated the skiff could take four hundred pounds of munitions.

"That would be forty, ten-pound kegs." Peter scratched his head.

Will looked aft at the one man dingy. "What will the dinghy hold?"

Peter stammered, "I...can't...leave the *Margaretta.* I have to stay on the boat."

"I know...I don't need you...just the dinghy. We can stow at least ten kegs on the dingy, tied behind the rowboat."

Peter said, "That'll work. High tide be coming in about midnight. That will help."

They carefully loaded kegs of black powder in the two boats and covered the oak kegs with waterproof tarps.

After the rowboat and dinghy were loaded, they ate bread and cheese. Cooking was forbidden on board.

Will's mind was preoccupied with the difficult task ahead, but Peter talked incessantly. Like most young men, he had Texas fever and wanted to know everything about Texas.

Will finished eating and said to Peter, "If the munitions don't get there soon, there may no longer be a Texas."

The boats started banging together about midnight. The tide came in and would reach its crest by three. According to Peter, the incoming tide would bring the boats up to within six feet of the dock. At high tide, Will would be able to hoist the kegs onto the dock. When the tide receded, the small boats would be eighteen feet below the wharf.

There was a full moon and nary a cloud in the sky—desirable conditions for navigating, but not good for smuggling highly explosive materials. Will climbed into the boat, took the oars, and Peter released the line. The skiff rowed away. The dingy followed like a duckling trailing its mother. Peter watched Will row out of the cove.

When Will reached the *Columbia*, he secured the boats. Peter had told him where he would be able to locate a wheelbarrow on the wharf. Will located it and hoped anyone aboard the *Columbia* was asleep.

He began the task of lifting one keg after another over his head and onto the dock. Repetition of the mundane task made each movement more efficient. He wanted to rest but couldn't until every keg was secure in his stateroom. As he pushed the last load up the ramp, Will noticed the tide beginning to recede. With his last bit of energy, he pulled the skiff and then the dinghy onto the dock and turned them over, bottom side up.

He slipped into his stateroom and double-stacked the kegs in the wardrobe closet. Exhausted, he collapsed on the bed and drifted off to sleep.

Twelve hours later, afternoon heat and humidity woke Will from a deep sleep. Hungry, he headed out for food. As he was locking his cabin door, a well-dressed woman was doing the same across the way. They turned at the same time.

She was startled when she recognized him and said, "So we meet again, Mr. Smith."

"Fancy meeting you here." Will tipped his hat to the woman he shared champagne and oysters with in Matagorda. "You're turning around, I assume?"

"I beg your pardon," she exclaimed, taking the comment as a disparaging remark.

"I meant, you're going back to Texas?"

"I'm here to shop." She turned and scurried away toward the gangway.

"I thought you were from here?" Will called out.

"You must have misunderstood." She hurried down the ramp without looking back.

Interesting, Will thought. *Now, she's trying to avoid me.* He followed her at a distance. The yellow parasol made her easy to spot. She stopped to admire a store window. Will stopped at a nearby food vendor's cart, which provided not only cover, but much-needed sustenance.

The mystery woman entered an unmarked shop with three brass balls hanging over the entrance. Will sat on a nearby bench and finished his bowl of gumbo. When she exited the shop, she appeared to be in a better mood. Her next stop was a ladies' boutique on Canal Street. It appeared she would be in the store for a while, so he returned to the food vendor's cart for more gumbo.

Will asked the food vendor, "What kind of shop is that? With the balls over the door."

"It's Ogden's Pawn Shop. A good place to pawn those fancy revolvers you're wearing." The cart vendor handed Will his seafood-laden gumbo.

After another bowl of gumbo, Will checked out the pawn shop.

A tiny man with a limp greeted Will when he entered. The store was long but narrow, less than twelve feet wide. The length seemed to go on forever. Musical instruments hung from the ceiling, and the shelves were cluttered with silver bowls and candelabras.

"Can I help you?" the owner, Ogden Johnson, asked.

Will looked around, "Do you have a small Derringer?"

"What caliber?" Ogden opened a cabinet door to reveal a dozen Derringers."

"May I see the shiny new one?"

"You have good taste. That's a brand new Navy issued fifty-four-caliber made by Henry Derringer. Never been fired." The pawnbroker peered over the counter. "I'd trade even for one of your Colt Patersons."

"Can't do that. How much for the Derringer?" Will motioned for the gun to hold.

"I've got to have fifty dollars. May I hold one of your Patersons? I've never seen one before."

The pawnbroker cradled the Colt Paterson like it was a newborn baby. He placed it on his workbench and then handed the Navy Derringer to Will.

Will cocked the Derringer "My gun's loaded," he warned.

Ogden asked, "May I take it apart to see how it works?"

"Make sure you can put it back together." Will pulled the Derringers trigger.

The pawnbroker was a gunsmith—he quickly broke the Colt Paterson down into its three parts. "You a Texas Ranger?"

"Yes. How would you know?"

"Samuel Colt only made two hundred and fifty of the Colt Patersons. All of them ended up with the Texas Rangers."

Will saw the low serial number on the new Navy gun. "How did you come by a Navy issued gun?"

"I never discuss where items come from." The pawnbroker laid Will's gun down on the counter and motioned for the Derringer back.

"Brand new—never been fired, serial number five." Will handed it to the pawnbroker.

"That's why I'm asking fifty U.S. dollars for it." The pawnbroker put the gun up.

"Would you take forty?" Will asked.

Ogden shook his head. "Far as I know, it's the only one that's ever been offered for sale." Ogden put his hands on the counter and looked Will in the face "Would you take forty for either of your guns?"

Will shook his head, reached into his vest pocket, pulled out some bills, and counted out fifty U.S. dollars.

"Anything else you need?" The pawn broker tucked the money in his pocket.

"I want a gold wedding band and a box of cartridges for this Derringer," Will said.

"Anything in particular you looking for in a ring?" Ogden placed the cartridges on the counter.

"Simple, like my mother's wedding band."

Ogden reached under the counter and brought up a tray of rings.

Will pointed at one that looked closest to his mother's gold ring. "How much?"

"Two U.S. Dollars for the ring." Ogden pushed the cartridges toward Will, "I'll give you twelve cartridges."

"Thanks…I'll take the ring." Will gave Ogden two dollars and put the ring in his pocket, loaded a cartridge, and tucked the new gun in his waistband. For a second night, he headed back to the *Columbia* to smuggle explosives.

Chapter Twenty-six

On the night of March 27, 1842, Will rowed in the second load without incident. He stored the kegs between his bed and the bulkhead, then covered them in tarps to make sure they couldn't be seen from the doorway. Tomorrow he would make the last trip, rowing in the lead bars and cartridge paper.

Church bells and seagulls mulling about were the only sounds on the riverfront. The obnoxious birds feasted on the riff-raff left by the receding tide. The bells reminded Will it was time to rise.

Will washed the best he could. Near noon, he found a small saloon with outdoor dining that offered a limited menu. Will ordered the Easter special, chicken and dumplings, and then ate under the shade of a giant oak tree. Will watched families in Easter attire—men sporting fashionable top hats, women in silk hats and bonnets, and children in new spring clothes—find their places for the Easter Parade to begin. Will smiled thinking about Bella and the possibilities of a family.

Will returned to his stateroom to prepare for the final run. He left time for a siesta, something he learned from Juan so he would be energized for his trip. He awoke and dressed in light clothes. Because of the considerable weight, he chose not to carry his guns and ammunition. He hid his guns in the wardrobe behind kegs of powder. Will was already in the skiff waiting when the afternoon tide rolled out. The dingy would be left with Peter; the skiff would be loaded with the last of the munitions.

Will brought the skiff alongside the *Margaretta* like an old salt and handed the line to Peter who was waiting for him. Peter walked the boat to the aft, secured it, and did the same with the dingy.

Will handed a sack to Peter. "Fresh bread and cheese."

"Much obliged… supplies getting low." Peter broke the crusty baguette and took a bite. "I've decided I want to go to Texas," he said. He lay the bread sack on the deck.

"Things aren't too good in Texas right now."

"Nothing could be worse than tending a boatload of bat shit for weeks at a time." Peter flung his arms. "I'm tired of the smell and being alone. If it weren't for my dog, I'd go bat shit crazy."

Will extended a hand. "Bat shit crazy?"

Peter pulled Will into the *Margaretta*. "You know, gunpowder is just bat shit, sulphur, and charcoal. If it blows, my ass is going to be blown all over this cove!"

Will smiled, "We can't let that happen, can we? When you planning to leave for Texas?"

"Soon as Captain Hebert relieves me next week, that's what I'm going to do."

Will wrote on a piece of paper. "Find Captain Jack Hayes, Commander of the Texas Rangers. He headquarters in San Antonio near the Alamo. He'll make you a Texas Ranger…that is if you have a gun and a good horse."

"Seriously, a Texas Ranger?" Peter looked at Will's note.

They loaded the skiff and said their goodbyes. At midnight, Will rowed out with one hundred five-pound bars of lead and fifty pounds of cartridge paper.

Once in the Mississippi, Will was confronted with a steady wind from the south. The howling wind blew water over the transom. Will stopped rowing, grabbed two of the five-pound bars, and dropped them in the river. The boat was about to sink. Will frantically dropped bars until the boat trimmed up enough to start bailing. Wet and cold, he shivered in the wind as he rowed on to the berth of the *Columbia*.

The cartridge paper rolled and wrapped in oilcloth survived with only a few of the pages damp. Seventy-nine lead bars remained. Twenty-one bars were sacrificed to save the lot. Lead could be found in Texas, but black powder was difficult to come by.

Will unloaded the boat and returned it and the wheel barrel. Then he headed to his stateroom, wiggled out of his wet clothes, and hung them on the railing to dry.

Monday morning, he woke to the sounds of the hustle and bustle of the ship's crew loading cargo. He donned pants to retrieve his clothes from the railing. Will noticed the mystery woman's stateroom door was open but went about his business of preparing for the day. Dressed, he opened the wardrobe to discover his guns gone and the gold ring missing.

Without hesitation, Will hurried to the stateroom across from his. The door was still slightly ajar. He opened it and found it unoccupied: no luggage or clothes. His mind raced, *She's done it again!*

He headed for Ogden's Pawn Shop where he found Ogden Johnson dusting his shelves.

Will asked, "Where are my guns?"

"How would I know?" Ogden laid his duster on the counter.

"If you bought them, you better hand them over, now!" Will came around the counter.

Ogden begged, "Please don't hurt me. I don't have them...but, I'll tell you where they are."

"Where is she?" Will grabbed a handful of Ogden's shirt.

"She's headed to Saint Louis on the *Queen*. It leaves at two."

"You better be right." Will let go of his shirt.

"She left here less than an hour ago. I wouldn't take them because I knew she stole them from you."

"Where's the *Queen of St. Louie* berthed?"

"Upriver... First Street Wharf," Ogden gasped.

Will ran north as fast as he could. When he arrived, a long line waited to board the *Queen of St. Louie*. The mystery woman was nowhere to be seen. Without a ticket, he couldn't get on board to search. He paced the length of the stern-wheeler frantically, hoping for a glimpse of her. Not seeing her on board, he went back to where the long line of passengers formed. Remembering how James Thomas got on the *Columbia,* Will got in line.

A stately carriage pulled up at the end of the growing line. A well-dressed gentleman drove the one-horse carriage. Will saw the yellow parasol. There she was, assisted down from the carriage by a man old enough to be her father. Will walked to the back of their carriage for a better view.

The man hollered, "Baggage boys!"

Three teenage boys appeared out of nowhere. One grabbed her matching luggage. The other two removed a large wooden trunk that had been tied to the luggage rack. The gentleman walked her toward the front of the line. Many in line seemed to know who he was and stood back. No one objected to their butting in.

Will made his move from behind with one last look to make sure it was her. He was certain the woman was the wicked whore he'd tangled with before.

"Excuse me, Miss, I think you have something that belongs to me." Will grabbed her right wrist.

She turned and screamed, "Let go, you bastard!"

Will reached into her skirt pocket and retrieved his Navy Derringer.

Surprised by Will's boldness, her companion yelled, "How dare you treat a lady that way."

The stunned baggage boys saw Will was armed and set the trunk down. "Mista, we don't want no trouble," they said and then ran.

"Are you her *ponce?*" Will looked at the man.

"I beg your pardon?" the man said.

A crowd gathered, and Will tucked the derringer in his waistband.

"Open the trunk." Will pulled her down and demanded, "I said open it!"

A man's wallet fell from her petticoat onto the wharf's deck. "That's mine!" The man recognized his custom-made leather wallet.

"You're lucky if that's all she took," Will said.

The man reached for his vest pocket. "My pocket watch is gone."

Will extended his free hand and said to her, "Give me his watch."

She reluctantly pulled the pocket watch from her bosom. She placed it in Will's open hand, and then grabbed his fingers and bit down on him like a wild animal.

The gentleman said, "You little tart. I helped you, and you stole from me?"

Will held her with both hands as she tried to break away. His right hand bled on her satin dress.

"Mister, would you open the trunk for me?" Will grimaced in pain. "You'll find two Colt revolvers. They belong to me."

The man cautiously opened the trunk's lid. Will's guns lay in the lift-out tray on top of an assortment of ill-gotten gains. As he held the woman with his bleeding hand, Will managed to strap on his guns.

"Where's the gold ring you stole from my stateroom?" Will raised his free hand, threatening to strike her.

"No! Please," she begged.

"Is this it?" The man held out a gold ring, "It somehow got attached to my gold watch fob."

"Thank you." Will took it and put the ring in his pocket.

"I should thank you for protecting me from this... no good whore." The man turned and climbed onto his carriage.

"You want to press charges against her?" Will called out.

"She has a ticket to St. Louis, purchased I'm sure with a worthless check, leaving me holding the bag," the man said. "So long as she leaves and never returns to New Orleans, I'll not press charges." He shook the reins and made a turn toward town.

Will knelt down on one knee to examine the trunk that was full of stolen goods. He heard a click and turned; a sharp blade protruded from the end of the yellow parasol. Will attempted to roll out from under the colorful umbrella that was now an instrument of death, but he felt a sharp pain in his back just below the right shoulder blade. He twisted and saw the woman holding her bloody parasol over him. Now flat on his back, she lunged the weapon towards his heart. Unable to move his injured arm, Will pulled the derringer from his waistband with his left hand, awkwardly thumbed the hammer back, and fired. The fifty-four-caliber ball was at such close range that it caused a massive exit wound to her upper torso. Her body crumpled on top of him.

Strangers pulled Will out from under the woman. A man on each side steadied him and walked him through the throng of gawking bystanders to a nearby doctor's office. The doctor saw the blood that covered him and thought Will was a goner. He quickly learned the blood was that of the dead woman who had tried to kill him.

Doc Puryear examined Will and knew what to do. Will's scapula bone had stopped the knife's blade from penetrating vital organs. The doctor was more concerned about infection from the bite on Will's hand.

"This is going to hurt, Mr. Smith." The doctor sat down on a three-legged stool. "Would you like a pint or two for your comfort? It's Kentucky's finest. Just a dollar a pint."

"One pint would do," Will grimaced as he tried to raise up on his elbows to reach for his wallet.

"Don't be moving around, we don't want it to start bleeding again." The doctor put a hand on Will's arm and asked, "Where's your wallet?"

"I've got three silver dollars in my right pocket." Will raised his buttocks.

The doctor retrieved them and called out, "Samson!"

"Yes, sir." A large black man came in from the foyer.

The doctor held up two silver dollars. "Run down to Boyer's and hurry back with two pints of his best Kentucky Whiskey."

Samson hurried down the alleyway. The doctor looked at Will. "The men who brought you and your arsenal said you blew a hole through your assailant the size of a melon. Is that right?"

"I don't remember much about the incident. It all happened so fast."

"You always carry that much firepower?" The doctor packed the bowl of his clay pipe with short-cut tobacco.

"When I'm ranging." Will attempted to sit up, "I usually carry a saddle-gun."

"You a hunter then?" The doctor lit his pipe and blew a large puff of smoke.

"I guess… you could say that." Will grimaced.

"What do you hunt?" The doctor puffed his pipe.

"Indians." Will stifled a cough.

Samson returned with two pint-bottles of whiskey. The doctor opened the first one and threw the cork out the window. The doctor handed Will the open bottle. "Sit up and drank as much of this as you can." He started to open the other one.

"Let's wait to open the second bottle. I don't think I'll need that much," Will protested.

The doctor pulled the cork, "The second one is for me. I can't have my patients drinking alone."

"How long's this going to take? I've got a boat to catch."

"That'll depend on you and how much pain you can handle." The doctor took a swig. "If you don't squirm and fight me, I'll be finished in five minutes."

Will stifled a another cough. "Then just do it!"

"Samson, I'm going to need you," the doctor called. "Lay face down...place your face in the cradle. Let your hands dangle off the sides of the table."

Will did as he was told. Samson came in and took a chair in front of the treatment table. Samson took hold of Will's hands. The doctor began the first stitch. It would take five more to finish. Now Will understood Samson's purpose in the doctor's practice.

A sling was fitted to prevent movement of the right arm. The doctor said, "The less you move that arm the faster it'll heal."

"Thank you, Doc." Will fumbled to open his wallet. "What do I owe you?"

"Your last silver dollar will do."

Will took a carriage to the *Columbia.* Visitors were waiting for him on the dock.

"It's about time you showed up. Delta and I was fixing to go looking for you." Peter picked up his sea bag.

"Who's watching the *Margaretta?*" Will strained to pet Delta with his good arm.

"Captain Hebert came this morning." Peter looked at Will who was shirtless except for the sling and bandages. "What happened to you?"

"Tangled with a wildcat, and I would just as soon not discuss it." Will looked at the sea bag. "Where you headed?"

"To Texas, with you, If that's alright?"

Will nodded. "If you can find me something to eat...I haven't eaten today."

"I can do that—if you'll take Delta." Peter handed the leash to Will.

"I'll be in my stateroom. I'll tell the first mate you're traveling with me; he'll show you where to find me."

Will slowly made his way up the ramp and finally reached his stateroom. He didn't feel well and spread out on the bed. Delta, sensing Will's distress, curled up at Will's feet.

Peter arrived with seafood gumbo and fresh-baked bread. Will woke to the smells, ate what he could, and when he finished, fell back to sleep. The events of the last few days had taken their toll.

Will came down with a high fever that made him delirious at times. Worried, Peter told the first mate about Will's condition. The doctor was sent for the next morning.

After examining Will, the doctor determined he had pneumonia and should be taken to a nearby hospital. Will was loaded on a horse-drawn ambulance for transport.

"Are you kin?" The doctor asked Peter.

"No, just a friend. We both work for du Pont."

"You work for du Pont, the richest man in America?" The doctor looked at Will then at Peter. "Why don't you ride with me?"

Will muttered, "No Peter, you have to stay...you need to get supplies to Texas...remember?"

"Sure, I remember." Peter bent over so Will could whisper in his ear.

"The munitions must get to Captain Jack Hayes. He'll be waiting for me in Matagorda...You have to make sure they get to him. The future of Texas depends on you."

"Don't worry I'll take care of it," Peter assured Will.

Will nodded and shut his eyes.

Peter touched Will's good hand and gently squeezed.

Will acknowledged the touch. "The *Columbia* will be leaving soon." Will tried to raise his head. "Please gather my things...as I won't be going to Texas."

Peter looked at the ambulance driver and said, "Hold up while I get his things."

Peter quickly returned with Will's possessions. He placed them in the wagon next to Will's stretcher and said goodbye.

Will struggled to speak, "Did you get…my saddle?"

"Your saddle, guns, and tack are in the wagon." Peter stepped back.

The ambulance moved out, followed by the doctor's carriage.

Will turned a year older during his recovery and rehabilitation. His hair and beard had grown longer. On the nineteenth of April, he boarded the *Columbia* for Matagorda. Will was still frail but was gaining strength each day. Again, Will had to postpone his plans to go to Santa Fe.

Still in love, the gold ring in his pocket, Will longed for Bella. He constantly thought about the intimate moments they'd had together.

But for now, Texas needed him more.

Chapter Twenty-seven

In Matagorda, Will bought a horse and headed for Austin. When he arrived, he noticed that the once busy center of government appeared abandoned. Vegetation now grew in its roadways. Raccoons occupied the President's vacant house. When in Austin, Sam Houston preferred the Eberly boarding house over the mansion built for Lamar. Will also chose the Eberly for short stays in Austin as his cabin was still in need of a roof.

Mrs. Eberly met him at the door. "Welcome home, Will." They hugged.

"Thank you, Mrs. Eberly. Do you have a room for me?"

"As you can see every door's open," Mrs. Eberly said as she pointed down the hall. "Pick any room you like."

"Where is everyone?"

"Sam Houston's Secretary of State and Peg-Leg Ward are the only Texas officials here." Mrs. Eberly shook her head. "Sam Houston has managed to scare everyone off…except the damn Indians!"

Will tried to jest, "You talk that way about your President?"

"You know I'm right! Besides, he ain't here, and I don't care if he ever comes back."

"Why would you say that?"

"He's constantly talking about moving the Capitol back to Houston. I overheard him complaining about how bad things are here with the

Indians raiding and the Mexican Army on its way. Times are hard enough, Will. We don't need our President talking bad about Austin."

Fenwick barged in, interrupting their conversation. He slapped Will on the back, "How's my brother?"

"Ouch!" Will turned toward his younger sibling.

"What's wrong?" Fenwick asked.

"Got a stab wound that hasn't healed." Will hugged Fenwick with one arm.

"Who stabbed you?" Fenwick waited for an answer that didn't come.

Will picked up his haversack. "Can you take care of my horse?"

Harvey came in, "I've taken care of your horse, so tell us who stabbed you."

Will started up the stairs to his room. His brothers followed, excited about Will's return. They continued to cajole Will about the stab wound, but he was determined not to tell them.

"How's Mother?" Will put his things in the armoire.

"About as good as can be expected," Harvey responded. "She thinks you're headed for Santa Fe to find Fayette."

"That was my plan, but with the Mexicans planning an invasion, and the Indians taking advantage of the situation, I best stay and fight with my brothers." Will looked at Fenwick then Harvey.

"We're with you Will, just tell us what to do," Fenwick said as Harvey nodded in agreement.

"Where's Mother?" Will asked.

"Next door at Lorenzo's. She's helping Margaret prepare for childbirth." Harvey smiled.

"Already?" Will raised his bushy eyebrows "Elnora's just barely a year old."

"Lorenzo and Margaret didn't waste any time!" Harvey rocked on his heels.

"When's she due?"

"Soon." Fenwick moved to the door. "Let's go surprise them."

The door at the Van Cleve home was open. Fenwick entered followed by Will and Harvey. "Look who's home!" Fenwick announced.

Lorenzo rose from his chair next to the canopy bed where Margaret was lying. Rebeckah sat in a rocker. Her eyes lit up when she saw Will. She waved her fingers gingerly as not to wake Elnora, sleeping in her arms.

Lorenzo embraced Will, "Welcome home."

Margaret raised her arms. Will leaned over and gave her a kiss. "How are you, sister?"

"I'm hurting Will...but I'm glad your home." Margaret held his hands.

"Look at your niece." Rebeckah stood and held Elnora up for Will to see.

Will hugged his mother, trying not to disturb the sleeping child. "How are you?"

"I miss your father terribly. This baby makes life bearable." Rebeckah touched Will's face, "When are you going to settle down with a good wife and have children?"

"In good time." Will kissed his Mother on the forehead.

Rebeckah motioned toward the door. "Why don't you boys go on outside? I'll holler if I need you."

The men retreated to the shade of an oak tree behind Lorenzo's cabinet shop—a place where they could talk of war and politics at an outdoor table.

Lorenzo straddled the end of the bench. "I got your letter, Will, about taking the family to Mustang Ridge. With an infant and Margaret expecting, we couldn't leave Austin. We all decided to take our chances here."

"Harvey and I weren't leaving without them," Fenwick said.
Harvey spit his chaw of tobacco, "Besides...Mother wasn't about to leave little sister."

"I understand." Will smiled, "Times like this a family needs to stay together."

Lorenzo turned on the bench, "Captain Hayes sent us three kegs of black powder and ten pounds of lead from San Antonio. It was delivered by two Rangers. The one named Rabedeux said he met you in New Orleans. That you asked him to accompany the munitions to Texas."

"Good; he made it with the munitions." Will smiled.

"He said you got stabbed while in New Orleans and was hospitalized," Lorenzo said.

"I was hospitalized with pneumonia. Not on account of the stabbing. I'm well now."

"Who was it that stabbed you?" Lorenzo leaned toward Will.

Agitated, Will raised his eyebrows and said, "A thief robbed me; tried to kill me. If you don't mind, I'd like to know what's been done to prepare for the invasion."

Lorenzo leaned back. "We've filled every man's powder bag and given them lead to make their own rounds. What's left is stored in the root cellar at the Eberly."

"How many men fit to fight?"

"Last count about sixty." Harvey pushed back from the table.

"You plan to take on the Mexican Army and fight the Indians with sixty militiamen?" Will pressed the palms of his hands down on the table.

"We have a few women like Mrs. Eberly who have guns," Fenwick said.

"Wouldn't y'all be safer behind the walls of Kenney's Fort?" Will looked at his brothers.

"We ain't leaving, Will," Fenwick said.

"Even if the entire Mexican Army attacks?" Will, exasperated, dropped his head.

Lorenzo shifted his weight. "Will…you have as much invested in Austin as any of us. We can't just abandon our homes. Staying put is our only option."

Will looked at them, knowing the issue was settled.

That evening, a baby boy named Cortes Van Cleve was born. Lorenzo chose the name: Cortes, the Spanish word for courteous.

Late in April of 1842, Maria Rowland sat quietly, knitting a Christening gown for her grandnephew. It was a warm spring day and all the windows were open. She heard a pop of a mule skinner's whip, and a familiar shrill whistle, followed by wagons creaking. The sounds came from the Rio Rancho below the Taos trading post.

"Bella, my husband is coming," Maria called out and quickly put her knitting away.

Bella looked at Maria, "How do you know?"

"Only my Juan can crack the whip like that… and it is his whistle." Maria clasped her hands and gave thanks to God for her husband's return.

Fayette shuffled in as fast as he could. "Three large wagons and riders are coming up the road."

"Fayette, please go tell everyone Juan is coming and to stand at the gate. We must give him a proper welcome."

The small entourage of family and workers were rounded up to greet John Rowland.

When asked, "Fayette, how do you know it is Señor Rowland that is coming from the Rio?"

Fayette answered, "If Momma Maria says it's him, I believe her."

Three empty freight wagons, each pulled by six Missouri Mules, entered the compound gate. They were followed by six well-armed riders. The red dust kicked up by wagons lingered inside the adobe walls. It choked throats and burned nostrils—temporarily blinding the eyes of the entourage. The corner of the baby's blanket did little to protect the infant's face. Bella took the five-month-old child she'd named William inside.

John climbed down from the wagon and went to the open arms of his wife. Friends and family gathered around the happy couple. Back slapping and embraces continued as the wranglers unharnessed the mules and horses.

Fayette watched from the store's porch. He saw Bella take baby William into the house. Protective of his little cousin, Fayette went to check on them. He found Bella bent over the crying baby, wiping dust and tears from its tiny smudged face.

"Can I help?" Fayette asked.

"Yes, please. Will you watch William while I get a wet cloth? This dust is horrible." Bella went to the kitchen.

The Rowland family entered the casa, speaking rapidly in Spanish. Fayette's Spanish vocabulary had improved to the extent he could follow most conversations. Maria asked the size of the Ranchero. Fayette didn't understand John's answer but saw that his Momma Maria was impressed.

"Enough land for all our family to farm?" Maria smiled at John.

"Sí, if they wish to come to California," John said softly.

Maria hugged and kissed John. She seemed happy. Fayette was happy for her but concerned for his future. Would he ever see his family again?

In the winter of 1842, John Rowland learned of the surrender of the Santa Fe Pioneers. Governor Manuel Armijo knew the Workman-Rowland caravan had left the territory before their surrender. Rowland or his partners couldn't have assisted the Texans anyway. Yet Armijo was convinced they were part and parcel of the Texas coup.

Padre Martinez on a visit to Taos told John, "The Texans who survived were marched to Perote Prison near Mexico City."

John worried that Will or other members of Fayette's family may have been on the ill-fated caravan from Austin. But he dared not inquire about them for fear of again being accused of spying on Texas' behalf.

Everyone at the trading post was caught up in the excitement of the move to California. John Rowland seldom ventured outside the walls of his compound, wishing to avoid any confrontations with the governor or Mexican Loyalists. He avoided talk of politics with customers.

The Rowlands were disappointed; old friends and some members of Maria's own family considered them traitors. Maria took comfort from John's assurance that new neighbors would welcome them to the San Gabriel Valley with open arms.

John Rowland had been away for seven months, but breakfast on his first day back was like he'd never left. The family came together as always, each in their same chair. John sat at the head of the table surrounded by Maria, Bella, Fayette, and Estevan. Maria's third cousin, Estevan Martinez, had started eating with the family shortly after Bella's baby was born.

Fayette listened intently to the questions asked about the trip. When asked how long it would take to get to the new home, John told them and then described the house he was building. Everyone at the table sounded as if they were going, including Estevan.

Fayette interrupted "What about me?"

"Do you wish to go to California?" John asked.

"I don't know what I want." Tears streamed down his face. "I'm just a ten-year-old-boy...what do I know?" Fayette got up and stormed out of the house.

Maria jumped up to go after him, but John gently touched her arm. "Please let him be. Fayette needs time to think. I will go to him, after I have eaten this wonderful meal you've prepared."

As Maria began to clear the table, John looked at Maria and stood, "Now I will go attempt to help a ten-year-old make the biggest decision of his life."

John found Fayette in the wool house. The boy was sitting on the floor among large bags of shorn-wool, petting Caleb. John laid his black hat on a bag of wool.

"May I join you, Fayette?" With some difficulty, John got down on the wool house floor. John took a deep breath. "What you said at breakfast, Fayette, is true. A boy your age shouldn't be making tough decisions. That's a parent's responsibility."

David Bowles

Fayette looked up at John and said, "My parents aren't here."

"I know, Fayette. Maria and I have tried to be your parents in their absence. In doing so, we have come to love you as our own. It breaks our hearts to think about what you have endured since the Comanche captured you." John stroked Fayette's back. "Fayette, you are one tough hombre."

"I don't feel tough." Fayette sniffled.

"Through no fault of your own, you have been thrown in the middle of some complicated situations that are difficult to explain." John shook his head. "Why things like this happen, I'll never know. But they do."

John explained. He hoped Nuevo Mexico would become a part of Texas. His unpopular views branded him a traitor and made his family outcasts. Because the territory was no longer safe for them, he was forced to find a place in California to live.

"I consider you and Caleb family." John hugged Fayette. "Maria and I love you as our son. Our hearts will break to say goodbye."

"Me too," Fayette sniffled.

"You may come with us if you wish. It will be a long journey over the mountains and through a dry desert. But once there, you'll think you're in heaven. The Missionaries who found the beautiful valley named it well: The Valley of the Angels."

"Sounds like Austin, except we have no Angels…just buffalo and Indians." Fayette stroked Caleb's fur.

"In this valley, oranges and grapes grow everywhere." John spread his arms and said, "You can ride up and pick the sweet fruit from horseback. Everything is green, even in the winter."

Fayette looked at him in disbelief.

"You understand that we can't cross the desert during the summer. There are many preparations that must be made. Fayette, you have months to decide. The decision is yours to make and no one else can make it for you."

"I want to go home…to Texas. My mother and sisters need me," Fayette sobbed.

John placed a hand on Fayette's shoulder. "When the wagons come in the summer, I will put you on a wagon to Independence."

That night, Fayette listened to John and Maria's bedroom talk.

"Fayette is just a boy. He can't go alone to Texas."

"He is not just any boy Maria. There is something about Fayette… he is special. He thinks like an adult. He made it from Austin, wounded and with no shoes…walking on rocks, ice, and snow. I don't know any man who could survive such a trip as that."

"I know, but he needs somebody with him. Someone to protect him." Maria rolled away from John.

John sat up in bed. "Maria, I know who can go with him."

"Who is it you want to take Fayette?"

"Peter Duncan mentioned he wanted to go back east. Peter doesn't want to stay here or go to California. We will send them to Independence together."

"Good. Now I go to sleep." Maria fluffed her feather pillow.

In the next room, Fayette liked the conversation he'd overheard.

Peter Duncan, the bookkeeper for the Workman-Rowland Partnership, was an acquaintance of their mutual friend and lawyer William Dryden. Peter had earned their trust and loyalty.

Rowland had hoped Peter would make the exodus to California, but Peter had no desire to go farther west.

Peter, a middle-aged bachelor, had taken a liking to Fayette shortly after the boy arrived at the trading post. He taught him about business, including weights and measures, as well as ethical business dealings.

Peter and Fayette would be able to travel together as far as Independence. There, Fayette would be left with John Rowland's friend, Lewis Jones, a prominent citizen and founder of Independence. Lewis would then contact Fayette's family in Texas without violating

John Rowland's agreement with Governor Armijo not to communicate with Texas or Texans. John and Maria Rowland slept well, knowing Peter would get Fayette safely back to his family.

Sam Houston was now into the sixth month of his second term as President of Texas. His predecessor, Mirabeau Lamar had left the Republic of Texas finances in shambles. Congress adjourned without appropriating funds for the military or the Santa Fe Expedition. Without authority from Congress, Lamar took $89,000 from the treasury to finance the ill-fated mission. Houston's administration was incensed, yet did nothing, not wanting to expose Texas' financial crisis to the world.

Captain Jack Hays' Rangers were the nearest thing to an organized army Texas had. Will found his longtime friend, Captain Jack Hays, in his small cluttered office in San Antonio.

"How are you, Captain?"

"Good…thanks to you Willie. I owe you big time. What could I ever do to repay you, Willie?"

"For starters, never call me Willie again."

Captain Jack got up and embraced Will. "It will be hard after all these years, but from now on, you are Will Smith, Texas Ranger." Captain Jack sat back down behind his desk. "I heard you were stabbed and damn near died. How in the hell did that happen?"

Will's face turned red. "I was stabbed in the back…the other favor you can do for me is to never ask me about it again." Will caught his breath, "And if someone should ever mention it in your presence, I ask that you shoot the son of a bitch."

Captain Jack laughed. "I guess that means you're ready to range again."

"That's why I'm here."

"I see you still have your pair of Colt Paterson's… and the Carbine." Captain Hays started filling out Will's enlistment papers.

Will pulled up his shirt to reveal the Navy Derringer. "I also have a fifty-four-caliber percussion Navy Derringer."

"How in the hell did you come by that?" Captain Jack motioned that he wanted to see it.

Will handed it to Captain Jack. He held it in his palm like it was his first-born child.

"Never seen a caliber this large in a Derringer." Captain Jack saw the USN Mark 5.

"Looks new. You ever fired it?" Captain Jack handed it back to Will.

"Just once."

"Make a big hole?"

Will nodded. "Especially the exit wound."

Captain Jack surmised Will killed his target. Instinctively he knew it had to do with the stabbing but didn't dare to ask.

Will was assigned to patrol the Nueces River from the confluence of the Frio River to Carrizo Springs. The one-hundred-twenty-mile length of his patrol was a two-day ride from San Antonio. His mission was to scout for Mexican troops and protect settlers from Indians. He failed to encounter any Mexican soldiers but did destroy an Indian village on the Frio.

Fifty miles northwest of Will's assigned patrol, Mexican General Adrian Woll passed through Uvalde Canyon undetected with twelve hundred troops on their way to capture San Antonio and raise yet another Mexican flag. On the eleventh day of September, 1842, after an intense two hour battle and a long standoff led by Samuel Maverick, John Twohig, and George Van Ness, San Antonio was again lost to the Mexican army. Three days later, General Woll marched two hundred and fifty captured defenders out of San Antonio to Mexico City. They were greeted by Texans from the Santa Fe Expedition at Perote Prison. They would not be released until April 1843.

The Texas Congress met to try and finance an invasion into Mexico. Ten million acres of public lands were appropriated for the purpose. President Sam Houston vetoed the enabling legislation, not wanting another war with Mexico. He feared a war could jeopardize any chance of annexation by the United States. Instead, he sent Dr. Ashbel Smith to Great Britain and France. James Reilly was sent to Washington to request help in peace negotiations with Mexico.

People who once supported Sam Houston now threatened the President. Despondent over the debt of his government and a new bride that wanted him home, Sam Houston seriously considered resigning. Only his friend and secretary, G.W. Terrell, could persuade him not to.

Appeasing those who wanted another war with Mexico, Sam Houston ordered Alex Somerville to muster up enough volunteers to retaliate. Will joined their camp in San Antonio. On the twenty-fifth day of November, 1842, seven hundred volunteers left San Antonio for the Mexican border.

The Texans easily took Laredo on the eighth day of December. The official punitive raid accomplished, Commander Somerville ordered the volunteers to disband. Only one-hundred-eighty-nine of the volunteers obeyed. The others elected William Fisher their Commander planning to invade Mexico on their own.

Will said "Commander Somerville, I will be pulling out in the morning."

"I'm glad you chose to obey my orders, Will." Commander Somerville looked up from his campaign desk.

Will asked, "Would you give Captain Hays a message for me?" Will stood at attention.

"Certainly, Will. I assume you'll be heading back to Austin?"

"No, I'm not, that's why I need you to give Captain Hays a message."

"Well, what is it?" Somerville asked.

"I appreciate his offer…but I'm going alone."

"Where you going?"

"Captain Hays knows. I would appreciate him advising my family."

"That's the message. You're going alone, and tell that to your family?"

Will nodded and said, "It was a pleasure serving with you."

"Likewise." Somerville stood and shook his hand. "Your service is appreciated."

Chapter Twenty-eight

*W*ill followed the Rio Grande for three days to a spot on his hand-drawn map marked Piedras Negras. He crossed the shallow waters of the Rio Grande into Mexico where the river was called Rio Bravo. A small cantina, the only public building, was open. A small scattering of adobe huts with thatch roofs surrounded it. He smelled food cooking from a hut behind the cantina.

A burrow tied to the hitching post swished its tail and brayed as Will tied his horse. Concerned but not afraid, Will moved to the left side of the six-foot-wide open doorway. He saw two round tables with no one at them. He quickly moved to the other side and saw a small Mexican man who was far too old to harm anyone. The proprietor kept his hands on top of the bar for Will to see.

"Bienvenido amigo," the proprietor said, and then in perfect English, "We are all friends here."

"You speak English?" Will looked surprised.

"I also speak French and Spanish. Sometimes when I get excited, I speak all of them at once. My name is Jean Louis Berlandier." He extended his hand across the makeshift bar.

"I'm William Smith from Austin...everyone calls me Will, Mr. Berlandier." They shook hands.

"Will, everyone around here calls me Frenchie. First-time customers get a drink on the house. What's your pleasure? We have mescal and tequila." Frenchie smiled.

Will and Frenchie exchanged stories about how they happened upon Piedras Negras, which meant Black Rock in English. Then Frenchie told Will that he was born in 1805 on the border of France and Switzerland to a French mother and a Swiss father. He came to Mexico twenty years ago and became a mapmaker. He lived in San Antonio when it was under the Mexican flag, but despising war, he moved to a place he thought would never be involved in hostilities.

"The natives of Piedras Negras are a peaceful people." Frenchie pointed at his other customer, "Mostly Indians, some descendants of the first Spaniards to arrive over one hundred years ago."

The old man finished his tequila and waved a friendly goodbye.

Frenchie looked at Will and said, "I pray your presence here has nothing to do with the war between our countries?"

Will pulled the gold ring from his pocket. "I'm heading to Santa Fe to marry my darling and hopefully find my nephew who was captured by Comanche Indians."

"Congratulations on the marriage… and much success in finding your nephew."

"You married, Frenchie?" Will slipped the ring back in his pocket.

"Yes…very happily."

Will looked around. "Where is she?"

Frenchie filled Will's glass "She is in Matamoros."

"That's a long way from here," Will raised his glass.

"That is why we're so happy." Frenchie made a toast, "Here's to happiness."

Will asked, "Frenchie, do you have any food?"

"Yes, today we have prepared roasted goat and beans. I'll have a plate fixed for you." Frenchie hollered the order in Spanish out the back door to a shack. When the cook, a pretty Señorita, brought his food, Will knew why Frenchie was there.

Will slept in a hammock, one of several tied between cedar trees on the shady side of the cantina. A cool breeze blew out of the north, reminding Will it was winter. He'd buy warmer clothes once he reached El Paso del Norte.

On the last day of December 1842, Will rode through Apache Canyon without incident. He saw smoke from the chimineas of the adobe dwellings as he spurred his tired horse on into the night. When the horse wouldn't go any further, Will dismounted and led it into Santa Fe. No lights were on at the La Posada. Will led his horse into the corral behind the hotel. He slept in the tack room.

Morning light shined through cracks in the wooden door. He heard a woman say in Spanish "Whose horse is this?"

Will opened the door and said, "The horse is mine. Where is Ramon?"

She shook her head of salt-and-pepper hair and pointed at the horse. "Yours?"

"Sí," Will pointed toward the hotel and asked, 'Donde esta Miguel Miranda?"

"California." She pitched feed to the chickens running toward her.

"Bella?" Will asked.

"Sí, Bella el niño a California," the women pointed west.

"El niño?" Will exclaimed. "Bella has a baby?"

The woman politely nodded her head.

"Donde en California?" Will asked.

She shrugged her shoulders and continued to feed the chickens while looking for their eggs.

Will learned from the new owners that Miguel Miranda had sold La Posada and moved his family to California with John Rowland and William Workman to a place near the San Gabriel Mission in the

"Valley of the Angels." He asked about a red-headed boy and was told that Fayette was put on a wagon train for Independence last summer. Will was relieved to know Fayette was alive and well. He hoped his nephew was back in Austin by now.

Is Bella's child mine? he wondered. He had to know.

Will followed the Old Spanish Trail to California. He had traveled through the mountains of Colorado Territory, Utah, and Arizona, and followed the trail through the desert to the San Gabriel Mountains. Will stopped on a high vista to take in the view of the valley below. Never had he seen such a lush green valley.

At the mission he found people toiling in the garden. They directed him to the new home of John and Maria Rowland.

Maria came to the door, "Yes, what is it?" She assumed the shaggy mess of a man was a peasant looking for work or a handout.

"Maria, I'm Will Smith from Texas."

Her lips trembled, for she assumed he was dead or in a Mexican prison. "Juan, come quickly," Maria called, "it's Will from Texas. He's alive."

John was now called Juan Rowland, one of the patróns of the San Gabriel Valley.

Juan knew it was Will from his distinct hazel eyes. "Will, we were afraid you were dead. Please, come inside."

"I'm too dirty to come inside," Will said.

"You come in as you are." Juan put his arms around Will.

"My horse—"

"I'll see that your horse is taken care of. You can wash up inside." Will nodded feebly as Juan helped him inside. Exhausted, Will crumpled to the floor. A curandero was summoned. She was the only healer in the valley.

Will was placed on a feather bed in a guest room where the elderly curandero woman of Spanish and Indian heritage nursed him back to health. She stayed beside Will's bed, chanting the healing words of her ancestors. He woke only to take nourishment or relieve nature's calls. The journey had taken its toll.

He had survived on deer jerky and hard tack for months and went without drinking water through the desert. No one knew what was in the curandero's broth. It tasted terrible, but it worked.

Three nights later, Will woke to the sounds of Maria and Juan talking.

"We must tell him, Juan!"

"When he is well. I will tell him."

The next morning Maria brought breakfast to Will in bed. "How are you this morning, Will?"

"I am much better, thank you. Please tell me about Fayette?"

"We offered a reward for him. A half-breed they call Mescal brought Fayette in. He was sick. The Comanchero cut his heels so he couldn't run. For more than a year, your nephew was with me. I fed him and nursed him back to health. I loved Fayette, and I miss him. Is he happy to be home?"

Will touched her arm "I wasn't in Austin, Maria. I came here from Laredo."

"That's a long way."

Juan came into the room. "It's good to see you again, Will."

"The feeling is mutual." They shook hands.

"Juan, Will doesn't know if Fayette made it to Austin."

"We loved Fayette." Juan put his arm around Maria.

Maria wrung her hands and said, "Now I'm worried, not knowing if he made it home."

"I'm sure he is safe," Will tried to assure Maria. He changed the subject, "Remember John, you promised to be my best man at our wedding." Will pulled the ring out of his pocket. "I brought the ring all the way from New Orleans."

From the look on their faces, Will knew something was wrong. "Are Bella and the baby alright?"

"Yes, but how did you know about the baby?" Juan frowned.

"Please tell me how they are? The baby is mine...isn't it?"

Maria spoke first, "Yes, and she named him William...after you. When you didn't come with the expedition, we assumed you were dead or weren't coming back."

"Where are they?" Will tilted his head.

Juan said, "She married Estevan Martinez. The family christened Will as Martinez."

"Bella said she would wait for me," Will moaned.

Maria clasped her hands together "She did wait for you, Will. Bella came to live with us in Taos. I delivered the baby that will be two years old the third day of April."

"That's my birthday!" Will's lips trembled as he eased into a chair. "Is Bella here?" Will looked at Maria for the answer.

"She grieved for you and asked me what I would do. Estevan knew the child was yours, but he loves him as his own. Not many men would do that. We encouraged her to marry for the baby's sake." Maria held her hands to her heart and cried, "Estevan is a good husband and father. She is now with his child, which will be born this spring."

Juan said, "William, I'm sorry...but Bella is a happily married woman. I'm sorry you have come all this way for nothing."

"It weren't for nothing...I made a promise and I kept it."

"William, you did what you said you would do. That is what being a man is all about."

"I'll get my horse and be on my way," Will said.

"Your horse is in no condition to ride anywhere. Please stay a few more days. You and your horse need more time to rest. Besides, I want to show you around the Rancho La Puente."

Servants brought in a bathtub and hot water. Will cleaned up, shaved off his beard, and trimmed his handlebar moustache. Maria brought him clean clothes to wear and burned the others.

Juan took Will for a ride in his new Spanish carriage. It had only two wheels, a hard top, and seats for two. Pulled by a well-bred trotting horse, it moved swiftly around the 49,000-acre ranch.

The Rancho La Puente was a partnership between William Workman and Juan Rowland. Each partner had selected their own home site, and each had built comfortable residences. Additional land was made available for other family members who'd fled Nuevo México.

Juan stopped at the new adobe home of William Workman. They had lemonade made from native lemon trees that grew on the ranch. Will saw and tasted his first lemon. The lemon tasted bitter, but he drank several glasses of sweet lemonade. The partners and Will reminisced about his escape and their nearly being imprisoned. They made a toast to William G. Dryden, who went to prison so they could remain free.

"Dryden should be getting out of prison soon. Padre Martinez wrote that he heard Dryden planned to settle down in Rio Grande, a Texas town near Matamoros, Mexico." William Workman looked at Will and said, "If you're ever down that way, would you look him up for us? Let Juan and me know how he's doing?"

"I'll do that," Will said.

A rider rode up and handed a sealed envelope to Juan Rowland. He opened it and read it as Will and Workman watched. Both men could tell Juan was deeply pondering the message.

"Uncle Juan...do you wish me to return with a reply?" The young rider was Ramon Miranda, Bella's brother. Will didn't recognize him.

"Ramon...please wait on your horse for me. We'll discuss it. I'll give you an answer soon."

Ramon nodded. He went to his horse, untied it, mounted it, and waited.

Will said, "That boy is Ramon, Bella's brother, isn't he?"

"Yes, it is Ramon." Juan took a sip of lemonade. "Maria went to see Bella and told her you have come all the way from Texas for her. This is a shocking thing for our family. Bella is excited you're alive and well. She wishes to see you and introduce her son to you." Juan pressed his lips together.

"She wants to see me?" Will asked.

"She is waiting at our house with Maria and your son." Juan glanced at Ramon, "I need to give Ramon your answer."

"Yes, I want to see them."

Juan nodded at Ramon. Ramon turned his horse and galloped off with the message that Will had accepted Bella's invitation.

Juan drove the carriage slowly as if there was no hurry. They were lost in their own thoughts. The only sound was the cadence of the well-bred trotter on a hard-packed road.

A quarter of a mile from the Rowland home, Juan broke the silence, "You don't have to do this if you don't want to."

"I want to see her...it's awkward." Will shook his head, "I don't know what to say to her after nearly three years."

Juan said, "I'm sure it is strange for her as well. You will find the way to express your feelings, and Bella will also."

When they arrived, Bella's family was on the veranda with her mother, father, and brother Ramon. Maria and Bella waited inside with the child.

Will remembered Bella's family. They were cordial towards him. Their understanding of his feelings helped the situation. Bella came out in a colorful fiesta dress that revealed she was again with child. She embraced Will and kissed him like a brother rather than a lover.

"How are you Will?"

"Good, now that I see you."

Juan motioned for everyone to go into the casa so that Will and Bella might talk in private.

Bella sat down on a wide bench swing that hung on a hemp rope from the veranda's large rafters. "Please sit by me where we can talk."

Will sat beside her—a bit uncomfortable at first. The swing gently rocked as both looked out at the lush green fields.

"I didn't know, whether you were alive or had found another." Bella held the ropes tight.

"I know it was hard for you, Bella."

"When I was pregnant with William, Estevan was always there for me. After the baby came, he stood by me in church. Everyone assumed he was the father." Bella sighed, "When William was christened we gave the baby Estevan's name, which is Martinez. We married in a private ceremony here on this veranda surrounded by family. "

"Are you happy...Bella?"

"Yes, I'm happy." Bella rocked the swing with her foot. "What about you, Will?"

"I don't know what I am at the moment, Bella. I came thinking only of you. I was excited about marrying you." Will pulled the ring out of his pocket. "I've carried this wedding band that I bought for you all the way from New Orleans."

"It is a pretty ring, Will. Someday you will find a woman who you wish to marry—"

"I wanted to marry you Bella...take you back to Texas...build you a house... have children."

"You remember when we say our goodbyes in Taos? I said if it was meant to be...it would be."

"Yes, Bella but..."

"It wasn't meant to be," Bella shook her head. "I'd never leave my family to move to Texas."

"Bella, you begged to go to Texas with me."

"I know...and I would have. If you had said yes." Bella turned toward Will. "That's what I mean when I say...if it is meant to be." Bella sighed.

They sat in the swing; Will moved it ever so gently. Neither one said a word. Maria came to the door with two-year-old William. Bella saw Maria waiting.

"Do you wish to meet your son?" Bella asked.

"Does he know who I am?" Will looked at her.

"Not yet, he is too young to understand." She stood. "In time when it is right, I will tell him."

Maria came out on the veranda, holding William who was dressed in a linen suit. She handed the toddler to Will. He sat down with his son. The boy didn't like being held by a stranger and wiggled out of his arms and off the swing. Will would have liked to have held him longer, but understood he was more interested in the horses tied to the hitching post.

Bella introduced her husband Estevan to Will. They greeted each other cordially. Will had nothing but admiration for the man who had taken in his own flesh and blood. Will told him so in front of Bella's family. Estevan had become the accountant for the large agricultural operation of the Rowland and Workman Partnership. They ate and drank wine from the Rancho Puente.

After a week of rest, Will headed back to Texas knowing his son was in a good place.

On the sixteenth day of September, 1842, Fayette arrived in Independence, Missouri accompanied by Peter Duncan. The next day, Lewis Jones, the founder of Independence, Missouri penned an eloquent letter that read:

> Your son La Fayette arrived here yesterday under the care of Mr. Peter Duncan, under whose charge he was placed by John Rowland of Taos, New Mexico – to be placed under my protection at this place.

Lewis Jones also wrote Elijah Stamps, Fayette's maternal grandfather in Talladega, Alabama. Elijah left immediately to get Fayette. Grandfather Stamps took Fayette to his home in Alabama.

Fayette's widowed mother, Angelina Stamps Smith, and sisters Caroline and Lorena, fell on dire straits after Judge James Smith's death. Angelina had no means to pay the debt of their property. Her husband had paid three hundred dollars and owed an additional three hundred dollars on the property.

Nine months after James' death, Angelina petitioned the Congress of the Republic of Texas for relief from the debt. Congress granted the request and President Sam Houston signed it. Angelina sold her property for five hundred dollars. Angelina's property would later become Hyde Park.

Fayette endured much pain and suffering during his eighteen months of absence from his family. He never fully recovered from having his Achilles tendons cut. For the remainder of his life, Fayette was unable to lift his feet and shuffled when he walked. Fayette was reunited with his mother and sisters in February of 1843.

The skills he'd learned while working at the Taos Trading Post garnered Fayette a job clerking at the Shackelford & Gould General Store in Washington-on-the-Brazos. His disability did not prevent him from working to help his widowed mother or serving the Sutler to Twigs Regiment during the Mexican-American War.

He enlisted in the Confederate States Army during the Civil War and was wounded at the Battle of Mansfield. Fayette married Elizabeth Gresham in 1855. They had three sons and two daughters. He became a successful merchant in Navasota, Texas. He never had contact with John or Maria Rowland again, but named a son Rowland after the good Samaritan who had returned him to Texas. Fayette and Elizabeth built a beautiful two-story Victorian home in 1888. The home still stands at 904 East Washington Avenue in Navasota, Texas.

Fayette died in 1906; Elizabeth in 1911. Both are buried side-by-side at Oakland Cemetery in Navasota, Texas.

Will returned to Texas and ranged for a while on the Mexican border. True to his word, he found William G. Dryden in Rio Grande

City—the man who went to prison to save Will's life. He was now the editor of the local paper. No doubt Dryden's influence was involved with Will becoming Sheriff of Starr County after Texas was granted statehood. Dryden enlisted Will's help in eliminating a few bad hombres who had taken over the town.

Will never married, but he spent the remainder of his life fighting border bandits on the Rio Grande.

The End

About the Author

David Bowles is a fifth generation Austinite. Both parents were early Travis County pioneers. His great grandmother, Elnora Van Cleve, is recorded as the first birth in Austin, Texas during the days of the Republic.

He named his dog Becka, after Rebeckah Mitchell-Smith his great-great-great-grandmother, matriarch of the family. The author and Becka live and travel in the Class A motor-coach they call home, telling and writing the stories of the *Westward Sagas*.

David grew up listening to the stories of his ancestors told by his elders. Their stories so fascinated him that he became a professional story-teller, spinning tales through the *Westward Sagas* as well as the spoken word. He is a member of the National Story Telling Network and the Tejas Storyteller Association. David entertains groups frequently about his adventures on the open road and the books he's written.

For information on David Bowles' appearance schedule
contact Holly@westwardsagas.com

Other books by the author are available for purchase at Amazon.com

The Westward Sagas series tell the stories of the lives of Scots-Irish families struggling to find happiness on the new frontier. Spring House begins in North Carolina in 1762 and paints a vivid picture of colonial life in the backwoods of the Carolinas. Adam Mitchell fought to protect his family and save his farm, but his home was destroyed by British troops in the Battle of Guilford Courthouse, and his corn fields were turned into fields of death.

In April 2007, National Indie Excellence 2007 Book Awards announced that Spring House *was a finalist in the Historical Fiction category.*

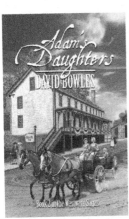

Adam's Daughters tells the story of Peggy Mitchell, a survivor of the Battle of Guilford Courthouse, grows up in Jonesborough, Tennessee during the tumultuous first twenty years of the nation's existence. Though haunted by memories of war, she matures into a strong, independent young woman who is courted by Andrew Jackson and who has a freed slave as her best friend. Her younger brothers and sisters become her surrogate children and students. Together the children of Adam and Elizabeth take on renegade Indians, highwaymen, and the hardships of an untamed land.

2010 International Book Awards finalist in Historical Fiction category.

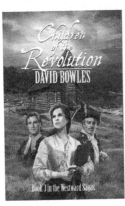

Children of the Revolution continues with the next generation of the Mitchell family. Peggy, the protgonist in *Adam's Daughters,* takes on a stronger role as she matures into a confident woman courted by British nobility. The book uncovers the untold reason North Carolina never ratified the U.S. Constitution. Adventure, intrigue, romance, and tragedy are woven into the story of the *Children of the Revolution.*

2013 North Texas Book Festival finalist in Historical Fiction category.